Writing IN THE AIR

ANTONIO CORNEJO POLAR

Writing IN THE AIR

*Heterogeneity and the
Persistence of Oral Tradition
in Andean Literatures*

Translated by
LYNDA J. JENTSCH

Foreword by
JEAN FRANCO

DUKE UNIVERSITY PRESS   DURHAM AND LONDON   2013

© 2013 Duke University Press
All rights reserved
Printed in the United States of America on acid-free paper ∞
Designed by Heather Hensley
Typeset in Whitman by Tseng Information Systems, Inc.
Library of Congress Cataloging-in-Publication Data
Cornejo Polar, Antonio.
[Escribir en el aire. English]
Writing in the air : heterogeneity and the persistence of
oral tradition in Andean literatures / Antonio Cornejo Polar
; translated by Lynda J. Jentsch ; with a foreword by Jean
Franco.
pages cm
Includes bibliographical references and index.
ISBN 978-0-8223-5417-8 (cloth : alk. paper)
ISBN 978-0-8223-5432-1 (pbk. : alk. paper)
1. Peruvian literature—History and criticism. 2. Bolivian
literature—History and criticism. 3. Ecuadorian literature—
History and criticism. 4. Literature and society—Andes
Region. 5. Culture in literature. I. Title.
PQ7551.C6713 2013
860.9'985—dc23   2013003134

CONTENTS

vii   Acknowledgments
ix   Foreword by Jean Franco

  1   INTRODUCTION

 13   CHAPTER 1
      Voice and the Written Word in the Cajamarca "Dialogue"
 13   The Cajamarca Chronicle
 31   Rituals of Other Memories
 46   A Perhaps Impossible Reading
 55   Identity, Alterity, History

 59   CHAPTER 2
      The Sutures of Homogeneity: Discourses of Impossible Harmony
 60   Garcilaso: Harmony Rent Asunder
 66   Social Depictions of the Inca
 71   From Garcilaso to Palma: One Language for All?
 75   Concerning Patriotic Speeches and Proclamations
 82   In Fiction: Three Novels
      Cumandá   84
      Torn from the Nest   89
      Juan de la Rosa   94
103   Celebrations

113   CHAPTER 3
      Stone of Boiling Blood: The Challenges of Modernization
114   The Ambiguities of a New Language
126   The Emergence of Dualisms

- 131 An Andean Modernity
- 136 A Hobbled History: The Indigenist Novel
- 145 The Subject Explodes
- 154 Underground Voices

- 165 OVERTURE

- 173 Notes
- 209 Index

ACKNOWLEDGMENTS

Foremost I would like to thank Cristina de Cornejo Polar for her unflagging support of this project and for asking Professor Ariel Dorfman to submit the manuscript to Duke University Press for consideration. Many, many thanks also go to Dr. Carlos Orihuela, a former student of Professor Cornejo, for suggesting the translation of *Escribir en el aire* in the first place and for spending countless hours comparing drafts of my translation to the original. *Un millón de gracias* to proofreaders Drs. Francine Masiello, Grace Márquez, and Janice Lasseter. My intention to make this translation as accessible as possible to the English-speaking reader would have been severely compromised without the research of my assistants, David Wendorf and Jonathan Warren, who found extant English translations of many primary and secondary sources and searched their pages for citations. Thanks also to Walker Grooms for his meticulous preparation of the index and to my dean, Dr. David Chapman, for his financial support of the same. I would be remiss in not acknowledging the help and encouragement of my colleagues Professors Mikle Ledgerwood, Kelly Jensen, Millicent Bolden, Patricia Romero, Dennis Sansom, and Francesco Ianuzzi. And to my family, of course, thank you for your unending patience and understanding.

LYNDA J. JENTSCH
Samford University
Birmingham, Alabama

FOREWORD

Antonio Cornejo Polar's book *Writing in the Air: Heterogeneity and the Persistence of Oral Tradition in Andean Literatures* initiates the reader into an area of literary criticism that moves us beyond the familiar grounding of the Western canon into areas at once more challenging and more subtly subversive.

The title, taken from a poem by César Vallejo written during the Spanish Civil War, is in Cornejo Polar's words a "call to orality" that "builds imaginary bridges in order to reconvert the written word to voice." The traumatic origin of the contest between oral and written cultures was "the sudden appearance of writing and the book as enigmatic instruments of conquest with no immediate ties to language or communication. The foundational event that signaled the entry of the book into the New World was recorded by chroniclers and occurred soon after the victory of the Spaniards in Peru when the priest Father Valverde approached the Inca ruler, Atahualpa, and offered him a breviary that the Inca threw angrily to the ground. It was not only writing that baffled the Inca," argues Cornejo Polar, "but also the mechanics of the book (opening it and turning its pages), major indications of the absolute miscommunication that underpins the story of a 'dialogue' as enduring as it is traumatic."

Throughout the colonial period and beyond, the confrontation was enacted and revised in the written histories of conquest, in the ritual dances and reenactments, and in the many dramatic works in Quechua or Spanish on the theme of Atahualpa's death. It was not only the subjugation of the indigenous that was reiterated but also the confrontation of oral culture with the written word, and "of an old system of verbal messages with the new communicative order based on writing." The event was both an interaction and a conflict that extends into the present, producing political misunderstanding and stigmatizing Quechua-speaking peoples as "alien to modernity." Cornejo Polar's study takes the reader through all the variations of this interplay between speech and written word, thus proposing a counterhistory that subtly questions the traditional categories of literary criticism and underscores the contrapuntal rhythm of Peruvian culture. One of those high points is the marvelous evocations of Quechua song in José María Arguedas's great novel *Deep Rivers*, whose protagonist, as Cornejo Polar argues, experiences "discontinuous times and plural cultures." It is most particularly in his account of Arguedas's novel that Cornejo Polar eloquently states his own convictions and belief in the possibility of nonhegemonic action "achieved through the construction of an intrinsically multiple and de-centered subject, discourse and representation." The book ends with a lyrical exposition of Vallejo's poem "'Pedro Rojas,' inspired by a comrade who wrote the message just before his execution." The poem begins, "He took to writing in the air with his best finger: 'Lib long, komrads! Pedro Rojas.'" Cornejo Polar's reading of the poem is offered in place of a traditional conclusion and attests to his own utopian desire, and he reads it as a vigorous assertion of humanity as the words battle the negative force of extinction. *Writing in the Air* is not just a book of academic criticism but a thoroughly committed account of a culture that was inaugurated by conquest but was never conquered.

JEAN FRANCO

INTRODUCTION

> He took to writing in the air with his best finger.
> —CÉSAR VALLEJO

> Now it's better but also worse.
> There are worlds up above and down below.
> —JOSÉ MARÍA ARGUEDAS

> Memory is best served by time.
> —MONTEJO/BARNET

> We are contemporaries of different histories.
> —ENRIQUE LIHN

> It seems we've already walked across more ground
> than we're covering now.
> —JUAN RULFO

> Whoever wants to see things deeply has
> to accept contradictions.
> —ANTÔNIO CÂNDIDO

In recent decades, both literary production and critical thought in Latin America have dealt sequentially with three major themes clearly related to more global and compromising sociohistorical situations and conflicts:[1]

1. Change, by means of the revolution that was "around the corner" in that splendid and beguiling decade of the 1960s, now the source of much nostalgia and sporadic cynicism, when imagination and plazas seemed to be ours, and ours the power, the

voice, and the capacity to invent love and solidarity anew. It was the time of the "new narrative," not only conversational poetry, experimental theater, but also street chants and the graffiti that painted all our cities in hope. The field of criticism seized the moment to accelerate and haphazardly modernize its theoretical-methodological arsenal.

2. Identity, national or Latin American, where we defensively sought refuge once again, as in the bosom of a primordial obsession, in order to explain the late arrival and fading of so many dreams, but above all to reaffirm (unfortunately more by way of metaphysics than history) the peculiarity of our being and consciousness and the fraternal unity of the peoples south of the Rio Grande. In those days, we valued both magical realism and testimonio, which, in their contrast, demonstrated the consistency and keenness of our America. At the same time critics hotly debated the relevance of constructing a theory sufficiently specific to the nature of Latin American literature.[2] Back then, the almost obligatory referential framework was the most hard-line (and less-than-perspicacious) version of dependency theory.

3. Recovery of heterogeneity, which defines our society and culture by isolating regions and strata and emphasizing the vast differences that separate and sharply contrast their various social-cultural worlds, and which, in their many historical rhythms, coexist and overlap even within national boundaries. It was—and is—the time to revalue ethnic and other marginal literatures and refine critical categories that attempt to explain this tangled corpus: "transcultural literature" (Ángel Rama), "other literature" (Edmundo Bendezú), "diglossic literature" (Enrique Ballón), "alternative literature" (Martin Lienhard), "heterogeneous literature" (as I prefer to call it), options that in part could be subsumed under the macroconcepts of "hybrid culture" (Néstor García Canclini) or "clashing society" (René Zavaleta), as well as the argument of "changing notions of literature" (Carlos Rincón) and the radical questioning, at least for certain periods, of the very concept of "literature" (Walter Mignolo, Theodor Adorno, Lienhard).[3]

It is interesting to reflect on how and why the search for identity, usually associated with images of solid and coherent spaces that stitched together vast social networks of ownership and legitimacy, gave way to the restless lament or the agitated celebration of our diverse, multiple, and conflictive configuration. In my opinion it was a process as unforeseeable as it was inevitable, especially because the more deeply we examined our identity, the more evident the disparities and contradictions in the images and the torrential, crashing realities that we identify as Latin America became. Surely that process did not originate within our borders. Thus, in the first decades of [the twentieth century], Latin American historiography performed the complex operation of "nationalizing" the pre-Hispanic literary tradition, as one sees in nineteenth-century colonial literature.[4] But the positivist underpinning of that historical thought, which interprets these processes as mono-linear, perfective, and self-canceling, cloistered that tradition in the depths of an archeological age and assumed that those literatures had come to an end with the conquest.[5] Not until long after that, the unusual union of Amerindian philology and anthropology highlighted the importance of native colonial and modern literatures and the need to include them as part of the entire historic process of Latin American literature, not just its first stage.[6] Clearly the corpus of our literature was distinctive in this way and could offer much to other marginal literatures. In addition we attempted a profound reformulation of its traditional canon.

This trajectory serves to underscore the fact that the present debate over the far-flung proliferation of our conflictive, contradictory literature is the consequence of the progressive and organic exercise of Latin American critical thought and its fluid relationship with its own literature. Several of us have pointed out that although the great epistemological project of the seventies failed (since in fact, a long-awaited "Latin American literary theory" does not exist), it was under its impetus that criticism and historiography found more productive—and more audacious—ways of dealing with a literature that is especially elusive because of its multi- and transcultural makeup.

It should be noted, too, that there came a time when Latin Americans' intense reflection on the plurality of their literature intersected with the categories belonging to poststructuralist criticism and postmodern thought in general. Decidedly "post" themes, such as the critique of the subject, the skeptical repositioning of the order and meaning of representation, the celebration of the dense heterogeneity of discourse, or the radical disbelief in the value and legitimacy of canons, to mention only the obvious ones, inevitably crossed with the Latin American agenda. This hybridization is curious (and should be treated in detail at a later date), first because of the frequency with which metropolitan postmoderns collect provocative references and citations from Latin American authors, from Jorge Luis Borges to Gabriel García Márquez, and eventually Carlos Fuentes, Mario Vargas Llosa, and Manuel Puig; second because the question of borders, peripheries, and the fringe continues to generate much excitement; and third because, paradoxically, "the postmodern condition," as expressed by the most advanced form of capitalism, would seem to have no better historical model than the crippled and deformed subcapitalism of the Third World. The irony here is obviously inviting, but I shall opt for (1) recognizing that poststructuralism has given us more refined and illuminating critical tools, but also (2) emphasizing that there is nothing so unseemly as trying to force—at times even ourselves—into "post" parameters by estheticizing a world of atrocious injustice and poverty. And, as a final caveat, the attempt to read all our literature under the paradoxical model of a criticism that does not believe in canons is just as unfortunate.[7]

Be that as it may, I would like to return to the theme of the destabilizing hybridity of Latin American literature. Initially critics tried to explain this through macrocomprehensive alternatives. Thus, for example, they attempted to delimit literary systems as "cultured," "indigenous," "popular,"[8] or otherwise, while underscoring internal stratification. Here critics tried to render an image of our literature as a boiling pot of blurred systems. This was a difficult task, above all because of an obvious lack of information and the deficit of theoretical-methodological tools appropriate for those subjects: the treatment of oral literature is a case in point. This is why it was preferable to probe multiform diversity within the first category: the "enlightened" system. In these matters one should remember that Alejandro Losada attempted a sort of regionalization that would clarify the differences among the literatures from the Andes, the River Plate, and the Caribbean. He also proposed examining the parallel functioning of highly differentiated subsystems.[9] At almost the same time Ángel Rama proposed distinguishing the literatures produced in large, urban centers open to transnationalizing modernity from those originating in provincial cities still imbued with rural customs and values and clearly less attentive to the demands of modernity. This exposition would lead him, on one hand, to elaborate the category of the "lettered city" and, on the other, to examine the intersection of modernity and tradition in transcultural literature.[10]

Clearly an analytical perspective, which separates out what is distinctive in order not to fall back on modes of globalization that are as abstract as they are false, seeks to encourage the study of a network of relationships interwoven with diversity. In fact, this is what Rama splendidly achieves with the term *transculturation*, which he takes from Fernando Ortiz's renewed and deepened anthropology. This is what I attempted upon observing the processes of how literatures that I called "heterogeneous," in which two or more social-cultural universes intersect, actually produce new forms of expression from the chronicles to testimonio, with gaucho, indigenist, and black discourses, the northeastern Brazilian novel, magical realism, and conversational poetry in between. This is also what Martin Lienhard proposes under the rubric of "alternative literatures," beneath whose "western" texture lie native forms of consciousness and voice. These three streams feed Carlos Pacheco's illustrative contribution on fiction and the effect of orality on transcultural literature.[11]

Is it possible, then, to guide the analysis of these literatures in new directions? This is what I intend to do in this book with respect to Andean literatures, but with the assurance that some of the proposals can be applied much more widely. As my subtitle indicates, underlying this is the concept of heterogeneity, a topic on which I have been working since the late 1970s. I would like to reiterate, however, that this category suited me well from the beginning to explain the "production processes" of literatures in which two or more social-cultural universes intersect in conflict (as in the case of Indigenism) by placing emphasis on the diverse and opposing relationships that emerge. I understood later that heterogeneity was infiltrating internal configurations, making them scattered, brittle, unstable, and contradictory within their own limits. At the same time I attempted to historicize what started out as the structural description of a process. This description contained a most fruitful paradox, since it found itself at an intellectual juncture in which the terms *structure* and *process* seemed inevitably contradictory, each pointing to different disciplines. In each case my focus is on the exceptionally complex nature of a literature (understood in its widest sense) that functions on the fringes of dissonant, sometimes incompatible cultural systems such as the one most dramatically produced in the Andean region. Since the horizons that this book attempts to scan are obviously vast and complex, I have pulled out three vital strands: discourse, subject, and representation. Of course these overlap deeply and mutually and are necessarily joined to others found not only in society itself but also in diverse discursive and symbolic settings.

As for discourse I have gone from the created schism and crude, compromising conflict between the voice of the agraphic Andean cultures and the written word of Western literary institutions to the spoken word transcribed in testimonio and the construction of the effect of orality in literary discourse, while analyzing bilingualism and diglossia. Evidently the construction of these discourses, which reveal the existence of opposing worlds and daring points of alliance, contact, and contamination, can be subject to an attempt to globalize that perturbing variety into a closed, powerful, and monologic authorial voice. But this can also serve to fragment diction and generate an exacerbated dialogism that abandons both the Bakhtinian polyphony it creates and the unpredictable and fickle intertextualities. On more than one occasion I have been able to read these texts as linguistic spaces in which discourses of greatly varying origin complement each other, overlap, intersect, or fight, each one searching for a semantic hegemony that is rarely achieved in any definite way. Upon examination it can surely be proven that within these dissimilar discourses there are also varied senses of time. In other words these discourses are historically dense because their internal social rhythms and time are arranged vertically, resonating in and with voices that can be separated from each other by centuries. Pre-Hispanic myth, sermons of colonial evangelization, and the most audacious proposals of modernization can coexist in a single discourse and confer upon it a truly perplexing historic depth. In this way the synchrony of the text, as a semantic experience that theoretically seems forced into a single block of time, can be deceiving. What I am proposing is that one can (and at times should) "historicize" synchrony, as aporetic as this statement may appear. Obviously this does not contradict but rather enriches the traditional option of making the history of literature into a sequence of artistic experiences, although in the case of Latin American literature's plural configuration such an alternative cannot be imagined as a single, totalizing historic trajectory. Rather it necessitates working with sequences that, in spite of their coetaneity, correspond to diverse historical rhythms.

As far as subject is concerned, experience and the modern concept of subject are clearly and forever linked to Romantic imagination and thought, especially in artistic and literary matters and their respective theoretical-critical correlates. An exalted and even mutable "I" firmly and coherently shows itself able to always return to itself; the "overflow of emotion" never exhausts the well from which it springs, in the same way that, for example, the almost obsessive topic of the journey in time or space never places in doubt the option of returning to the point of origin.[12] Like it or not,

Romanticism became, in these and other matters, the common-sense basis of modernity. This is why Walter Benjamin, who passionately probed the meaning (or meaninglessness) of modernity, dedicated his doctoral dissertation to early Romanticism and its construction of the image of the self-reflective and autonomous subject.[13] Thus, a discussion of the identity of the subject and the perplexing possibility that it may become a space full of internal contradictions and more relational than self-sufficient leads to nothing other than the Romantic image of the "I." We should add here that as for the identity of social subjects, Marxist concepts of social class did not displace Romantic formulations such as those concerning the "spirit of the people." This did not happen because class was imagined as an internally coherent totality. In some ways the category of social class, in the simplified interpretation I have just summarized, has the same function as the Romantic idea of the "I" in the modern debate over social identities. It is not irrelevant that in militant iconography and rituals the proletariat identifies with the simple image of the raised fist. What I have frequently found in my research is precisely the opposite: a complex, scattered, multiple subject.

Here it is imperative to mention that in Latin America the debate over the subject and its identity goes back in time and activates a premodern way of thinking. I am referring to the medieval theological and juridical discussion concerning the condition of the Indian. In this discussion remote and somewhat eccentric scholars, flanked by Aristotle and the Church Fathers, would concede or negate the human condition of the inhabitants of the Indies (animal, savage, man) or at best would scrupulously measure the degree, magnitude, and consistency of our barbarity. I have no irrefutable proof, of course, but I suspect that the obsessive probing of American identity has much to do with that debate, whose context was not Spain, but the colonial state of the Indies, which destroyed the subject and perverted all the relationships (with itself, its fellows, its new masters, the world, the gods, the future, and its dreams) that made it what it now is. In many ways the colonial condition entails precisely this: denying the conquered their identity as subjects, breaking the bonds that used to confer that identity, and imposing others that disrupt and disjoin—with intense severity. Clearly this does not invalidate the powerful emergence of new, future subjects and a respect for the profoundly reshaped remains of former ones.

Nevertheless, even in these cases, the subject that springs from a colonial situation is placed in a web of multiple and cumulatively divergent crossroads: the present is no longer anchored to memory, becoming a repository more of incurable nostalgia or seething rage than of formative experiences; the other meddles in the desires and dreams of intimacy and converts these into an oscillating and at times ferociously contradictory space; and the world and one's relationship to it change, just as these frequently incompatible relationships are superimposed one on another. I am attempting to sketch out both the clashing nature of a subject, which precisely because of its essence is exceptionally changeable and fluid, and the character of a reality composed of fissures and overlays, gathering several epochs into one and stolidly taking the risk of fragmenting the discourse that both represents and constitutes it. I intend to neither lament nor celebrate what history has done. I want to free myself from the shackles that impose the false imperative of defining once and forevermore what we are: a coherent and uniform identity, complacent and ingenuous (the ideology of *mestizaje* would be a good example), which has more to do with metaphysics than society and history. In other words I want to escape from the Romantic—or, more generically, modern—legacy that demands that we be what we are not: strong, solid, and stable subjects, capable of configuring an "I" that remains unchanged. And then cautiously explore horizons where the subject renounces the magnetic power that resides within, meant to deactivate all dissidence and anomaly, and comes to recognize itself in not one but several faces, even in their most vivid representations.

One could take this argument as a somewhat naïve or even perverse strategy to convert necessity into virtue, an underhanded celebration of the breaking down of a subject subdued and dominated by the colonial regime. Not so. It should be more than evident that the conquest and colonization of America was a meticulously atrocious act, and atrociously realized, but also that, in spite of all our condemnation and imprecation, those events did happen and forever mark our history and our consciousness. Out of that trauma comes a modern America capable of expressing a permanent lament for all that was lost to the self-willed enthusiasm of those who see in past intermixtures the potential to universalize the experience. Thus, for example, the epic "cosmic race" and the modest, but effective, "new Indian."[14] And all this without taking into account the asinine raptures of the Hispanizers that still stalk our shores and continue relishing the "feats" of the conquistadors. Despite the temptation to psychologize, it seems to me that trauma is trauma until it is no longer assumed as such. In short, can we really speak of a Latin American subject that is either unique or totalizing? Or should we dare speak of a subject formed by the unstable fissures and intersections of many dissimilar, oscillating, and heterogeneous identities? I wonder why it is so difficult for us to accept the hybridity, the ill assortment, and the heterogeneity of a subject thus configured in our space. Just one answer occurs to me: we introject as our only legitimacy the monolithic, strong, and unchangeable image of the modern subject, based on the Romantic "I," and we feel guilty, before the world and ourselves, when we discover that we lack a clear and distinct identity.

But I have grown more and more suspicious about the matter of identity being too closely tied to the dynamics of power. It is, after all, an intellectual and political elite, with all its inherent desires and interests, that converts an exclusive, comfortable "we" into a broadly inclusive, ontological "we" that may well disfigure all those voiceless individuals forced into this process. This "we" is, of course, that intensely desired "identity." I am being ironic. I do not know if the affirmation of a heterogeneous subject implies a pre- or postmodern stance, but in either case it is curious—and uncomfortable—that there has been such untimely interweaving of a centuries-old experience finally rendering the image of a subject that is not afraid of its multivalent plurality. I sense that this is not so much a matter of subscribing (or not) to the "postmodern condition," which is really none of our concern, as it is the acceptance or rejection of the existence of several modernities in any one of which the subject could take root and find nourishment in various historical and cultural soils without losing its true nature in the process. Again, a heterogeneous subject.

But the subject, whether individual or collective, is not built within and for itself. It is formed, virtually, in relationship with other subjects, but also (and most notably) through and in its relationship to the world. In this sense mimesis is finally freed from its historic constraints of re-presenting the reality of the world or, as a correlative to this, being a "control of the imaginary" on either a personal or social level.[15] Rather, as a discursive construction of what is real, the subject defines itself in mimesis just as it proposes that an objective world be ordered and evoked in terms of the independent reality of the subject that, nevertheless, does not exist except as uttered by the subject. Obviously I am in no way postulating that reality does not exist, but that the material of discourse (sadly reality does not speak for itself) is a rocky crossroads between what is and the way the subject constructs it, either as a peaceful dwelling place, a contentious space, or a purifying but desolate "vale of tears": a singular and final shore or a passage to other transmundane dimensions. In other words there is no mimesis without a subject, but there is no subject that can be constructed outside of the mimesis of the world.

Latin America, and the Andean world especially, is subject to extreme violence as well as extreme disintegration. Here everything is mixed with everything else, and the most startling contrasts are juxtaposed, face-to-face, on a daily basis. This viscerally dislocated, intense social framework imposes its own codes of rupture and fragmentation on verbal representation. Unfortunately what should be a bright path toward human and social abundance (the same ability to live in one as in any other homeland)[16] is in reality the repeated carrying out of injustice, abuse, and wide-ranging discrimination, the machinery of unbearable misery. There is nothing more basely treacherous than estheticizing in writing a meticulously and radically inhuman reality. So if I attempt a demythification of not only the monolithic, one-dimensional and prideful, coherent subject but also the harmonious discourse of a single voice whose only response is its own echo and a representation of the world that forces it to constantly turn on the same axis, and if I seek a parallel justification of the profound heterogeneity of these categories, it is, of course, because they are literary, but also because they aptly express ideas and life experiences. I do not wish to celebrate chaos: I am simply and plainly pointing out that, inside and outside of ourselves, there exist other, much more authentic and worthy existential alternatives. But they are worthless, naturally, if individuals and peoples cannot work them out in liberty, with justice, and in a world that has become their dignified dwelling place.

At one point I was tempted to undertake an exhaustive study by treating many other topics and organizing them along rigorously historical lines. Fortunately I soon recognized that neither my abilities nor the very material under my reflection could stand up to such a commitment. After all, there is nothing wrong with a book about heterogeneity being heterogeneous itself. I therefore opted to select certain decisive points in time and tried to place them within their pertinent problematic universes. Chapters 2 and 3 are especially fragmented because of the variety of topics they treat and certain analytical changes in perspective. I truly regret that my greater knowledge of Peruvian literature has led me to treat it more than those of Bolivia and Ecuador. My consolation is that, in the main, the problems (and even texts) are broadly Andean in nature.

I should add that absolutely coincidental circumstances caused me to write this book over a span of five or six years, during which time I taught at various universities: primarily Pittsburgh and San Marcos, but also Berkeley, Dartmouth, Montpellier, and Alcalá. In every case, my obsession with the topic caused me to offer courses and seminars related to it, which helped me define this book in wider terms. I am most grateful for the invaluable help of colleagues and students at these universities and other friends (mentioned in the text) with whom I consulted. There were also dozens of conversations with participants in conferences, symposia, and seminars where I had the opportunity, time and again, to speak about a topic that continues to touch me viscerally. And finally, because destiny seems to have placed me in the First World, I have discovered that I myself am irremediably (and happily?) intermixed and heterogeneous.

CHAPTER 1 Voice and the Written Word
in the Cajamarca "Dialogue"

Understanding Latin American literature as a complex system of multifaceted conflicts and contradictions carries a principle obligation: to examine the basic duality of literature's structural mechanisms, that is, orality and writing. This problem precedes and is deeper than bi- or multilingualism and diglossia in that it affects the very materiality of discourse.

In literary production, orality and writing have their own codes and histories and are based on two strongly differentiated rationalities, with a wide and complicated zone of interactions separating them.[1] In Latin America this zone is exceptionally fluid and complex, especially if one rightly assumes that its literature is not solely the one that the lettered elite write in Spanish or other European languages, and the one that can become quite unintelligible if its links with orality are severed.[2]

It is certainly possible to distinguish the many shapes that the relationship between oral and written literature may take, several of which have been treated exhaustively by philologists, especially the conversion of oral discourse into written texts (for example, Homeric poetry).[3] In other cases, however, as in Amerindian literatures, classical philological instruments seem to be insufficient.[4]

THE CAJAMARCA CHRONICLE

I would like to first examine what could be called "ground zero" of this interaction, or the point at which orality and writing do not merely reveal their differences but evidence their mutual estrangement and their reciprocal, aggressive repulsion. This point of friction is documented and, in the case of Andean history, even has a concrete date, setting, and cast of characters. I am referring to the "dialogue" between Atahuallpa Inca and Father Vicente Valverde in Cajamarca on the afternoon of November 16, 1532.

This is not the origin of our literature, which goes back to the lengthy history lived and breathed long before the conquest, but it is the most visible beginning of the heterogeneity that has characterized Peruvian, Andean, and, in large part, Latin American literary production ever since.[5] Obviously in other areas of the Americas there are situations similar to the one acted out by Atahuallpa and Valverde in Cajamarca.

For my purposes let us put aside for the moment the commentaries concerning the inevitable miscommunication between two people who speak different languages. Neither is it very helpful to analyze the job well or poorly done by Felipillo (or Martinillo), one of the first interpreters utilized by the conquistadors. My focus is on the clash between orality, formalized here by the supreme voice of the Inca, and writing, which in this case becomes incarnate in *the* book of the West, the Bible, or a text derived from it, all of which sets in motion an extensive and complicated series of acts and repercussions.

I shall first describe the event according to the chronicles, then briefly examine its vestiges in several ritual dances and songs and, more thoroughly, in "theatrical" texts that, despite their common theme being Atahuallpa's execution, consistently include sporadic references to the topic I intend to study.[6] Nevertheless I need to clarify why I give such importance to an event that in principle seems to have no other relationship to literature save that it has been the point of reference for many chronicles and other, later texts.

At issue is a broad concept of literature that assumes a complete circuit of literary production, including the reception of the message and attempts to explain the problematics of orality, to mention just two basic points.[7] But above all it has to do with something much more important that to this day continues to leave its mark on the richly textured fabric of our written culture and the whole of social life in Latin America: the historic destiny of two ways of thinking that from their first encounter repelled each other because of the very linguistic material in which they were formalized. This presages not only a series of more profound and dramatic confrontations, but also the complexity of processes of transcultural overlapping. With the Cajamarca "dialogue" both the great discourses that for five centuries have expressed and constituted the abysmal condition of this part of the world and the inevitable dissonances and contradictions among the various literatures produced here are *in nuce*.

In other words, Valverde's and Atahuallpa's gestures and words may not be "literature," but they compromise its very material on the decisive level that distinguishes voice from written word, thereby constituting the origin of a complex literary institutionality, fragmented in its own base. It could be said that they allow for the interplay of several discourses, especially the Bible (which, even in its sweeping universality, also seems to relate to the intertext peculiar to Andean literature), the longstanding discourse of imperial Spain, and the one that from then on came to be globalized as "Indian" (obviating even more Andean ethnic differences) with its signifiers of defeat, resistance, and revenge. Together they contain the seedbed of a never-ending story.

These gestures and words serve to condense the historical-symbolic memory of the two sides of the conflict and therefore are so frequently reproduced in the imaginaries of their literatures. At the same time they constitute the emblem of the tenacious Latin American preoccupation that the pertinence (or not) of the language with which it represents itself includes the image of the other.

There are few testimonies of those present at Cajamarca. All are, obviously, from the Spanish side. As cases in point, I offer these: "When Ataba-liva had advanced to the center of the open space, he stopped, and a Dominican Friar, who was with the Governor, came forward to tell him, on the part of the Governor, that he waited for him in his lodging, and that he was sent to speak with him. The Friar then told Atabaliva that he was a Priest, and that he was sent there to teach the things of the Faith, if they should desire to be Christians. He showed Atabaliva a book that he carried in his hands, and told him that that book contained the things of God. Atabaliva asked for the book, and threw it on the ground, saying: — 'I will not leave this place until you have restored all that you have taken in my land. I know well who you are, and what you have come for.'"[8]

> The Marquis don Francisco Pizarro, having seen that Atahuallpa was coming, sent Father Friar Vicente de Valverde, first bishop of Cuzco, Hernando de Aldana, a fine soldier, and don Martinillo, an interpreter, to go and speak with Atahuallpa and to require him, by God and the

King, to subject himself to the law of Our Lord Jesus Christ and the service of His Majesty, and to tell him that the Marquis would treat him as a brother and would not consent to there being committed outrage nor damage in his land. The Father having arrived at the litter on which Atahuallpa was being carried, spoke to him and told what he had come for and preached about our Holy Faith, this being declared to him by the interpreter. The Father was carrying a breviary in his hands, from which he read what he was preaching to him. Atahuallpa asked for it, and he gave it to him closed, and since he did not know how to open it when it was in his hands, he threw it to the ground. . . . After this Atahuallpa, calling them scoundrels and thieves, told them to go away, and that he was to kill them all.[9]

[And a friar from the order of Santo Domingo carried] a cross in his hand, wishing to tell [the Inca] the things of God, and he said that the Christians were his friends, and that the lord governor loved him dearly and that he should enter his dwelling in order to see him. [Atahuallpa] replied that he would not advance further until the Christians returned all they had stolen from him. Leaving this discussion to one side, the friar with a book in his hand began telling him the things of God that he needed to know. And [Atahuallpa] did not want to accept them. But he asked for the book and the friar gave it to him thinking that he was going to kiss it, and he took it and threw it down. And the priest turned round shouting and saying, "Come forth, come forth Christians, and attack these dogs our enemies, who do not want the things of God. Because this cacique has thrown the book of our holy law on the ground!"[10]

Seeing this, the Governor asked the Father Friar Vicente if he wished to go and speak to Atabaliba, with an interpreter. He replied that he did wish it, and he advanced, with a cross in one hand and the Bible in the other, and going amongst the people up to the place where Atabaliba was, thus addressed him: "I am a Priest of God, and I teach Christians the things of God, and in like manner I came to teach you. What I teach is that which God says to us in this Book. Therefore, on the part of God and of the Christians, I beseech you to be their friend, for such is God's will, and it will be for your good. Go and speak to the governor, who waits for you." Atabaliba asked for the Book, that he might look at it, and the Priest gave it to him closed. Atabaliba did not know how to open it, and the Priest was extending his arm to do so, when Atabaliba, in great anger, gave him a blow on the arm, not wishing that it should be opened. Then he opened it himself, and, without any astonishment at the letters and paper, as had been shown by other Indians, he threw it away from him five or six paces, and, to the words which the monk had spoken to him through the interpreter, he answered with much scorn, saying: "I know well how you have behaved on the road, how you have treated my Chiefs, and taken the cloth from my storehouses."[11]

. . . Father Vicente Valverde, of the Order of Preachers, who later was Bishop of that land, with the Bible in his hand and together with Martín, an interpreter, made their way through the crowd in order to be able to speak with Atahuallpa, to whom he began to tell things about Holy Scripture and that Our Lord Jesus Christ commanded that among His people there be neither war nor discord, but rather full peace; and that he in His name thus requested and required the same of him . . . at which these and many other words that the friar told him, he was quiet and without answer; and saying again that he look at what God commanded, which was written in that book in his hand, marveling, in my opinion more at the writing than at what was written there, he asked for the book and opened and turned its pages, looking at the printing and order of it, and having seen it, he threw it among the people, saying with great ire and a flaming face, "Tell them to come hence, for I shall not leave here until they give account and satisfy and pay for what they have done in my land."[12]

Scholars have shown that the conquest's first eyewitnesses were not entirely reliable (especially with regard to cultural behaviors and artifacts of the Tawantinsuyu) and were barely understandable through amateur and sometimes biased interpreters. Furthermore this was a case of a bilingual "dialogue," mediated by one of these interpreters and in whose transcription (to confuse the matter even more) reality might well have been mixed with dialogistic stereotypes from classical historiography or chivalric novels, although I sense that these interferences and those from the *romanceros* became more pronounced as time progressed.[13]

In any case there is a definable common theme in these testimonials: Valverde, through an interpreter, requires that the Inca be subject to Christian beliefs and the rule of imperial Spain and gives him a sacred book (presumably the Bible or a breviary) that Atahuallpa in the end throws on the ground. With subtle differences in the renderings, this act provides the rationale for the unleashing of the conquistadors' violent military machine. Although it is clear that no historical retelling is an exact replica of what really happened, there is all indication that the versions noted here seem to "reproduce" events that did indeed happen, as well as some of the exact words that were spoken.[14] But even if one were to doubt the veracity of the narration out of excessive skepticism or for other reasons (Inca Garcilaso de la Vega roundly refutes it and Martín de Murúa alludes to the fact that each one relates the episode according to his interests), the subject matter that the Cajamarca witnesses recount possesses sufficient symbolic consistency to be retold countless times (from the colony to the present) in chronicles and other accounts produced by those who could draw upon both written and oral tradition. Obviously the cited texts originate in the former, but the understudied oral tradition is most probably based on a much more varied array of sources.

It is impossible to present here an exhaustive compilation of all later versions, but most of them clearly expand upon and/or stylize the material in the first accounts, although the fact remains that their roots are not only found in the written tradition but also in the oral, which seems to take a parallel path.[15] Examples of expansions are found in texts by Agustín de Zárate or Francisco López de Gómara, who "transcribe" (or rather imagine) Father Valverde's long speech: a prolix recounting of Catholic dogma and the King's ordinances derived from the text of the *requerimiento* drafted by Juan López de Palacios Rubios in 1512.[16] Despite its length it is useful to cite Zárate's version:

> Then the bishop, Fray Vicente de Valverde, came forward with a breviary in his hand and expounded how One God in three persons had created heaven and earth and all that was in it, and had made Adam, who was the first man on earth, taking his wife Eve from his rib, whereby we were all engendered, and how by the disobedience of our first parents we had fallen into sin and could not achieve the grace of seeing God or going to heaven until our Redeemer Christ was born of a virgin to save us, as a result of which He received His death and passion; and that after His death He was reborn in glory, and remained in the world for a short time before rising to heaven, leaving in His place Saint Peter and his successors who lived at Rome and whom we Christians called popes; and how the popes had divided the whole world between the Christian princes and kings, entrusting each with a task of conquest; and that this

province of Atahuallpa's had been assigned to His Majesty the Emperor and King Don Carlos, our master; and that he had sent Don Francisco Pizarro to represent him as governor and inform Atahuallpa on behalf of God and the Emperor of all that he had just said; that if Atahuallpa chose to believe and receive the waters of baptism and obey him, as did the greater part of Christendom, the Emperor would defend and protect him, maintaining peace and justice in the land and preserving his liberties as he did those of other kings and lords who accepted his rule without the risk of war; but if Atahuallpa were to refuse, the Governor would make cruel war on him with fire and sword, and lance in hand.[17]

Atahuallpa's response is rendered by Francisco López de Gómara as

Atahuallpa responded very angrily that, being free, he did not desire to become a tributary nor hear that there might be another, greater lord than he; nevertheless, he would be glad to be a friend to the emperor and make his acquaintance, because he must be a great prince, since he sent as many armies as they said throughout the world; he said that he would not obey the Pope, because he gave away what was not his and would not leave his father's kingdom to someone who had never seen it. And, as for religion, he said that his own was very good and that he was contented with it and neither wanted nor was obliged to question such an ancient and well proven matter, and Christ died and the Sun and Moon never died.[18]

The not-so-ingenuous process of stylization is made obvious by comparing the above text with Jerónimo Benzoni's, which derives from it: "When the king had heard all this, he said that he would live in friendship with the monarch of the world; but it did not seem, to him, incumbent on a free king to pay tribute to a person whom he had never seen: and that *the pontiff must be a great fool*, giving away so liberally the property of others. As to the religion, he would on no account abandon his own; for if they believed in Christ who died on the cross, he believed in the Sun, who never died."[19]

No doubt such textual sequences depend heavily on not only the literary-historiographic codes employed but also the transformations in Spanish oral memory and the receptivity of the narrator for native oral memory.[20] These are obviously related to the ideological and social interests implicit in the subject of the text. For example, the approval or disapproval of the conquistadors' behavior, especially by Valverde, usually shifts from the direct expression of this judgment to the "objective" narration of the events, or vice versa.

Such is the case in the chronicle by Pedro Cieza de León, who condemns Father Valverde's action ("so that [the Inca] could understand, he should have said it in a different way"), adds information about the fear motivating the priest's actions, and extrapolates a general judgment about clerical behavior ("the friars here only preach where there is no danger"), thus casting doubt on the veracity of the long discourse that Pizarro's chaplain was to have pronounced.[21] Likewise Miguel Cabello de Balboa, who also has a critical attitude (he complains that Valverde mentions the Gospels "as if Atahuallpa knew what Gospels were or was obligated to know"), prefers the version in which the Inca lets the breviary fall by accident.[22] It is also noteworthy that Martín de Murúa opts not to linger on parts of the Cajamarca episode ("and so I shall not speak of them") because there are other versions that already do so. But still, he points out the utter senselessness of the Dominican's behavior.[23]

I underscore several points of this expansion and/or stylization since it affects the chronicles' representations of Atahuallpa's reactions to the book. As we have seen, in the eyewitness versions the event is recounted with extreme brevity. The shortest one (by Pedro Pizarro) simply tells that the Inca asks Valverde for the book and immediately throws it down. The most elaborated version (Francisco de Xerez) adds only that the Inca cannot open the book (also stated by Pedro Pizarro), that he finally manages to do so, and that "without any astonishment" he finally casts it on the ground. In another elaborated version (Miguel Estete), the testimony changes and the Inca "marvels" at the book, although obviously more at the "writing" (understood as the "printing and order" of the book) and not at "what was written there." Of course their basic common sense obliged the writers of the first accounts to avoid even the slightest reference to reading, although in those circumstances perhaps they could have actualized the image of the "speaking book."[24] Above all what remains is a testimony both direct and dramatic (in its terrible consequences) of what I call "ground zero" of the relationship between two cultures, one oral and the other written.[25] This is represented by Atahuallpa's difficulty in understanding not only the written word but also the mechanics of the book (opening it and turning its pages), major symbols of the absolute miscommunication that underpins the story of a "dialogue" as enduring as it is traumatic.

Later chronicles elaborate on this point with more complex imagery. They tend to omit the basics (the Inca's difficulty in opening the book, perhaps because by then this may have appeared excessive) and instead insist on his attempt to "listen" to what the holy text "says." Although the chasm between orality and writing still exists, these versions clearly emphasize the book's signifying function: whereas previously it was a question of "marveling" at an object, now the focus is on "understanding"—or not—what it means. If in many versions the Inca throws down the book because he does not "hear" a "voice" that confirms what Valverde has told him, all of them stress—with inevitable but biased references to reading—his *looking* at it almost as if this were an act that should lead to deciphering the written word. In any case there is quite a gap between the Inca who does not know how to open the book and the one who looks at it and curiously turns its pages. Cieza offers little explanation, noting only that Atahuallpa took the breviary and "looked at it and looked again, leafing through it several times. Not liking so many pages, he threw it up in the air without knowing what it was."[26] López de Gómara, for his part, points out that the Inca asked, "'how did the friar know that the God of the Christians had created the world?' Friar Vicente answered that the book said so, and gave him the breviary. Atahuallpa opened it, looked at it, and leafed through it, and telling him that it told him nothing of the sort, threw it on the ground."[27] Zárate confirms this version, although he openly includes the idea of writing: "He asked the Bishop how he would know that what he had said was true, or where could it be understood. The Bishop said that in that book it was *written* what was the *writing* of God. And Atahuallpa asked him for the breviary or Bible that he had in his hand; and when he gave it to him, he opened it, turning the leaves over and over, and said that the book said nothing to him nor did it speak any word, and he threw it on the ground."[28]

The most elaborate version is clearly Murúa's, which establishes that since the Inca considered the Spaniards to be gods (as per Andean religious consciousness), with the book's silence he realized the truth and became enraged at the bizarre nature of what Valverde was telling him, which was alien, unintelligible, or "heretical" for that worldview. Moreover, the same chaplain would have been deceitful upon affirming that Atahuallpa would "hear" what the book had to tell him. The text is ambiguous: "When Atahualpa was looking at the book and leafing [staring at] the pages to listen to it, and did not hear one word, he was displeased and angered at how differently he had been addressed from what he had expected and understood of the messengers whom he considered to have come from the Creator and Viracocha. And when he realized that he would not find what he was hoping for and furthermore that he was being asked for tribute and submission to someone he did not know, he threw the book to the ground with contempt."[29]

Clearly, although what stands out most is the aporetic account of "listening to the book," the insistence on documenting that the Inca looks at and leafs through (*ojea/hojea*) the text tangentially includes a concept of reading not present in the first chronicles, with the exception of Estete's.[30] However, the result is the same: the book says nothing to the one who synthesizes native cultural experience and, along with his people, becomes subject to a new power based on the written word and edged out of a history constructed upon written language. In one way or another the Spanish chroniclers suggest that the Inca "failed" with respect to the alphabet, and it is obvious that his "ignorance" of that specific code classified him and his people as barbarians or, in other words, as passive objects of legitimate conquest. Of course the power of the written word and the right to conquest have both political and religious meaning. If, as Sabine MacCormack points out, for Atahuallpa "the book had to be an object, not a text," there is no doubt that this object was sacred, since it was speaking to him of gods.[31] Consequently his "failure" had a sacred, religious, or divine dimension defined by his inability to "understand" the word of God that was generously being offered him. Being ignorant of the written word, Atahuallpa is ignorant of both the King and God: two sides of the same unpardonable sin.

Nevertheless many of the conquistadors present in Cajamarca were illiterate, and others practiced the medieval habit of reading aloud. Consequently, though it seems paradoxical, Atahuallpa and his retinue were not an exception or rarity among the Spaniards, though their behavior with respect to writing is nevertheless a source of derision and punishment. Furthermore in Europe at that time (and in decades to come), the written word did not hold sway over voice, and in many ways the latter incarnated power, even within the confines of religion. Still in the Andes and in the form of the Inca and Valverde's emblematic "dialogue," writing assumes the full representation of authority. This indicates that in the Andean world the association between writing and power must be depicted within a very concrete circumstance: the conquest and colonization of one people by another, radically different one, which causes conflicts between voice and written word to take on a much deeper significance of rupture and belligerence than would normally develop in a homogenous society or between relatively similar societies. In short, writing in the Andes is not only a cultural matter. It is in addition and above all an act of conquest and domination. This should be the context that frames all reflection on this topic.

Bearing this in mind, one's imagination could be stirred by a reading of this episode that goes in the (almost) opposite direction of the one above: not as the story of the Inca's failure with respect to the book, but rather the story of the failure of the book itself.[32] Ironically this interpretation is not entirely different from that of the Spaniards, who could not really expect the book to function as text. Rather, for them the magical-religious power of its "letters" or even its "paper" should have rendered the Inca "astonished," according to Xerez. In effect the book appears at Cajamarca not as a means of communication but as a sacred object, worthy of reverence and able to produce revelations and resplendent miracles. Mena points out that Valverde thought Atahuallpa was asking for the book in order to kiss it, thereby extrapolating the Christian custom of kissing the holy book into the indigenous context. But this very extrapolation lays bare the belief that this book could indeed create miracles: in this case Atahuallpa's instantaneous conversion. MacCormack notes that "for unlettered people, such books were objects of reverence rather than reasoning, let alone debate. Indeed, Valverde's book, whatever its content had been, was written in Latin and thus could not have been read by Pizarro and his men. How then could the Inca expect to read it?"[33]

The same author asserts that at that time "unlettered people were prone to view the written page with superstitious awe, as being endowed with speech, even inhabited by spirits," which makes it believable that the conquistadors could think that the book would, indeed, "speak" to the Inca in order to convert him.[34] Of course this argument does not explain Atahuallpa's behavior or that of the Indians in Cajamarca, who only later made writing an object of worship, but it does reinforce this other and inverse interpretations of the events. The book as a bearer of divine power (and obviously as text) failed resoundingly in the Cajamarca plaza: it neither said nor did what the Spaniards seemed to think it would say or do on that occasion. One should also remember that Iberian accounts recall the reconquest of the Peninsula as they describe over and again the miracles that favored the conquistadors, taking these as irrefutable proof of the religious nature of their wars.[35] The transformation of St. James the Moor Slayer into St. James the Indian Slayer is well known.

Be that as it may, it is most significant that two of the three great Indian chroniclers do not dwell on the Cajamarca episode and do not mention or barely allude to the "dialogue" between the Inca and Valverde. Joan Santa Cruz Pachacuti dedicates a few lines to it, without alluding to the book at all,[36] while Diego Titu Cussi offers this brief version: "those two Spaniards showed my uncle [Atahuallpa] a letter or a book, or some such, I don't know what, saying that it was the *quillca* of God and the King. But my uncle, as he felt affronted by the spilling of the *chicha* [an action of the Spaniards related earlier in the text], which is what our drink is called, took the letter or whatever it was and threw it down saying, 'How do I know what it is you give me there? Move along, go away.'"[37]

Omitted reference to the book points to Santa Cruz Pachacuti's pan-Andean (*colla*) historical consciousness rather than one from Cusco, while Titu Cussi's main concern is that Atahullpa usurped the throne that rightly belonged to his paternal ancestor. For both of these native writers, then, the events at Cajamarca had no decisive significance. These two chronicles weave complicated dialogic strategies (acceptance and resistance) vis-à-vis Spanish power, which downplay the events.[38] In either case their silence means that we have no versions couched in the indigenous tradition, except for the one by Felipe Guaman Poma de Ayala.[39] The *Nueva crónica* treats the matter, but the written version sheds no new light on the plot as set forth by most of the Spanish chroniclers:

> He came forward holding a crucifix in his right hand and a breviary in his left and introduced himself as another envoy of the Spanish ruler, who according to his account was a friend of God, and who often worshipped before the cross and believed in the gospel. Friar Vicente called upon the Inca to renounce all other gods as being a mockery of the truth. Atahuallpa's reply was that he could not change his belief in the Sun, who was immortal, and in the other Inca divinities. He asked Friar Vicente what authority he had for his own belief and the friar told him it was all written in the book that he held. The Inca then said, "Give me the book so that it can speak to me." The book was handed up to him and he began to eye it carefully and listen to it page by page. At last he asked, "Why doesn't the book say anything to me?" Still sitting on his

throne, he threw it on to the ground with a haughty and petulant gesture. Friar Vicente found his voice and called out that the Indians were against the Christian faith.[40]

It is no coincidence that in this episode Guaman Poma's prose explodes with words such as "to say" or "to ask," so that the writing constantly harks back to the act of speaking and places it foremost in the reader's consciousness. I cannot say for certain that in this fragment the expressions derived from the verb "to say" are more prominent than in others, but it is intriguing that this account of the confrontation between voice and written word was written by an Indian who recurrently—almost obsessively—evokes orality.

The reader has likely noted that most of the chronicles are basically homogeneous in their structure and plot, although details and judgments as to the value of the Cajamarca episode vary, even to the point that some indigenous versions barely mention it. Garcilaso is the great dissenting voice. He is careful to prove the validity of his sources (directly, the oral tradition of the first conquistadors and Father Valera's chronicle, and indirectly, indigenous tradition preserved in *ñudos* or *quipus*) and emphatically discredits the popular version (based on error, adulation, and Pizarro's prohibition to write "the truth of what happened"). But this well-kept historiographic framework is clearly and directly at the service of a very pointed interpretation of the incident at Cajamarca as part of the fulfillment of a divine plan: the evangelization of the Indies.

What Garcilaso tells is that the Spaniards, "not bearing the prolixity of the discussion" between Atahuallpa and Valverde, attack the indigenous nobles in order to "snatch the many jewels" that they were wearing, at the same time stripping an idol of its gold and silver covering in a tumultuous scene. In his fright Valverde drops the cross and breviary and pleads for the Indians' safety, but his cries go unheeded: a massacre ensues, and Atahuallpa is taken prisoner. Thus, for Garcilaso, the Inca "neither threw the book nor [even] took it in his hands" and limited himself to speaking to Valverde through an interpreter. In this conversation Atahuallpa did not deny the sovereignty of the Emperor and "changed [his] irate and bellicose attitude . . . not just into meekness and gentleness, but great submission and humility," all an irrefutable manifestation of a providential plan: "It is certainly to be believed that this was a manifestation of divine mercy, for with this and similar marvels which we shall often observe at many points of this history, we shall see how God was disposing the spirits of those heathen to receive the truth of His doctrine and His Holy Gospel."[41]

Without analyzing Garcilaso's complex version, I would like to highlight several points. First, Garcilaso is especially interested in pointing out that there was no conquest as such, because the authority of the King and the truth of Catholicism were (or were able to be) freely accepted by the Indians. This insistence is even more emphatic in Guaman Poma and other Indian chroniclers with the addition that the heroic height of the conquest is reduced to an explosion of greed on the part of the Spaniards, unable even to wait until Atahuallpa and Valverde's "dialogue" ends. Second, this passage reproduces one of the essential tensions present in the *Royal Commentaries of the Incas*, that is, the tension between the call to tell the whole truth and the equally strong call to totalize events within a general interpretation of history. In this case the interpretation is teleological and providentialist, as if the writer had unintentionally proposed to prove that history is, above all, a discourse that bestows global order and meaning to material that it constantly tries to capture but that in the end is always elusive and ambiguous.[42]

Finally I would like to point out that Garcilaso's version drastically reduces the importance of the book and places the drama at Cajamarca wholly within the realm of pure orality. Disagreeing with the meaning of other chronicles, the *Royal Commentaries* conceives the catastrophe as an act of greed and constructs a space where dialogue (again, without interference from the written word) would have been possible. It is no coincidence that Garcilaso stops to consider the precautions that Atahuallpa took to make sure that the interpreter did his job well (including speaking in Felipillo's native Chinchaysuyo language), even though in the end the translation proved to be "barbaric."[43] He also insists on the sound evangelizing spirit of the "good Friar Vicente," even though he advises that his oratory was "very dry and harsh, with no nectar to soften it nor other flavor whatsoever."[44] In a certain sense, if writing is taken away from the scene, its bilingualism proves to be a minor hurdle: it seems that *spoken* Quechua and Spanish do not repel each other in the way that orality and writing definitely do.

It is significant that the *mestizo* Garcilaso's experiential and ideological project has to minimize the presence of writing in this episode in order to imagine an alternative reconciliation between Andean and Spanish world orders. This is somewhat paradoxical, however, as Garcilaso will finally try to reach this ideal harmony through his own splendid writing, a writing that proposes to be a link between voice and written word and a translation from Quechua to Spanish. One must remember that Garcilaso tends to rest his historical discourse on what he heard from the lips of the first conquistadors and members of Inca imperial nobility, which produces a continual transfer from orality to writing, often complicated by the underlying act of translation. Alberto Escobar has shed considerable light on Garcilaso's role as "interpreter" and how this is realized—and not only on the linguistic level—in the *Royal Commentaries*.[45]

As we have seen, Garcilaso is very critical of the behavior of the one who acts as interpreter (*lengua*) in Cajamarca. This topic is the crux of the account by Juan de Betanzos, a Quechua-speaking Spaniard married to a *ñusta* (princess) from the same *panaca* (royal clan) as Atahuallpa. His version takes special care to clearly define the failure of the translation ("book" is translated as "painting," for example), and to this effect he partially replicates it in a text that in the end is as confusing as the translation probably was:

> While he was engaged in this conversation, Fray Vicente de Valverde approached him. He brought with him an interpreter. I fully believe, because of what those lords said who were right next to the Inca's litter, that the interpreter did not know how to relate to the Inca what the priest Fray Vicente told him. They said what the interpreter told the Inca when the priest took out a book and opened it. The interpreter said that that priest was the son of the Sun, and that the Sun had sent him to tell the Inca that he should not fight, he should obey the captain who was also the son of the Sun, and that was what was in that book and the painting in the book said that. Since he said painting, the Inca asked for the book and, taking it in his hands, he opened it. When he saw the lines of letters, he said, "This speaks and says that you are the son of the Sun? I, also, am the son of the Sun." His Indians answered this and said in a loud voice all together, "This is Capa Inca." The Inca repeated in a loud voice that he also came from where the Sun was. Saying this, he hurled the book away.[46]

Unlike other versions, Garcilaso's rendering of what happened at Cajamarca was not widely regarded, and what remained in the Andean imaginary was the story generically designed by the other chroniclers, with the Inca throwing the Bible on the ground and Valverde calling the Spaniards to war to avenge such an outrage. For me it is not a question of judging the historical veracity of one version against another. Rather my point is that the chronicles in which the book appears as a "character" in the Cajamarca encounter cannot help but image it as an explicit or tacit symbol of the substantial lack of communication that underlies—and undermines—the inaugural and premonitory "dialogue" between the voice of Inca Atahuallpa and the written word of Father Valverde.[47]

On a political-military level Valverde's actions could be read as a religious ruse used to justify the violence of the conquistadors, the sacking of the imperial riches, the execution of the Inca, and finally the subjugation of the Tawantinsuyu. After all, it was clearly foreseeable that Atahuallpa would not accept the requests or the orders of the cleric and that his "rebelliousness" could be an excellent first chapter in the chronicle of a death (the Inca's, and that of his empire) foretold. It seems to me, however, that Father Valverde's behavior, with all its senselessness and fanaticism, is nothing more than a clumsy version of the absurd ritual of the requerimiento: an intentionally unintelligible pronouncement that demands of the Indians, on pain of merciless reprimands, an immediate, absolute, and total obedience on both political and religious grounds.[48]

Aside from the matter of writing, Valverde's oral discourse has dark, sectarian, and irrational overtones that under other circumstances would be utterly grotesque. Only pure fanaticism explains how it could occur to anyone that the abstruse mysteries of the Catholic faith would be accepted all at once and on first hearing. Even worse, the certification of the requerimiento implies that fanaticism was not an exception practiced by a few, but was at the very core of a vast and triumphant culture, which imposed itself on the Andean world beginning with the Cajamarca episode. One must understand this authoritarian and dogmatic relationship and the pattern of sociocultural behavior that continues to influence the most basic aspects of Andean life to this day.

The chaplain does not seem to be especially worried about being understood or not but above all wants to exercise his authority as a representative of God and the King (evangelization and conquest were interchangeable terms), both incarnate at that moment in the sacred text, be it Bible or breviary. Ironically, but inevitably, one must note that Valverde would have found no humor in Atahuallpa's actually reading the Bible. The spiritual climate of the times, full of mistrust generated by the Counter-Reformation's stance on the reading of sacred texts, guarantees that the book given to the Inca was not really a text but an object of reverence and adoration: a sacred object.

In addition, and omitting the fact that the book was written in Latin, the overlooked but important reality is that not only was the Inca illiterate, but almost none of the Spaniards who captured him, beginning with Pizarro, could have read it even in Spanish, although clearly this is a question of two different types of illiteracy: one of "primary orality," while experiencing a globally agraphic culture, and the other relative to ideological mechanisms that distanced writing from individuals and social groups not belonging to a lettered culture, as this prestige was enjoyed almost exclusively by its upper crust.[49]

The crux of the matter lies in the conflict between an oral culture and a written one that has biased the written word toward the sacred and overburdened it with more esoteric than symbolic dimensions to the point of splitting off writing from the system of communication. This estrangement implies the idea of the book as fetish and harks back to primitive historical experiences, which we can still recognize in some etymologies that associate the written word with magic, at the same time invalidating another secular, humanistic tradition that makes the book (like the classic "book of nature") into an object of and for human knowledge.[50] What happened at Cajamarca is a power ritual, mediated and constituted by the book: its "dialogue" would have functioned only in terms of order and submission. In November of 1532 this "dialogue" did not come about, and the rupture, because of the Inca's "disobedience," took on tragic dimensions: he who refuses to respond with the sole word to which he has a right (the perverse right to say only "yes") should and must die. And in effect, shortly thereafter the Inca is murdered.

Essentially then, writing appeared in the Andes not so much as a system of communication as a symbol of order and authority, as if its only possible meaning were *power*.[51] The physical book is much more fetish than text and much more an expression of domination than an act of language. As such, it leaves out indigenous orality, the orphan of a materiality that could roundly confirm its own truth, the diluted voices that memory gathers up with no real interest, almost contemptuously. In other words, the written word's initial triumph is, in the Andes, the voice's first defeat.[52]

Here one must remember that the early indigenous consciousness bestowed upon the conquistadors a divine nature (*viracocha*),[53] not only because their presence evoked myths that spoke of ancient gods returning by sea, but also because the conquistador was made into a strange and powerful being by a combination of traits and behaviors, among them his mysterious ability to communicate through inanimate objects such as the oft-cited "white cloths." Titu Cussi, in his 1570 *Ynstruçion*, puts the inventory of the marvels that transform the conquistador into viracocha in the mouths of the messengers that take the news of the Spaniards' arrival to Atahuallpa and later repeat it to Manco Inca in Cusco. With respect to writing the messengers say, "And also they called them that [viracochas] because they had seen them speaking alone with some white cloths as one person to another and this was called reading books and letters . . . and we have even seen them with our own eyes speaking alone with white cloths and name some of us by our own names without saying it to anyone, just by looking at the cloth in their hands."[54] Guaman Poma synthesizes this idea saying, "[The Spaniards inspired awe among the Indians because] all day and all night [they] talked to their books and papers, which were called *quilca*."[55]

Predictably, this deceit would not last long, as Titu Cussi himself noted; nevertheless writing remained vigorously joined to the idea of power.[56] And it is through the power of the written word that the chronicles would fashion the image of Cajamarca, a true "primordial scene," according to Max Hernández, of the Andean culture and people.[57] Soon thereafter part of the Cusco nobility and some of the chiefs of other ethnic groups would also begin to make use of the strength of the written word in various ways: to defend their rights in long accounts to colonial authorities or the King himself, to record what needed to be remembered, or to reshape their identity in the mirror of a writing in which they began to recognize their new condition.[58] Titu Cussi dictates his *Ynstruçion* and has it written out "because man's memory is thin and weak and if we did not turn to letters *in order to avail ourselves of them in our time of need*, it was impossible to be able to ever remember all our long and important dealings."[59] From this appropriation (or expropriation) of the written word would arise noteworthy texts from that of Guaman Poma, as laborious in his Spanish as in the difficult utopia he proclaims, to Garcilaso Inca's, no less strained in its wish to bring together in harmony a history torn asunder.[60] There arises, above all, a new, writing subject, capable of using the written word in Spanish or Quechua, whose very presence, though intermittent and subordinated, substantially alters the order and limits of the lettered space of the Andean nations.[61]

RITUALS OF OTHER MEMORIES

The catastrophe of Cajamarca forever marked the memory of the Indian peoples and remained emblematized in the death of Atahuallpa: act and symbol of the destruction of not only an empire but a world, although this was understood on a social level only with the passage of time. In fact at first, in addition to their deification of the invaders, the residents of Cusco thought the Spaniards to be the restorers of their supremacy, which had been threatened by Atahuallpa's order to have Huascar executed. In the meantime, other Andean ethnic groups established alliances with the conquistadors in order to free themselves from the recent expansion of the Inca Empire and return to their status prior to their incorporation into the Tawantinsuyu. Only when the true nature of the conquest is uncovered and the macroethnic image of what is "Indian" is constructed does Atahuallpa's death acquire, even to this day, a sense of pan-Andean tragedy.[62] Fittingly, Hernández defined the events at Cajamarca as "our primordial scene."[63]

The account given by the chronicles is determined as much by its adherence to the historical genre in its most Western, in this case Spanish, form (whose norms and conventions mestizo and indigenous authors try to follow with surprising and revealing results) as by its narrative and written state. On different levels, history and written narrative follow an obligatory, linear, and finite order that parcels and serializes the event, makes each of its instances irreversible, and establishes a fixed ending. In effect, although even etymologically the chronicles allude to time, this is a time frozen both in the past and in the discourse that evokes it, with a beginning and end marked by the finite nature of written narration.[64] A chronicle can be read in many ways, each time revealing new and contradictory meanings, as proven by the subtle hermeneutic interpretations drawn from the *Royal Commentaries* or the *Nueva crónica*, but it is impossible to add new events or modify its empirical contents. Its end point is also the end time, the expiration of the alliance between writing and history.

In this sense, the story of Cajamarca can only conclude with Atahuallpa's execution, understood in the only way that *this* history permits: as a fact taking place at a determined time, and quite immutable. But on the fringes of this discourse or outside its bounds there are other, contradictory versions, all of which show the cultural variety of possible historical consciousnesses or the many ways that the different social-ethnic subjects have of remembering what happened and conferring upon it reality and legitimacy by simply remembering it. We are speaking here of versions that, in addition, are not expressed through written narration but rather in ritual dances or representations that somewhat abusively tend to be called "theatrical."

Manuel Burga has studied the conversion of *taquis* such as the *comparsa* (a choral drama) of the Inca/Captain into dances that, representing in ritual what happened at Cajamarca, express the ill will between Indians and Spaniards (or later, ordinary Indians and *mistis*) and the inversion of roles that originally had ceded greater esteem to the Inca and later tended to highlight the power of the Captain, Pizarro. This in turn is related to the resolution—or not—of the contradictions specific to each town where these dances are performed as part of collective celebrations lasting several days and coinciding with each Andean community, village, or city's annual patron saint festivities. In some towns these contradictions seem to have been resolved under the questionable symbolic syncretism of the national flag.[65]

I have neither the capacity nor sufficient information to analyze dance as a discourse having precise meaning, but certain points cannot be ignored. The memory that underlies the comparsa of the Inca/Captain produces something akin to a "cliffhanger," as the account concludes before the death of the Inca, which not only makes the episode less tragic and reaffirms the festive spirit of the celebration but—and above all—opens up the possibility that the story could end in different ways.[66] In fact, as documented by Burga himself, the dance normally concludes with the Inca's capture. But an inverse denouement is also possible: either the Inca captures the Captain or both of them are taken prisoner by the opposition forces.[67] There are several testimonials to the latter denouement, but the best known recalls that the famous outlaw, Luis Pardo, enjoyed impersonating the Inca, in which case it supposedly was he who defeated the Captain and finally took him prisoner.[68] Nevertheless, the peculiar connotations of this case should remind us that even with much less famous personages it was and continues to be possible that, on any given occasion, it may be the Inca who overcomes Pizarro.[69] This was surely the custom when the surviving indigenous aristocracy oversaw such festivals.

The comparsa of the Inca/Captain tells then, *another* story, not only because it frames it differently by obviating (exorcising?) the Inca's death, nor because it modifies or has the power to modify the action, but rather—and fundamentally—because it does not speak about unique, definitive events with a single voice, nor does it cancel them out as part of a chronology that grows shorter and shorter. As expressed in the collective dance, the story stays open and therefore can lead, quite legitimately, to several possible denouements. In fact, as ritual, the choral drama does not so much evoke the story as renew it symbolically, and upon "repeating" it in an ever-changing present, it neither prefigures nor ordains an outcome. In a certain sense anything is possible—except forgetting the cyclical celebration of the ritual that actualizes over and over again the confrontation at Cajamarca. The historical narration of the chronicles seems to become lost in the movements of the dance and the collective festival in which it is inscribed, as if it were dissolved in another kind of matter (not in writing but in the sway of bodies) and another space (not the private one of writing-reading but the public one, out in the streets and plazas). Under these conditions and, of course, coming from a different cultural rationality, the linearity, parceling, and finitude of Western written history makes little sense. The story that the choral drama tells does not falsify this history: it puts in its place another that has its own legitimacy and its own distinctive formal conditioners. In short, writing history is not the same as dancing it.

Unfortunately Burga does not transcribe the words of the songs that make up this ritual, although one must recognize that here words have a somewhat accessory value. But there are "theatrical" texts that incorporate segments of the taqui or in some way are parallel to the meaning of the Inca/Captain dance and serve to complement and transform it. These texts deserve greater attention than we literary scholars have given them. The following pages are devoted to them.

It would be wise to first offer some general information about these texts. In the mid-1900s various specialists in Quechua literature released manuscripts that contained "dramatic" texts concerning the death of Atahuallpa, but about which there was only old and unclear data. Shortly thereafter several anthropologists presented studies of contemporary "stagings" of these works in numerous Andean towns and cities and in some cases (just a few compared to the number of papers on this topic) transcribed the manuscripts on which this long, collective, highly ritualized festival is based. In the following, I shall treat this significant, but limited corpus.[70] In several cases the texts are not very trustworthy: the transcriptions are often done without much fidelity or care, and all are based on very late manuscripts, some of which are damaged.

I shall not attempt to resolve the problem of the chronology of these texts, which should be left to the best specialists in the field, but note that they have been performed (with many variations) for centuries, although the oldest manuscripts date from the second half of the nineteenth century. Most scholars of Quechua literature point to 1555 as a starting date, based on the information given by Bartolomé Arzanz in his *Historia de la villa imperial de Potosí*, in which he tells that in that year and in that city great festivals were carried out, including the presentation of four Spanish works and some indigenous ones, the last of which was probably titled *Ruina del Imperio Ingal*. Its subject matter is "the entry of the Spaniards, their unjust imprisonment of Atahuallpa, Thirteenth Inca of this Monarchy; the omens and remarkable signs that were seen in the Sky and Heavens before they took his life; tyrannies and shame perpetrated by the Spaniards on the Indians; the enormous quantity of gold and silver he offered in exchange for his life; and his death by their hand in Cajamarca."[71]

This description applies quite well to texts in Quechua and/or Spanish that exist (under different titles) to this day, all on the theme of Atahuallpa's death, but the date (1555) seems to be too early.[72] Burga opines that the first representations of the Inca's death date from the end of the seventeenth century or the beginning of the eighteenth.[73] In any case, what is important here is not a precise date of origin but how long this *wanka* (translated by Jesús Lara as "tragedy") has been represented, making it our most ancient Andean text.[74] Its uninterrupted social and literary life continues to this day.[75]

It is unclear, however, if the texts that have survived truly have this origin and are thereby associated with the pre-Hispanic representations about which Garcilaso and other chroniclers speak;[76] if they are tied to catechizing and thus to the *autos sacramentales*;[77] or if they reformulate, with Andean subject matter, the Moorish-Christian choral dramas whose dispersion in the New World is widely known.[78] It is very probable that they treat the ritual or festive confrontations between Indians and Indians dressed as Spaniards as documented by Burga around 1660 as well as the ancient choral dramas of the Inca/Captain noted above.[79] Without rejecting any of these possibilities, I choose to read these texts as discourses belonging to several, conflictive subjects, within a process whose most recent chapters do not invalidate those that came before.

Consulting many known texts for his latest research on this topic led Teodoro Meneses to distinguish between a "theatrical cycle" (which he associated with the tradition of the acculturated and secularized *autos sacramentales* of the "colonial Quechua theater") and a "folkloric" cycle.[80] But upon consideration of essentially the same corpus, Meneses reached the conclusion that the differences among the texts do not derive from their belonging to different cycles, but rather from the variable social use that each version has enjoyed (despite the fact that the Chayanta manuscript discovered by Lara seems to differ in part from other known texts in this respect).[81] Obviously until serious philological work is done to establish at least an approximate image of what classical philology called the *stemma* and its range of variants, only modest and unverifiable generalizations can be made in this area. One would also need to become familiar with texts that cultured Bolivian writers might have written in Quechua on the same topic, as well as any translation to this language that would have made a Spanish drama widely known in the Andean region.[82]

What does indeed seem likely is that these texts contain certain elements rooted in orality as well as others that would be impossible outside the framework of writing. I believe there is sufficient evidence that these dramatic discourses were written during a period in which writing had not completely displaced the norms of oral expression. One might even suppose that certain portions come directly from oral sources, since they invariably incorporate ancient dances and songs. Just a few examples would be the formulistic and repetitive style of speeches 2 through 33 in Meneses' version,[83] the laments of the coyas and pallas in this and other manuscripts, and the war chants and dances that probably formed part of the action "*en scène*."[84] In this case this wanka would not have the scripted characteristics of the corpus known as "colonial Quechua theater" and would be more strongly Andean and less trans- or acculturated, which would not exclude the possibility that at times other social subjects would have left their mark on these texts.[85] It is clear, moreover, that these representations, although "theatrical," have not cut their ties with ritual.

To complicate things further, I suspect that each version contains its own distinctive *archeology*, as if it were accumulating formal and meaningful strata that correspond to its spatial-temporal actualizations that naturally have social and ethnic content. As proof I offer the Oruro version retrieved by Hernando Balmori, where there are evidently fragments so old as to be considered formulistic, but also others that are very modern.[86] The parody inherent in some segments is undeniable in the half-mocking, half-fearful mimicry of the behavior, language, and "rituals" of an army well known by the spectators (the 1940s Oruro version) to put down popular uprisings, especially among peasants and miners. "General" Pizarro's orders always follow the formulae of the military manuals of the time: "Men, fall in; right shoulder, arms; forward, march. Men, present arms."[87] In this context the repeated mention of the Inca being "shot" by the Spaniards is totally believable, as are other brusquely interpolated sections that derive almost word-for-word from history texts used in elementary and secondary schools.[88]

In a certain sense literary history here does not so much tack one text onto another as condense itself in each text in the form of partially superimposed strata. I sense that the order of this process, which in the end explains what is repeated and what changes, is based on the expectations, needs, and interests of those who watch or participate (and all do) in a representation that is never just theatrical, even when the performance is undertaken by specialized groups or when professors, students, or neighbors with varying degrees of education are in charge of the script or direction.[89]

I believe that the reading of each version of the wanka creates a sort of text map, establishing both the various areas in which social subjects of differing backgrounds act and, within those areas, the interference of other subjects that have left their mark on the stratification of meaning. This is not unique to our case, but here the conflicts are much more acute: the worldview and languages that dispute textual space come from different cultures and can represent brutally conflicting social interests. This would map, then, plans for a battle in which each subject wins or loses dimensions of the text, and that reproduces the confrontation that the very text represents dramatically. Frequently this reproduction has a denouement that runs counter to historical experience: the majority of the versions of the Inca's death, at least as they have come to us, show a relative hegemony of indigenous consciousness and contain with greater or less clarity its strategies of resistance and recovery. Comparing these texts with their Mexican and Guatemalan counterparts, Nathan Wachtel shows that Andeans stand firm in their disconnect between what is indigenous and what is Spanish, contrary to the union that characterizes the others; this underscores their messianic dimensions.[90]

The multiplicity of subjects that compete in the text is only partially constrained by the fact that the conservation (and modification) of the manuscripts is bound to the traditions of each community, where there are people charged with their care and the preparation of their periodic and celebratory mise-en-scènes.[91] In recent decades, however, it has become more common for groups of "professionals" or prestigious "actors" to perform in various locations, which favors rapid changes in local versions. It is also possible that there have been varying degrees of interference from the powers that be, presumably uncomfortable with certain aspects of the performance. Nevertheless, in the corpus in question the fundamental initiative remains in the hands of the ethnically and socially subordinated strata.

It is enlightening that in the version retrieved by Meneses, Atahuallpa's death sentence (which recalls the Andean version where the Inca is beheaded) appears in the explicitly grotesque speech of an eccentric "preacher priest":

> Persignum asignatis incuentatis in nomine toti veritates es tempus brujabil non tentatis. It is doctrine for that reverend Father brother "shaved-head" that in his rules and antiphons he wrote the rules for castrating monkeys, according to several true authors; how ugly to see a woman with emanations. (1) By order of the Governor don Francisco Pizarro the king Atahualpa Inca of Peru is to be beheaded. (2) As well for having usurped the kingdom from his half-brother and legitimate heir Huascar. (3) As well for having cast on the ground the book of the holy gospels, as ordained by god's law ... (7) Reverend Father it is beautiful when the carnation touches the innocent butterfly mother Eve was in the garden and it was over and done, I beg pardon from my hearers for my errors and my poor explanations that leads me to coarseness, I beseech my hearers and the innocent butterfly.[92]

The radical incongruity of this speech underscores the absurd nature of Spanish "justice." This segment breaks abruptly with the norms of the rest of the text, and there is every reason to believe that it is an interpolation. However, I believe that the speech's meaning has little to do with disrespect to the original text, and everything to do with the expectations of a social subject needing evidence that the Inca was condemned without reason or justice. The expectations are stronger here because this version offers a diminished image of a maddeningly passive, groaning Atahuallpa, demanding compensation.

It appears that it is a copyist (or "actor" whose irreverent recitation is later incorporated into the text) who cannot accept this image of the Inca and counterbalances it with a grotesque configuration of the one condemning him has inserted this delirious segment. This does not necessarily imply a conscious and deliberate process, but rather a rupture in meaning by way of a discourse that, despite its farcical nature, succeeds in repairing a great deal of the semantic inner workings of this version. It also implies that at one point the text expressed themes and expectations of other groups, perhaps especially the evangelizers, which are subverted by the carnivalesque outburst of the "preacher priest."

In addition, although there are no stage directions to this effect, there is every indication that Atahuallpa's death sentence is a written text read by the preacher, which makes it possible that his burlesque lines were to be interpreted as placing what is *written* within an *oral* framework that subverts its meaning and, in the end, the writing itself. Its wild disorder, its coarseness, its daring allusions to the body and sex, and its religious irreverence are all equally festive and critical signs of the best carnivalesque tradition that ridicules what the written text says and breaks down the rational, closed order of the written word.[93] While writing speaks here of death, the orality that surrounds it recovers the primary instincts of life. There are no testimonies to the performance of this speech, but the fact that it survives in a late manuscript seems to indicate that it enjoyed social acceptance.

Something similar could be said of the final scene in which the King of Spain (sometimes written "Ispaña") condemns Pizarro to death for having executed a virtuous sovereign.[94] In a different way, this scene speaks to the interests of several users of the text: from the indigenous masses that wanted the guilty party condemned and the heterogeneous sector that argued over the legitimacy of the conquest to certain Spanish groups tied to the interests of the Crown and in conflict with the first conquistadors and their descendants, who needed to discredit the "feat" of Cajamarca and realized what the scandal of regicide meant, above all when Garcilaso's image of the Inca as a paternal sovereign had permeated many consciences.[95] The reader will note that the mere mention of these hypotheses puts into play various times and worldviews that are linked and mixed in a single version.

Following are several fragments showing the intervention by the "King of Spain" from Lara's manuscript:

Oh, Pizarro, Pizarro,
what an abject traitor you are!
Heart born for pillage!
Why did you cut off

the head of this Inca?
Did you not see
that in his country he governed
his innumerable subjects
in the midst of good fortune and happiness
with his ever gracious word?
Did you not hear
His ever peaceful voice?
It was like a song of happiness.
    [Pizarro dies]
Take him then.
Go and deliver him to the fire and may
all his descendants perish with him.
And order his house destroyed.
Of this infamous warrior
nothing should remain.
This is as I command it.[96]

From a different point of view, the scene in which Pizarro is sentenced to death by his king recalls the mindset of the chiefs who, like Guaman Poma de Ayala, accepted the substitution of the Inca by the King as the governing axis of the world and arbiter of justice in a new world order, while not imagining that this apex of power would interfere with the Andean social hierarchy. This remittance to "Ispaña" for the justice that restores the moral balance of the world is imaginable only from a perspective that assumes the cosmic refounding or historical-political cosmology best expressed in the *Nueva crónica*. How is it possible to shift the burden of indispensable justice to the metropolitan power if there is no underlying, difficult compromise between the acceptance of colonial reality and the stubborn desire for autonomy? This is why I think that certain parts of the wanka concerning Atahuallpa's death have roots in the time when Guaman Poma imagined his utopia.[97]

Other less compelling denouements of the tragedy reveal more generic social expectations, such as the promise of a permanent remembrance of the Inca or the announcement that precious metals would be "hidden" in the hills so that the Spaniards would either not find them or suffer in their quest, seem to correspond to an extended pan-Andean consciousness.[98] In the Oruro version Balmori noted a brief reference to the resurrection of the Inca in the song of a ñusta: "Eternal Lord, surely come, and the young powerful Inca, bring him back to life."[99] According to the author (who takes Vellard as his source) these mythical contents are central to the version performed around 1940 in La Paz. Here the final scene was "a true Epiphany which included an epilogue of the Resurrection and Triumph of Atahualpa,"[100] which harks back to the myth of Inkarri.[101] Wachtel believes that parts of these works are messianic in nature.[102]

Especially interesting is the version Wilfredo Kapsoli retrieved in Pomabamba, where the ceremony is heavily dominated by the misti sector. The landowners play the role of elegantly dressed conquistadors, and the Indians make up Atahuallpa's armies. The text is similar to the others but differs from them in its insistent praise of the Spaniards' valor and generosity (in baptizing the Inca and saving him from Hell), in its incongruity in representing Atahuallpa's inner character (which goes from ordering the Spaniards to worship the Sun one moment to asking to be baptized the next), and in a few significant details (for example, Atahuallpa sins by throwing down not only the Bible, but, in another scene, the crucifix as well). All of this leads to an exemplary denouement. Valverde, who seems to be speaking more to the audience than to the actors, says, "Stop, infidels! Hear the voice of Heaven through my mouth; do not mourn your King, may his death abjure his sin. As consolation he was given the water of holy baptism that redeems his error. Infidels, imitate this example!"[103]

But in this same representation there is a final episode, not mentioned in the text because it is only mimed: Quispicondor, whose costume and actions imitate the aspect and movements of this bird of prey, devours the entrails of the dead Inca and, according to the text cited by Kapsoli, causes "hilarity among the spectators."[104] I have no answer for the many hard questions that arise from this episode. Is being devoured by the condor hyperbole for punishment ("devoured by vultures") or rather a sign of victorious and hopeful transfiguration (from Inca to condor)? And is the spectators' laughter mocking the defeated Inca or jeering the mistis who err in thinking him dead?[105]

It is notable that among all these texts that point to oral and public representation, there is none without a written "script," even if, as Juan Zevallos affirms, in the communities of Cajatambo the written anchor is contingent and invisible. Here the senior members of the audience, without looking at anything written, correct the mistakes that the "actors" make, and the whole audience protests angrily when there is a deviation from the hallowed model, so that the whole performance has to be stopped and the action retraced until it takes its original shape, according to the demands of the old folks' implacable memory. This is a case in which oral memory has an extraordinary function, but it makes one think that there was an original text, similar to those preserved in other communities and used "for rehearsal only."

One might ask where and how memory works to guarantee the secular survival of the wanka about Atahuallpa's death. Considering that some modern manuscripts contain altered and seemingly meaningless versions, one might be tempted to think that in the Andean world oral memory, which protests when it goes unrecognized in the performance, is much more faithful than the memory of the written word, all of which goes back to the agraphic nature of the Quechua culture.[106] But for me this matter is even more complex.

As they have come to us, these texts carry with them very clear indications of their oral roots, as one can see in the solid survival of formulistic style and most of the characteristics of Walter Ong's "psychodynamics of orality."[107] This has to do with the fact that we are dealing with "theatrical" representations, that is, discourses that, even if they have a text, are actualized in pure orality. Whatever the function of orality, the fact is that the wanka has had for a long time (in my opinion, since its origins) a written materiality, but written within the tradition of an oral culture that contributes specific attributes of composition permeated with orality. Although comparisons can be dangerous, Paul Zumthor's thesis concerning the long coexistence of voice and written word in medieval Europe, with the open or underground preeminence of the former even over texts in book form, could explain many of the problems presented by texts and representations concerning the death of Atahuallpa.[108]

From this perspective, the "rehearser" might be the hinge between writing and orality and the cultural entity that makes their difficult coexistence possible, even in our day. I imagine the "rehearser" as a variant of the interpreter appearing in the chronicles, capable of transferring meaning between two languages. In this case, however, the importance of bilingualism is somewhat blurred by the exigencies of converting the written word into orality, which is especially demanding when the "actors" and a majority of the audience are illiterate. It is impossible to know for sure to what degree the "rehearser" respects the text and what capacity for memorization the "actors" have, but clearly this key person preserves the text that serves as the basis for the rehearsals and at any time may be charged with copying it. It is probable that on these occasions there are voluntary changes, or other modifications springing from the inattention or the precarious literacy of the copyist.[109] In this sense, one might think of writing as the open weave of discourse, preserving it for posterity but at the same time allowing seemingly contradictory modernizations (the language of school books or military manuals, as in the Oruro example) and eventual or definitive losses of its linguistic meaning (as in the versions retrieved by Roger Ravines, Mily Olguín, and Francisco Iriarte).

The fact that the most recent copies show a great degree of deterioration could be interpreted in two different ways. On one hand one might think that the representations are slowly losing their collective meaning and instilling less commitment in the community, which is what Ravines suggests when he notes with respect to the manuscript retrieved in Llamellín that nowadays some "actors repeat [their speeches] without actually understanding them."[110] On the other hand one could also consider a rearchaizing process of disjoining the precise linguistic meanings of the more generic ritual meaning from the action being represented. If this hypothesis, which I take up below, is true, those participating in the performance would understand the global significance of the action more than the exact meaning of the text. This matter needs more study, but clearly similar problems present themselves when the texts are bilingual and some or all of the audience is monolingual in Quechua, which at times is the present case and was probably the norm in the past. Under these circumstances meaning is more bound up in the action — and in what it symbolizes globally — than in language. Let us not forget that we are speaking here of "theatrical" texts and that in them meaning is always found beyond mere words.

This textual deterioration, in Quechua as well as Spanish, deserves a much more detailed analysis than I am able to undertake. There are, however, several key points to be noted. In the texts' chain of written transmission, gradual and cumulative omissions and transformations must have occurred, in addition to breaks that have substantially altered the discourse. Also, there is no reason to believe that the language of the hypothetical original texts was particularly meticulous. As for the fragments in Spanish, there is a clear and definite interference from Quechua, but also a mixture of cultured and archaic Spanish with more popular and contemporary language, where there is an attitude of respect for the former, but at the same time a marked ignorance of its norms.[111] I cite as an example Pizarro's speech in the Llamellín version: "Valerosos adelides hijos de un beneble marte cuyo pedio generoso pueblan en aquesus manes al arma al arma tocad caja guierra, guera contra el ynfiel munarca matad todos estos canalla leones y ferones."[112]

One should also remember the texts studied by José Luis Rivarola, one from the end of the sixteenth century and another from the second half of the seventeenth, both written in precarious, "motoso" Spanish by high-ranking Indians.[113] Here the broad interference from Quechua hinders, but does not impede, their comprehension ("este su serbidures le desea en puena compañía de ysa mes señoras"), while Pizarro's speech is much more obscure, and at times unintelligible, as are—to the point of being completely indecipherable—many other fragments of similar origin. It is reasonable to assume that the difference comes from the fact that the former are originals whose errors are their authors,' while the latter are the result of a long chain of copyists accumulating poor transcriptions of a text written in obsolete Spanish. In the end it appears to be the work of someone who is barely familiar with the language of the text he is reproducing (*guierra*/*guera*), and it is even possible—exaggerating just a bit—that his activity is more one of drawing signs than writing letters. In any case, one might imagine a copyist with a minimum of formal education who nonetheless takes on the task of transcribing a text that contains affectations (adelides = adalides) and archaisms (aquesus = aquesas) that he does not pretend to understand. The act of copying a text that for the copyist himself is largely unintelligible complies with a long-standing ritual that, on one hand, has to do with the veneration of power and prestige of the written word and, on the other, the collective need to preserve a text whose representation is part of the symbolic-imaginary life of the community. It is shocking to think that this ritualism, which is essential for community cohesion, is at the same time an (almost) indecipherable message.

As I imply above, these texts continue to be represented and accepted by social groups seemingly capable of transcending their linguistic opaqueness in order to find a passionately ritualized, symbolic meaning beyond the words. In more than one sense these texts straddle the ambiguous and conflictive space between Quechua and Spanish and between orality and writing. While residing at the intersection of two histories and two cultures, these texts also reveal that the written word (although still largely mysterious) has imposed itself ever so slightly over voice, but at the cost of being transformed almost to the point of unintelligibility. Since in the end these representations are realized in and through the spoken word, the almost magical attachment to the graphics of lettered people could well be a sign of a captive (and captivated) imaginary but also—and paradoxically—a gesture of resistance and recovery: the written word may say little or nothing, but through it one can hear a voice, one's own, reverberating as if in the town square. Above I suggested that, hypothetically, this could be a rearchaizing process. It is possible to reaffirm that the recitation of now unintelligible texts is actually a ritual action that goes back to a time when writing was not indispensable, and that, in the very production of the wanka, the weight of the written word has profoundly disturbed the dynamics of the original orality. I might have been tempted to propose the idea that this writing, isolated here like an archipelago of sounds, has a mysterious relationship with pre-Hispanic indigenous "writing": colors and knots whose meaning is tied to the separation, the void, between one and the other.

It is noteworthy that the most modern text, the only one dated and showing the author's name, is presented with the help of a "commentator" who not only "narrates the events in a colorful manner but whose account is put forth as the plot thread" of the drama.[114] The prestige and importance of the commentator in this later version, together with the fact that his account is not set down in the dramatic text, could make one think that this unwritten voice was also at work in earlier versions, serving to clarify and make up for the obscurity of what was happening "en scène." In any case, it is curious that a "commentator" appears in a representation whose text offers no great problems in linguistic comprehension.

In these representations, then, orality and writing seem to have both competitive and complementary functions and should be judged not so much for the fidelity with which they reproduce certain models but rather for their urgency in symbolizing contents of multiple and changing collective worldviews that recognize that the death of Atahuallpa tells a very long story (implied metaphorically and metonymically) and is not an event frozen in a distant past. That story is *their* story. This is a complex process of inserting profound and multiple meanings into a historic event: the death of the Inca encapsulates the global experience of the Andean people. Assuming the imperatives of the Quechua worldview or its subsets and with respect to events that did not stop with Cajamarca, the wanka of Atahuallpa's death has a definitely historical dimension. Unlike the Western "historical drama" that exhausts itself in the staged repetition of uplifting or moralizing events, it serves as a paradigmatic configuration that takes on new tragic situations—and new expectations of justice—as if the fixed, determined event had been transformed into a fluid, porous, and continually renewed sign. In one sense the fidelity of the wanka has to do—through the story of Atahuallpa's death—with the whole story of the Quechua people.[115] Hence the power of its longevity throughout the centuries.

I must clarify that this in no way means that these texts and their representations are mere contingencies to these worldviews. There is, as we have seen, a social force that demands respect for the tradition assumed to be legitimate, which has everything to do with textual fidelity. This force is not sufficient, however, to preserve as inalterable either the writing or the representations of the wanka. With some extrapolation one could use a speech by Soto in the Llamellín version to confirm this. Turning to the Inca (although the statement is meant for Felipillo), the conquistador warns him, "no altirsis el descorso," a bungled sentence (a possible reading of which might be "do not change the discourse"), but emblematic.[116] This might be deconstructed somewhat imaginatively in order to underscore that *descorso/discurso* seems to allude to both language and the passage of time, and in this case the demand is to not alter either history or the discourse that recounts it. At the same time, the very statement demands a fidelity that it unwittingly damages: *altirisis/alteréis*. In the end nevertheless, there is no contradiction: history remains faithfully unaltered, but rather than a history frozen in its tracks, it bubbles effervescently. From this perspective it is true that the Inca was garroted, beheaded, run through with Pizarro's sword, shot, and drowned, and that his entrails were devoured by a condor. His many deaths are historical because in the wanka Atahuallpa is also a whole people (with its infinite deaths and its complex mechanisms of imagination and memory). Placed between voice and written word, the wanka cannot "suspend" the death of the Inca as a dance might, but neither can it configure it as a unique, definitive act as the chronicles do. He dies, to be sure, but time and time again, in a demise so prolonged (in César Vallejo's words, "But the corpse, alas! kept on dying") that it holds within itself five centuries of a whole people's oppression.[117] In fact the death of Atahuallpa moves from being an action to taking on flesh as a sign.

We are dealing then with both a symbolic space charged with drama not only because of its subject matter, an emblem of immeasurable suffering and certain vindication, and, at the same time, the extreme tension that exists between repetition and change. This is the crux of all history, to be sure, but it is especially volatile in Andean consciousness and language. Naturally, and the wanka is also exemplary here, this tension inserts itself into the greater conflict of the colony (and its aftermath), made up of intersecting identities and alterities (changing signs according to individual perspective) that ever since have been obliged to coexist and fight, ceaselessly attracted and repelled, in the Andean space. So then the wanka is an incomparable testimony to the avatars of a dialogue that proves its impossibility at the same time that it is realized. As we shall see, the representation of noncommunication is in an oblique way an act of communication, but one that is incomprehensible outside either a historical process that comprises different temporalities, each with its own rhythm, or the ambience of a radical social-cultural heterogeneity that embraces the torn, yet fertile, ebulliently protean state of its intermixed subjects.

A PERHAPS IMPOSSIBLE READING

The chronicles place the sacred book of the West, the Bible, at the center of the events of 1532. As we have said, this book becomes charged with religious and political motives, because Father Valverde interprets the text, creating a single discourse of imperial power. The Andean representations of the Inca's death, on the other hand, allude to two texts: the religious one spoken of in the chronicles and, more strongly, a "letter" from the King or Pizarro to Atahuallpa. This second text, which includes religious language, receives more attention than the first. We are dealing here with a discourse whose primary meaning is power, as is obvious in Balmori's version, which first calls it a "letter," then a "commission," and finally what it really is: an "order."[118]

The letter evokes the first encounters between Indians and Spaniards previous to Cajamarca, but it is significant that the orality of the former is transmuted—in the memory expressed in the wanka—into writing. One can imagine that this transformation corresponds to the ambiguous fascination that the Quechua culture felt toward the written word, immediately incorporated into a mysterious and powerful order capable of turning the natural order on its head. In more than one version, and especially Lara's, the impossibility of deciphering writing is associated with the conviction that the foretelling of the empire's destruction is about to be fulfilled. As paradoxical as it is dramatic, then, the written word (or rather the silence of the written word) becomes inscrutable in its intentions. So it is in the following speech:

> SAIRI TUPAC: Waylla Wisa, lord who sleeps,
> what a white *chala* that is.
> Give it to me, perhaps I can
> divine its warning.
> No; I cannot come to understand
> what it means.
> It can say nothing good.
> In my dreams I have seen Tukuy Jall'pa
> And have heard from her lips that she loves
> those bearded enemies.[119]

Or more clearly still:

> KHISHKIS: Waylla Wisa, sorcerer,
> How can we interpret
> this impenetrable thing shown us.
> But perhaps, if our Mother Moon
> shone on me, I would come
> to comprehend what this *chala* enfolds.
> I already knew that the enemies
> were to come.
> For more than four months now
> our Mother Moon, in my dreams,
> three times over told me
> that our lord's existence
> was close to its end,
> that it would soon be concluded.
> I no longer have need to see this *chala*.
> My whole being is crushed
> and my heart destroyed.
> Affliction already falls upon us,
> our day of misfortune has arrived.[120]

There are less dramatic indications of this fascination with writing. Frequently, an obviously oral message is dressed in the most codified rhetoric of official writing. In Balmori's version Almagro states that he must speak with the Inca because he is carrying a message from the king saying, "I come with this order from my illustrious king of Spain: if this order is not obeyed we shall take the king's head or his crown. *God save Y[our] H[ighness]*."[121]

This text recalls the recourse to writing and reading in the "writs" that Herod sends to his sages and those he receives from them and from the Magi in the *auto* entitled *La adoración de los Reyes Magos*, originally performed in Cusco and recently published by Margot Beyersdorff.[122] But indicated above all is the fact that written language is associated firmly, immediately, and consistently with power: although indecipherable, or precisely because it is just that, it contains threats of destruction that will surely be carried out. In addition, written codes begin to interfere with those of orality and even imitate them in a sort of metaphor for the absolute sway that the written word holds over voice. This is the conflict between orality and writing, to which the wanka is the superlative testimony: a conflict never totally resolved in performance because of the chance and circumstantial prevalence of one or the other that harks back to a single, basic text, even when it has deteriorated to the point of saying almost nothing.

The wanka gives evidence of a curious blend of two communicative technologies: the letter goes and comes among dignitaries of the Inca court by way of a perhaps unnecessary messenger. In most versions one supposes that the dignitaries form part of Atahuallpa's retinue and are close to each other, but the letter is always transported by a royal functionary or a *chasqui* whose action on stage (according to the only testimony that we have) consists of running a few steps "in a zigzag pattern, representing [a] long march of twists and turns, with a leap to the final arrival point."[123] If this distance were nonexistent both in the staged fiction and the referent to which it alludes, the chasqui's presence and action would clarify the drama of the many failures of those who try to decipher what is written. In any case, even if such blocking is justified in the performance's fictitious space, the exaggerated movements of the bearers of the text emphasize the somber need to associate the new communicative order based on writing with the old ways of the messengers, as if the "letter" had to depend in some way on those taking it from one place to another, although in the end all effort is futile and the punishment inexorable.

Additionally, there is reason to suspect that the winding paths taken by the Inca's correspondence are degraded in the late Cusco version of the *Auto de los Reyes Magos*, in which a "black" character leans over so that the owners of the written word can write the messages they are sending each other on his back.[124] The technology of writing both makes those who do not have command or understanding of it into pure physical supports in the transmission of meaning and inscribes the graphics—almost like scarification—on the bent-over back of the illiterate bearer. In the next chapter, I analyze a related "comic" version.

Even more interesting is how the Indians "read" the letter from the king or Pizarro. Of course, the point of departure is that all efforts to decipher it will be futile, but in this process one discerns the systematic, naturalizing interpretation of the West's cultural object par excellence. The paper is called *chala* and the ink "dirty water," while the graphics are almost always "translated" as signs coming from nature.[125] Several key texts follow:

> WAYLLA WISSA: Who knows what this *chala* says.
> It is possible that I'll never
> come to know.
> Seen from this side
> It is a swarm of ants.
> I look at it from this other side
> and I see footprints
> left by birds
> on the muddy banks of the river.
> Seen this way, it looks like *tarukas*
> turned up-side down
> with their feet in the air.
> And if we look at it just this way
> it's like bowed llamas
> and *taruka* horns.
> Who can understand this?
> No, no; I cannot possibly,
> my lord, comprehend it.[126]

Also:

> REY INCA: Oh, what a white *chala* this *chala* is! From here it looks like the tracks of a snake that's slipped; If you look hard, other parts are like the eyes of my *ñusta*, so round, so round; looking at it from this other

side it's like Huaylla Huisa's road, so winding, so winding; what *chala* is this that I cannot understand, that I cannot decipher!

PRIMO INCA: What *chala*, what *chala* is this? From this side it looks like a rooster's foot spread out in three points; from here it seems like the round, round box of Huaylla Huisa; from this other side they look like a hill of black ants. With what black water is this *chala* sprinkled, that it cannot be understood, that it cannot be penetrated?

APU INCA: What white *chala* is this? I cannot solve it, nor in any way understand it: From here it looks like the tail of a snake that reappears; seen from here it's like little birds fighting; as if sprinkled with black water this white *chala* appears. I cannot understand it at all I cannot resolve it at all.[127]

With respect to the Gospels, the reaction is similar:

INCA: Oh Felipillo I do not understand,
and I do not know what it says, do these
little worms speak?
Here I see nothing else.[128]

The Pomabamba version is more tragic. Here his consternation clouds the Inca's thought and senses and even makes him mute, a compacted symbol of the imposition of the written word over voice:

INCA: This neither reveals nor says anything to me. These little bird scratchings and worm tracks do not inform me. My head does not understand, my eyes do not see. My ears do not hear, my tongue does not taste, my heart does not feel, my mouth does not speak.[129]

These "reading" exercises, in which graphic signs refer to shapes of the natural elements that they seem to represent, obviously have a purely fictitious dimension with respect to the moment and the events into which they are placed.[130] This creates an ambiguous space. For example, since I link it to the denouement of the story and feel the anxiety of the Inca dignitaries, my reading tends to be dramatic, while Balmori sees the long scene presenting the Indians' efforts to decipher the letter as "comic."[131] It might be part of a long tradition in which the incomprehension of a message creates comedy,[132] but in this case it seems to me that the comic effect is clouded for several reasons: first because what is undecipherable is a death threat (which will be carried out) and second because its contents are known "en scène" and by the audience through words such as those uttered by Almagro (Oruro version) and translated by the interpreter (*lengua*) into the Quechua language.

It is difficult to trace the ancestry of these fragments. In Western terms one might presuppose the existence of a written, or even a "literary" perspective, because such consistent, spirited, and imaginative translation techniques may seem unlikely among people encountering writing for the first time. Neither should we ignore the fact that even key metaphors, such as paper = chala, left no trace in either the colonial or modern Quechua lexicon. They are literary figures that function only within this textual and imaginary space. Thus one could believe that the repeated representation of indigenous incomprehension of writing might include a sense of mockery or disdain produced by a subject unsympathetic (at least in part) to the Quechua people. Even more complicating is the fact that the sarcasm toward Indian ignorance does not necessarily have to come from a Spanish point of view. *Ladinos* were very aggressive with unlettered Indians: Guaman Poma says that the Indian who does not learn to read and write in Spanish should be taken "for a barbarous animal, a horse [*cauallo*].[133] It is not impossible that this estimation may have slipped unconsciously toward the past.

The above hypothesizes that the wanka texts conceal a profound and contradictory stratification: the various voices that compete in the text and make it ambiguous establish themselves in different social, historical, and ethnic realms and sound the depth of one discourse composed of many discourses. This depth is relative to the accumulation of historical experiences and assumes as its primary condition the representation of Atahuallpa's death as a sign of centuries of oppression. In any case, the word that would mock the ineptitude of the Indians is transformed by other words that speak to the tragic, unjust destruction of their own just world order. The cries of the coyas and pallas are the best example of this other meaning, which finally acquires semantic hegemony.[134] Remember that in several versions Pizarro is condemned to death.

But the wanka includes other episodes about the deciphering of written language. In versions that repeat the account found in certain chronicles, the Indians try to "hear" (or feel) what the written word "says." It is probable that its staged or visual state determines the dramatic need to put into action and emphasize the written word's strangeness and the impossibility of translating it to an oral culture. In most cases the representation of the incompatibility of orality and writing is limited to the Inca's attempt to "hear" the book, but on certain occasions this matter takes on more complex dimensions, because either there are gestures related to more than sight and hearing or members of the imperial retinue repeat (and therefore collectivize) these gestures. Following are several examples, the most direct from Meneses, including this brief stage direction: "Then the Inca puts the letter to his ears and immediately throws it down violently."[135] Pomabamba and Llamellín extend this version: "He receives the book; then he raises it to his ear, his eyes, and his head."[136] And "The Inga takes the book, opens it, and *put it all over his body*."[137]

The Inca verbalizes this action in the Chillia version:

Speak to me now because I want
to know all secrets,
and if you do not speak to me visibly
tell me in my understanding.
It is possible that you do not want
to reveal the secrets to me;
if to my forehead you do not wish,
then speak to my ears?
you still say nothing
perhaps to my breast?
well this does not speak with me,
not to my forehead,
nor to my breast,
nor to my ears,
nor to my sight,
then this is worthless to me?[138]

In his description of the performance in Carhuamayo, Luis Millones notes that Valverde gives the Inca a bundle of papers that Atahuallpa smells, puts to his ear, tears with his teeth, and finally throws in the air. Since the stage directions in the transcribed text are very direct (the Inca "receives and examines [the book] at length and with the curiosity of his escorts, they look at each other and he passes [it] among his generals, wanting help in deciphering"), one must suppose that the notations belong to the "actor" who played the part of the Inca in the celebration studied by Millones in 1984.[139] This is most likely an indication of an *ad libitum* or a certain onstage virtuosity, which follows an already established tradition.

Just as we have seen in the Carhuamayo version, the Manás version makes the Inca's movements collective. Here Atahuallpa "puts the Book over the eyes and chests of the Sinchis and ñustas," without getting any results.[140]

I shall not go back to the discussion as to whether the indigenous "reading" is comic or dramatic, although it would be fitting to examine it here, because it underscores the radical incompatibility between orality and writing as a global framework for the representation of the events at Cajamarca. To return to Ong, oral thought is "agonistic," emphasizing the importance of bodily action.[141] From this point of view it is impressive how the cited texts (and many others) "theatricalize" the collision of the written word with orality. The "staging" of the wanka facilitates the presence of the spoken word, not only out of the obvious need to transform it all into a public voice, but also because the movements and expressions of the characters allow the representation of body language, which cannot be divorced from oral expression. In the end the body is the great signifier of orality.

Regrettably very few manuscripts annotate the physical expressions that accompany the actors' speeches. But working with Balmori's version in particular, Lore Terracini notes that if linguistic communication fails in performance ("the master feigns deafness; the oppressed is relegated to silence"), on another, nonlinguistic level "the semic act is realized as knowledge of power and praxis of violence," which results in the relegation of the vanquished to an infrahuman position.[142] Looking at the global dynamics of the representations, with their emphasis on the capture and death of the Inca, this description is on target. Nevertheless, that other language of gestures and expressions of arrogance and power appear to be shared in the wanka by both parties in conflict, and frequently by the spectators as well. In other words, if the sense of the global action places power and violence in the victors' camp, the body codes offer similar information for both conquerors and conquered, although the denouement obviously defines the triumph as being of the former on this level as well. In the end, as Terracini notes, the conquest of the Americas was a form of not only political but also semiotic aggression.[143]

In addition to body codes bearing meaning, one must consider other aspects of the performance. There is little or no scenery, but both costumes and props deserve a more detailed analysis.[144] In photographs of the Oruro performance some conquistadors are dressed as such, others wear uniforms that seem to be styled after those from the wars of independence, while still others are in modern military uniforms, all of which may be explained by the unique, cumulative sense of history that the wanka expresses. In these cases, the Inca and his imperial dignitaries wear black sunglasses, and the women cover Atahuallpa's corpse with black umbrellas or parasols. One is immediately tempted to risk a hypothesis: since dark glasses and umbrellas block or darken the sun, they could symbolize the silencing or defeat of the indigenous gods (the Sun) by the conquistadors' gods. But this is purely intuitive on my part.

In one way or another, the powers of (a mostly Quechua) voice display great vitality in the public representation of the death of the Inca, while writing is merely objectified in the silence of the letter or book and generates disruptive answers that are also on the side of orality. The performance of the wanka implies an inversion of the discursive circumstances of the chronicles, clearly inscribed in writing (except for the drawings included in some indigenous chronicles) and barely evocative of the realm of the spoken word.[145] But it also supposes a definite deviation with respect to its own written base: if its precarious conservation shows an almost religious respect for the written word (though it is distorted, being the unknown tongue of the other), voice imposes its own conditions and expands its social capacity as a call to assembly. By abandoning the private space appropriate to writing, orality claims its own terrain—the public sphere—and emits its meanings from there.

Another noteworthy case: in Lara's monolingual Quechua version, the conquistadors merely go through the motions of talking without uttering a single word, their speeches only heard through the lengua's translation.[146] This silence could certainly be interpreted as a result of the language choice of this version, which would make it impossible—and unbelievable—for the conquistadors to speak in Quechua. Nonetheless this argument is invalidated to a point by the "colonial Quechua theater," whose nonindigenous characters speak in Quechua, which opens up the possibility of another interpretation: the silencing of the Spanish voice at the moment of this great intercultural confrontation could be taken as the imaginary revenge of those who neither read nor write. The invader's voice is cut off, he becomes mute "en scène," like the correlate of the Indians' inability to read: in the imaginary of the wanka it is they, the illiterate ones, who are the only ones that speak: a belated revenge, as per the Chayanta manuscript, but a symbolically potent one.

IDENTITY, ALTERITY, HISTORY

All the above obliges one to explore the discursive circumstances and nature of the "theatrical" representations of the Inca's death and contrast them with those found in the chronicles. Although one can trace the ebb and flow of these texts, in the sense that some chronicles are sources (or well-disguised copies) of others, the chronicle is a closed discourse that refers back to the person of the author as legitimization of its meaning and truth. It is not unusual, therefore, for the chronicler to incorporate his own experience into the weave of the discourse as a way to guarantee the authenticity of what he is saying, just as it allows him to duplicate his presence and insist on his authority. In other words, chronistic discourse cannot move outside the space configured for it by its author, thus respecting the finite nature of all written expression, although various and distinct voices, including those of oral informants, may find resonance within the text. It is no coincidence, then, that there are very few anonymous chronicles and, as far as I know, none that is the collaborative effort of two or more authors.

But these texts are also confined in another, less obvious but equally significant sense: the story of what really happened (although we know that discourse never copies events) is the limit of their discourse, at times stretched to the outermost reaches of either what had to or could happen according to Holy Scripture or the Western imaginary of the time. The mermaids that Columbus saw were quite believable from this perspective, for example.[147] Moreover the most imaginative (or distorted) chronicles conform to a rigid mimetic concept, are accommodated within the space of the "reality" that they pretend to represent, and, with respect to this space (and the consciousness of their time), generate the conventions regarding what they are permitted to *say*. Or, from a different angle, their legibility is under the protection (and dominion) of their time's Western conception of history and truth. At bottom this is the fidelity imposed by the genre. I might add that the Indian chroniclers are careful to comply with these requisites, even translating forms peculiar to their culture into those acceptable to the Spaniards, though in the end this process can demonstrate — as in the case of Guaman Poma — magnificent originality.

As scriptural products the chronicles cannot escape the linear space of written language and the frame that inevitably encloses it with a grip that becomes more iron-fisted as it materializes into the book that paces back and forth within the confines of its covers. Michel de Certeau's study associating the linearity of writing and the chronology of history, both impossible in a West without a precise beginning and end, leaves little doubt concerning the scope of the memory that the chronicles can evoke: events, definite and unrepeatable, that occurred once and for all and remain inscribed in immutable graphics.[148]

On the other hand the wanka is inscribed within another, very different discursive realm. In the first place it appears as a text open to the uninterrupted collaboration of many "authors" who continue to modify it. Even though these modifications are partial, they result in the reformulation of its global interpretation in that they change the system of signs that correspond to meaning. Naturally, then, the presence of the "author" fades or disappears and is substituted by the impersonal action of subjects who feel no need to identify themselves, because knowingly or not they are bearers of a collective consciousness. In any case the text does not rest on an individual's experience, nor is it so legitimized. Rather, through a radically different process, it finds its validation in social expectations and the collective acknowledgement that can guarantee its survival as a given community's celebratory/ritual/theatrical behavior. In addition, one should remember that none of the versions is in the form of a book (except the most recent editions) and that all are anonymous.[149] If any name appears, it is the copyist's.

Finally, if the wanka represented history as seen with Western eyes, it would have at most the first, but never the last word. One might say that it resounds solely as the memory of an event covered by layers of images and symbols that evoke it with extraordinary freedom. This gives the genre a primordial function: the event is neither narrated nor described, but spoken by invented, "theatrical" voices that are obliged not to repeat a supposed, original dialogue but generate another that effects a present, vitally concerned audience. Again, the chronicle appeals to a lone reader, while the wanka is in its essence a public act, but one not taking place in formal theaters but as a collective ritual. In the performance it is not the "actors" who are primary, but rather the space shared in communicating with a community that feels that it is being represented and whose story is the wanka's very subject matter. We must add that this story reveals nothing new but rather confirms a story that everyone knows (the capture and death of the Inca in Cajamarca).[150] But this episode is temporally ubiquitous: it is there in the past, but also here in the present, charged forever with new experiences and meanings, and even pregnant with content that speaks of a future that will correct the cosmic disarray begun by the conquest.

We are not speaking here about the obsolete reality/history dichotomy on one hand and fiction on the other, nor a purely generic opposition between chronicle and "theater." We have said that historical-chronistic discourse contains a great deal of fiction but also insist that the fiction of the "drama" contains a great deal of truth: not so much a factual, empirical, or verifiable truth, but rather—and decidedly—the truth of a consciousness of history as an experience that is lived out collectively. Neither are we trying to separate what is Spanish in the chronicles from what is Andean in the wanka, not just because there are indigenous chronicles (and even those that are not are still impacted by their indigenous referents), but because the representations of the Inca's death, even though they may be rooted in pre-Hispanic "theatrical" experiences, also have unabashedly Spanish ties. No wonder their subject matter is the collision of two societies and cultures. In the end, although the Cajamarca chronicles and the Andean representations of the Inca's death both have the first confrontation between Indians and Europeans as their main plot and their basic theme is the radical incomprehension that separates one from the other, the great meaning that the two discourses revolve around is the building of a new, historical process whose effects are wide ranging. Chronicle and wanka are part and parcel of that history, one that reconstructs the identity of the subjects that live it.

But we err if we try to summarize the discourse of these dichotomies, obviating their differences as if they were parallel, but homologous. They absolutely refuse this conflation, having mutually belligerent and even incompatible natures in spite of their eventual, but traumatic, interrelationships. Suffice it to say that the chronicle is the realm of the written word, which wholly assimilates and transforms the voices of oral tradition, while the representations of the Inca's death conversely stem from sometimes haphazardly written lines but are realized in the voice's full dimension. As an example of this belligerence one must remember that within the wanka, there are frequent exchanges of insults between characters of different social groups, where one expels the other from *its* world.[151] This aggression is mutual and therefore establishes an unusual common space: one of contradiction. The story that begins in Cajamarca is, in its strongest sense, the story of a contradiction whose scope depends on the action of the opposites that constitute it. In this case, as unlikely as it may seem, historical and discursive totality is woven by and with these contradictions.[152]

Bakhtinian dialogism alone does not elucidate this literature. It is dialogistic, to be sure, but full of a profound and discordant polyphony that includes the potentialities of the voice (which resounds in the text of the wanka—as well as the chronicles—and claims victory as it is performed) and the written word (which interferes with the music of the spoken word and recalls other writings), all within a sociocultural ambit that so mixes the discourses that in the end none is intelligible by itself. When such radical opposition forces a face-off between orality and writing and between the mutually incompatible, discordant rationalities of history, the only option left to critical thought is to assume that opposition as an object of knowledge, a radical contradiction, or stark contrast. Otherwise, only one side of the story is told, and that side has no meaning in and of itself. For too long we spoke of the "literature of the conquest" or the "literature of the colony" as if they were exclusively written in Spanish. Later the "literature of the vanquished" was added as a separate system, when in reality we are dealing with a single entity whose identity is strictly relational.[153] Here the true object is this intersection of contradictions composed of a history that inextricably overlaps varied and opposing times, worldviews, and discourses. Ever after our literature has conquered and appropriated the written word within that space—the space of the "lettered city"—one feels, even now, an impossible desire, a longing for voice.[154] "Pedro Rojas" ("He took to writing in the air with his best finger") by Vallejo comes to mind, for example.[155]

At bottom this debate between voice and written word is nothing less than the formation of a subject beginning to understand that its identity is also the destabilizing identity of the other, a mirror or shadow with which one merges—somber, torn, and conflicted—as a way to either alienation or fullness.

CHAPTER 2   The Sutures of Homogeneity
Discourses of Impossible Harmony

The tragic contradictions that are the essence of the Cajamarca accounts and the Andean representations of Atahuallpa's death should not be read solely within the space created and bounded by these discourses. The tension between them, extreme in the intersection of orality and writing and the radical incompatibility of the historical consciousness that each expresses, is inscribed in a much larger context with a force so dynamic that it has traversed five centuries and configured the many social subjects that coexist in the Andean world today.

I would now like to examine the inverse of the profound heterogeneity studied in the previous chapter and work with the discourses (and behind every discourse there is a desire) of homogeneity. By looking at the other side we can clarify what we understand to be the defining character of Latin American—and especially Andean—literature and the paradoxical and complex web of confrontations that undergird it.

At bottom, if each wanka is a battleground of meanings that overlap, compete, and self-cancel, and many chronicles reveal irreparable internal ruptures (as in the case of Garcilaso or Guaman Poma), and if the relationship between the two genres is based on the most unyielding conflicts, then the examination of the opposite discourse, focused on homogeneity, can only make its contradictions more profound. This becomes more complex and problematic when we try to make harmonious what is unequal, divergent and inflammatory.

The great homogenizing discourses are from the nineteenth

century at emancipation, when one imagines a community integrated enough to be recognized—and to recognize itself—as an independent nation.[1] This is a question that does not pertain to the colonial regime, which does not require imagining a common, shared space but rather demarcating the limits between power and the great mass of vassals subdued by the rights of a just conquest or imperial order. The desire for autonomy soon begins to grow among those on the front lines, whose task is expropriated by the colonial bureaucracy, while at the same time creoles and mestizos feel that they are being overlooked in their own land. For their part, torn between resistance and rebellion, disconcerted Indians form survival strategies and begin to make underground plans for the utopian restoration of ancient times: the construction of a new order.[2]

The voice of a mestizo, Garcilaso, will be one of the first to attempt the configuration of a convergent and harmonious space. I shall first study the arduous, homogenizing discourse of the Inca and then go on to examine the way the life and work of Garcilaso de la Vega serve to construct the symbolic image of an integrated nation in the nineteenth and twentieth centuries. Finally, by utilizing several texts from the nineteenth century and a few from the twentieth, I shall try to clarify certain vital aspects of the (sometimes deliberately delayed) homogenizing discourse of these times.

GARCILASO: HARMONY RENT ASUNDER

Garcilaso's entire work is based persistently and obsessively on his identity as a mestizo. Better still, it is a complex semiosis destined to produce the legitimacy of that personal and social being, beginning with the legitimacy of his own writing, proposed as the harmonious articulation of all that is varied and mixed: in sum, mestizo writing. And it surely is in many ways. While linking Hispanic and Quechua traditions, it presupposes the constant decanting of Quechua orality into a written Spanish that is meant as much for his distant Peruvian relatives as the peninsular court and the cultured Renaissance reader.

But the validation of Garcilaso's mestizo writing, specifically in the *Royal Commentaries*, does not have to do solely with the duality of his "sources" or even with preserving the respect that he owes any of his ancestors. It is essentially a question of constructing—or self-constructing—both the subject that speaks in the text and the space in which he does so. To be credible as a trustworthy historian, Garcilaso meticulously sculpts a speech capable of bestowing authority on a discourse that is fairly dissident when compared to others that had treated the same or similar referents. In the end the plausibility of his alternative visions was based on the inevitable condition of forging a subject who would have the right and the reason to write what he wanted to write.[3]

Of course, the *Royal Commentaries* contains a subtle, varied, and complex historiographic strategy, but all depends on what I call the self-construction of a subject that relates (and produces) history. According to José Durand, when one reads Garcilaso, "there comes a point at which history becomes autobiography before our very eyes."[4] This is true, but one must not forget that this is an autobiography that, more than relating personal situations, tends to clarify the ethnic makeup (and the discursive possibilities) of the author. On the other hand, as a subject for enunciation, the Inca possesses an extensive array of discursive strategies. Without taking into account the various names he used throughout his life, Garcilaso speaks at times as the faithful servant of his Majesty, at times as a doubly noble mestizo, at times simply as a mestizo, at times as Inca, and at times as an Indian. These are personal depictions that allow for internal variants and are neither always nor necessarily exclusive. Indeed, Garcilaso's primary impulse is to unite them under a single aegis.[5] This ambitious goal is achieved through the use of his most obvious device: the image of the mestizo.

One must also remember that the first ethnic definition to appear in Garcilaso's work, essentially through the internal need for self-identification, is that of "Indian." I am referring to the curious interpolation of this qualifier in *La traducción del indio de los Diálogos de Amor*, which was modified without losing its ethnic content to *La Florida del Inca*, which Durand interprets as Garcilaso's expression of pride in his "state as a new man."[6] One might add here that the shift from "Indian" to "Inca" may well signify the incorporation of noble or class content into the original ethnic matrix. It seems clear to me, however, that "Indian" and "Inca" function almost as hyperbole of the oddity of being mestizo, but under an ambiguous code that demonstrates both modesty and pride, and at once and above all warns the reader that this is a different kind of discourse: a discourse of an*other*. One could say that the self-definition of the mestizo as a scripted Indian or Inca is a way of underscoring the alterity of this discourse and of the one who transmits it.

The fact that neither the translation of the *Dialogues* nor *La Florida* requires the autobiographical authorization needed by the *Royal Commen-*

taries and the *General History* should not make us forget that Garcilaso intentionally enmeshes all his works with cross references (especially in his prologues and dedicatories), so that when autobiographical legitimization is questioned in his last two books, it is already solidly reinforced by the image of an author who has defined himself long since as Indian/Inca as well as a scholarly writer and an amenable and trustworthy historian. In my opinion there has not been sufficient study of the complex process that conjoins all of Garcilaso's books and generates a macroauthorial space in which sharply defined variants do not extend beyond its laboriously conceived boundaries.

In any case, even if we were unaware of the facts of his biography, the writer of the *Royal Commentaries* can be no more (or less) than a mestizo. In fact, the ultimate meaning of his discourse would be inexplicable outside of this: the subject and his writing. Recall Garcilaso's beautiful and righteous declaration of his mestizaje: "The children of Spaniards by Indians are called *mestizos*, meaning that we are a mixture of the two races. The word was applied by the first Spaniards who had children by Indian women, and because it was used by our fathers, as well as on account of its meaning, I call myself by it in public and am proud of it."[7]

This declaration of his mestizo state (even bolder in the next section when he tells how in the Indies the word is uttered with contempt) is part of what enables the writing of the *Royal Commentaries*, itself a dual text just as unusual as the mixed-race man who writes it at the turn of the sixteenth century.[8] We should also underscore that in the above excerpt the father has an important role: he is proud to call himself a mestizo because this is what he is ("we are a mixture"), but also because that is what his Spanish father called them ("the word . . . used by our fathers"). From this point of view the prologue to the *General History of Peru* implies a new angle on his filiation: the Spanish disappears from the "we" implicit in the mestizo category and there is a fraternal welcoming of Indians, mestizos, and creoles: "To the Indians, *mestizos*, and creoles of the kingdoms and provinces of the great and wealthy empire of Peru, from the Inca Garcilaso de la Vega, their brother, compatriot, and countryman, health and happiness" (Garcilaso, *General History of Peru*, prologue).

It would be tempting to correlate Indian with brother, mestizo with compatriot, and creole with countryman, but in reality the economy of the phrasing seems to turn on the term *mestizo*, which embraces the Indian and the creole (that is, all America), while the affective meanings of the second enumeration come together. In other words, when he emphatically declares himself to be mestizo and associates himself as brother to both Indian and creole, Garcilaso assumes a multiplied representativeness and places his discourse in a multifaceted space. We might say that Garcilaso considers himself an author(ity) of multiple writings and proposes to install himself at a utopian crossroads where a "pan-optical," globalizing, and totalizing ideal may be realized.

One may ask, however, if the realization of this project is possible or, more precisely, if Garcilaso is capable of it. Although at times it alarms him, Garcilaso clearly sees the mestizo condition in terms of union and synthesis. Here he resorts to various strategies, from the assimilation of neo-Platonism, a philosophy in which he found a conceptual basis appropriate to thinking of himself as a function of a harmonic convergence of dissimilar, oppositional forces, to the sometimes faulty assuredness of a providential sense of history. Thus Garcilaso pictures the reign of the Incas not in opposition to the conquest but rather—as the classical world was to Christianity—a propitiatory prologue to the evangelization of the Indies. So, like stages in God's great plan, which goes from the barbarism of distant epochs to the natural reason of the Incas and from natural reason to the divine revelation offered the Indians with the conquest, the end of the empire and the subjugation of its people by the Spanish are stripped of all drama. Historical discourse can run on unabashedly, suturing tears and welding ruptures with nothing less than divine reason. This also helps to fill the gaps in Garcilaso's own self-image.

Nevertheless, although powerful, these and other conceptual devices do not always function effectively. I shall not reiterate here the ambiguity or the constant waverings of Garcilaso's prose, obvious indicators of the instability and unresolved conflictedness of his proclaimed mestizo state. I shall consider just one text, seemingly irrelevant to this question, that can be read somewhat imaginatively as a hidden metaphor for the failure of this desire for harmony:[9]

> In 1556 in a corner of one of the mines of Callahuaya there was discovered one of the stones that occur with the metal . . . for it was riddled with large and small holes that ran right through it. In all of them points of gold could be seen as though molten gold had been poured over it: some of these points projected from the stone, others were level with it, and others were inside it. Those who understood mining said that if

it had not been extracted, the whole stone would in the course of time have turned to gold. In Cuzco the Spaniards regarded it as a marvellous thing. The Indians called it *huaca*, which, as we have said, has among other meanings that of a remarkable thing, something admirable for its beauty or also something abominably ugly. I saw it with both Indians and Spaniards. Its owner was a rich man who decided to come to Spain, bringing it as it was a present for King Philip II. . . . I heard when I was in Spain that his ship was lost with a great deal of other treasure. (Garcilaso, *Royal Commentaries of the Incas*, 535).

Very much in keeping with his style, Garcilaso shows how the Spaniards view this strange stone ("[they] regarded it as a marvellous thing"), and likewise the Indians ("called it *huaca* . . . a remarkable thing"), creating a sort of underground and intermediary translation. In this context the huaca is exactly the same as the Spaniards' "marvellous thing," thereby confusing both views in a single meaning: marvellous thing = huaca = remarkable thing, all this within the wishful harmony where what is double is really one. The cost of this may mean the semantic emptying of the Quechua word, which becomes, while still maintaining its rhetorical function, an attractive but useless hinge joining identical elements. Here, as on other occasions, Garcilaso's discourse valorizes both Indian and Spanish views but immediately subsumes them (removing the conflict from their mutual alterity) into a complacent, totalizing category. In a sense the verbal production of synonymy dissolves the duality of the perspectives that birthed it.

Predictably, Garcilaso wants to give his own testimony and makes a point of saying "I saw it with both Indians and Spaniards." Why, if *huaca* and "marvellous thing" are synonyms (or almost so) does the Inca make explicit his double vision, so to speak? In addition if "to see with" were interpreted simply as "to look at in the company of," and if this note were nothing more than another way of expressing his dual parentage and giving voice to both his ancestors, the urgency to be so precise would still be quite impressive. I imagine that what is happening here is that his triangular translation is unsatisfactory even to Garcilaso himself and he feels obliged to insinuate that in reality, Indians and Spaniards view the stone differently because it tells them different things. All indicates that the frustration comes from the fact that in this excerpt, but not in others where he insists emphatically on it, Garcilaso has erased the sacred meaning of *huaca*.[10] If he had made it clear, "marvellous thing" and "remarkable thing" would have obturated their synynomy: marvels speak here to the caprices of nature, which attracted both the Renaissance elite and the coarse conquistadors with Medieval mindsets, while the "remarkable thing," the huaca, can only refer to (as it does in indigenous consciousness) the surprising mystery of the divine presence in certain of the world's sacred spaces.[11] In this way the homogenizing convergence so carefully woven into the explicit discourse of harmony unravels in the barely implicit, underlying discourse where what is varied, contradictory, and heterogeneous threatens to reinstall its troubling hegemony.

But the excerpt prods one to go even deeper. We should remember that Garcilaso notes that "those who understood mining said that if it had not been *extracted*, the whole stone would in the course of time have turned to gold," a sentence that must be read as related to the one that begins the chapter: "Spain is a good witness to the wealth of gold and silver that is *extracted* in Peru," as well as the one that concludes the story of this exceptional goldstone with its loss in the sea. Perhaps it is not too audacious to think that the text unwittingly narrates the (im)possible story of the Inca empire depicted in the goldstone that would have turned to solid gold had they left it where it was, while lamenting—or eulogizing—both the rupture of a process that was moving along splendidly toward its golden age and its fateful end, lost in the same deep waters that brought the conquistadors.

But since the logic of meaning here opens itself up to plurisemic error, is there not, underlying this entire account, a longing for a possible, golden unity that history finally destroyed? Along with this essential and impeccable unity, the image of harmony laboriously constructed by the Inca's mestizo discourse can be appreciated more as the painful and useless ointment applied to an open wound than as the expression of a joyous syncretism. Understood in terms of violence and impoverishment and as the mutilation of the completeness of a being that the conquest tore to pieces, mestizaje, the greatest of Garcilaso's signs advocating harmony between two worlds, finally (in the very discourse that holds it up) reasserts its equivocal, precarious, and deeply ambiguous state that does not convert union into harmony, but rather into forced, difficult, painful, and traumatic coexistence.

Texts such as this (and there are more obvious ones) erode the conciliation carefully propitiated in the mestizo author's writing and expose the precariousness of the aporias that the Inca was never able to fully resolve. Garcilaso's proposed reconciliation ends neither in the Indies nor in Spain. Perhaps, like the goldstone that was also "mestizo," it sinks into a sea that forever drowns the fullness and purity of the gold symbolic of an identity without conflict that, though impossible, creates the longing that the Inca can never hide. It is no coincidence, then, that Garcilaso's work ends not with an image of synthesis and fullness but rather the opposite: the execution of the "good prince" Tupac Amaru I, in order to "tell to the end of our work and labor the most painful of all that has happened in our land and we have written it all [and this is most important] as tragedy" (Garcilaso, *General History of Peru*, 1169).

Since at least the first decade of the twentieth century, by contradicting the tragic sense of Garcilaso's work as a tenacious, brilliant, yet useless attempt to coherently articulate the many traditions collected in it and make them marginally compatible, the lettered elite constructed the official image of the Inca as "the first Peruvian": standard bearer of the greatest symbol of a nation that, at least in its intentioned discourse, needed to reconcile its two streams into the personage of an exceptional mestizo. Raúl Porras Barrenechea, with his repeated designation of Garcilaso as "a Spaniard in the Indies, an Indian in Spain," correctly sensed the incurable division in Garcilaso's life and work.[12] But Durand was the one who most consistently questioned the idyllic image of the Inca as an emblem of harmonious fullness when he underscored the essential tragedy of both Garcilaso and his discourse by noting that "the Inca wants to glorify his two lineages, but any glory he grants them is steeped in bitterness."[13]

SOCIAL DEPICTIONS OF THE INCA

Garcilaso is not just his persona, his texts, and a person who produces texts. He is also the rather unstable social figure discovered after multiple readings. It is the collective construction of this figure and the meaning given it that I shall now examine. Here one should remember that the images with which each social subject configures the community to which he or she belongs are varied and uneven, especially those of certain paradigmatic personages whose memory—cultish to the point of being sacred—functions as an efficient, validating symbol and argument for a community image, especially on the national level. One of these, not only for Peru but also for the entire Andean world and even "Mestizo America," is Garcilaso, perhaps because, in addition to the importance of his work and the nature of his biography, there is the complexity of his significance as a "cultural hero," which allows several different readings. After all, the density of Garcilaso's writing and the ambiguities and contradictions that define it are powerful inducements for a vast array of often-incompatible interpretations.

Unfortunately the *Royal Commentaries'* reception in the Andean world is yet to be fully revealed. Although we know of setbacks due to the religious and imperial censorship of the day and something of its influence on certain key moments in history (the Inca nationalism of the eighteenth century, the great revolution of Tupac Amaru, and the years of emancipation, for example), there is still work to be done on how deeply they are inserted and re-elaborated in Andean consciousness.[14] At those particular points Garcilaso's works raised the vindictive and even subversive spirits of Indians, mestizos, and creoles alike. But later a different image appeared, one that continues to be both hegemonic and a subject of debate to this day. This is the image constructed by the intellectual elite of the turn of the century, especially through the studies of its most prestigious member, José de la Riva-Agüero, one of whose major points is the configuration of the Inca as a symbol of the harmonious fusion of the races that constitute Peru and, consequently, as an emblem of a harmonious nationality reconciled in and with all its diverse components.[15] Somewhat paradoxically this patriotic canonization of Garcilaso seems to partially explain the fact that his version of the Inca period is the most widely accepted, although it also implies a condemnation of the Colony and the Republic, which was outside of (or meant something else in) Riva-Agüero's ideology. It is interesting to note that in present-day Peru, and thanks to the widespread diffusion of Garcilaso's version throughout the educational system, 84 percent of all students believe that the *Tawantinsuyu* was the "happiest" time in the nation's history.[16]

Riva-Agüero synthesized the matter in 1916: "The influence and authority of [the] *Royal Commentaries* in Peruvian history was, for two hundred years, all-embracing. . . . But in the mid-nineteenth century the expected and even desired reaction, instead of containing itself within the limits of the calm objectivity indispensable to scientific research, became so extreme, out of hand, and unruly that it has become necessary to attack its unjust excesses."[17]

Clearly, Riva-Agüero was referring to the stance both of some Spanish scholars, singularly Menéndez Pelayo, and of certain Peruvian historians who, during the nineteenth century and the first part of the twentieth, questioned the historic value of the Inca's works. In large part, due to the enormous influence of Menéndez Pelayo, they doubted the veracity of the *Royal Commentaries*, which the latter claimed were not history, but utopia.[18] The situation changed radically in 1910, thanks to the vigorous vindication of the historical nature of Garcilaso's works, especially the *Royal Commentaries*, in the doctoral dissertation written by Riva-Agüero, one of the most prestigious intellectuals of his day.[19] This vindication is decisive within the framework of Peruvian and Andean historiography but, by its nature, does not so much concern Garcilaso's image as it affects the historical nature of his discourse. Using then-modern heuristics that clearly defined its substantial wisdom and minor errors, Riva-Agüero emphatically legitimizes Garcilaso's discourse not only as a trustworthy historical expression but also as one of immense national importance.

With incisive intuition, Riva-Agüero establishes that Garcilaso's sources and loyalties favor his credibility as an historian, since they provide him information that is close to both events and their protagonists. At the same time — and this is where the paradox comes in — they interfere because, being their direct descendants, they express the interests and idealizations of the story's protagonists. This ambivalence clearly influences the scholar's method for "discovering the truth" that underlies the *Royal Commentaries*. He goes about removing the three layers that idealize, hide, or deform it: the *quipucamayos*, the Inca relatives that informed Garcilaso, and naturally, the layer that he himself created "out of love for his country and his blood." Impeccable as positivistic heuristics (which understands the writing of history as an expression of a single, verifiable, and objective truth), Riva-Agüero's recommendation stretches the *Royal Commentaries* to the point of their becoming an *other* text, but it serves to remove any doubts about the seriousness of this work, whose explicable, subjective digressions only needed clarification in order to both authorize it as canonic within high culture and history and to place it at the center of national historiography. It remains curious, however, that Riva-Agüero does not include among the idealizations to be discarded those that come from Garcilaso's Spanish loyalties.

But if in his 1910 dissertation Riva-Agüero barely touches upon the "life and character" of the Inca, leaving the latter's symbolic depiction in the background, in his "Elogio del Inca," which was and continues to be the most important text concerning Garcilaso's meaning on a social level, the emphasis is placed directly on the image of this personage. As such its interpretation as a great national sign and emblem clearly rises to the surface. He insists, "Garcilaso [is] the highest and most complete personification of Peruvian literature . . . from his blood, his character and the circumstances of his life, to the content of his writings and the gifts of imagination and the unmistakable style with which he embellished them, [it all] converges to make him the perfect representative and symbol of the soul of our land" (Riva-Agüero, "Elogio," 6).

Naturally this representativeness comes first from his being mestizo, but this mestizaje is repeatedly referred to in terms of a harmonious synthesis. For instance: "He is the complete synthesis and necessary product of the coexistence and confluence of mental, hereditary, and physical influences that determine Peru's peculiar physiognomy" (Riva-Agüero, "Elogio," 58). Or more clearly still, "And since hope, to stay alive, must be born of or sustained by remembrances, let us salute and revere, as a good omen, the memory of the great historian in whose personality were lovingly *fused Incas and Conquistadors*, who with solemnity opened the doors of our own literature and was the magnificent precursor of our true nationality" (Riva-Agüero, "Elogio," 62, Cornejo's emphasis).

A necessity for imagining one harmonious nation in light of an inaugural figure such as the Inca, the idea of homogeneity not only insists on the peaceful and constructive convergence of the two "races" that entered into contact during the conquest but also substitutes the conflictual meaning of this word with an expression of harmonious fusion. In effect, the word "conquest" almost imperceptibly loses its first denotation of combat and conflict and shifts toward a semantic area as unforeseeable as it is necessary: the erotic. Born out of love and not destruction and death, the homeland comes to be the sum and oneness of all that is varied and different. Mestizaje is its illustrious representation.

This is, however, a unique mestizaje, one that joins two nobiliary ancestors: "Off-spring of the imperial [Inca] line and one of the first among the new and invincible *viracochas*" (Riva-Agüero, "Elogio," 21). The text of the "Elogio" presents stunning genealogical scholarship about Garcilaso's paternal branch, almost reaching a state of ecstasy when referring to the Inca's relative, the Marquis of Priego, as "Spanish grandee of highest class and antiquity, Lord of Aguilar de la Frontera, overseer and oldest son of the illustrious house of Cordoba, Marquis Consort of Diego D. Alonso Fernández of Cordoba and Suárez of Figueroa, decorated General, veteran of Argel, San Quintín and Flanders . . . one of the highest nobility of the Kingdom" (Riva-Agüero, "Elogio," 30).

In contrast, although he insists on the fact that the Inca's mother belonged to the Cusco nobility and accepts her concubinage with Captain Garcilaso, Riva-Agüero clearly places the irremediable inequality of this relationship at the forefront.[20] He describes the situation: "And the *poor girl* Isabel Chimpu Ocllo, stem of a *minor and ruined branch* of Atahualpa, a *mere* niece of Huayna Capac . . . *was nothing more than the concubine* of the proud Garcilaso, although one supposes that he esteemed and respected her greatly" (Riva-Agüero, "Elogio," 9, Cornejo's emphasis). And then: "Between campaigns [Captain Garcilaso] had relations in Cusco with a young Inca princess, the *ñusta* Isabel Chimpu Ocllo, granddaughter of the former Monarch Tupac Yupanqui, *one of the timid flowers that comforted the fierce Spaniards.*"[21]

As one might expect, Riva-Agüero points out that Garcilaso's mother "had to yield her position" to a Spanish lady (whom he describes with his irrepressible genealogical obsession as the "sister-in-law of the brave Leonese gentleman, Antonio de Quiñones, close kinswoman of the former governor Vaca de Castro and of the lineage of Suero de Quiñones") and defines the Captain's marriage as a "commensurate union."[22] Having made all these provisos, the splendid image of the conquest as an act in which "Incas and Conquistadors were lovingly fused" begins to crumble internally. If on one side are the "proud" and "fierce" Spanish, and on the other the "poor" and "timid" Indian women, it is because at bottom there is no way to hide the "disproportion" of the relationships out of which was born—with an irony that the explicit discourse seems not to perceive—the symbolic founder of the nation. In the face of brutal reality, then, the homogeneity of mestizaje barely survives on the nobiliary vertices of the two social pyramids, one of which imposes itself without concession on the other. The tender acceptance of "conquest" as amorous embrace vanishes and the other, the true conquest (and its consequences), once again beats its war drums. To hear them one only has to read the inverse of the discourse of harmony.

Riva-Agüero's view of the Inca is decidedly and fanatically aristocratic but, its excesses notwithstanding, establishes a solid stereotype whose weft holds that Garcilaso is a symbol of a harmonious mestizaje and by extension the very essence of being Peruvian, and whose warp underscores the exceptional nature of this doubly noble mestizaje. The first of these interpretations has even taken root in the world view of some indigenists like Uriel García who, directly or indirectly, favor an integrative mestizaje, while the second, albeit diluted, often reappears in the work of Garcilaso scholars who do not necessarily agree with all of Riva-Agüero's thoughts.[23] In sum, the discourse of national homogeneity has perhaps no clearer expression than in Riva-Agüero's version of Garcilaso, although paradoxically this is a version that clearly distinguishes Spaniards from Indians and aristocracy from commoners and, consequently, builds its great synthesis upon the unbridgeable abyss between them.

FROM GARCILASO TO PALMA: ONE LANGUAGE FOR ALL?

In the *Royal Commentaries*, interspersed with the astonishing "discourse of abundance,"[24] which extols the great fecundity of European fruit trees in America, Garcilaso narrates a "comic tale": two Indians are charged with taking the first fruits of a splendid melon harvest to Lima, and the foreman warns them not to eat any because the letter that they are also carrying "will tattle." Along the way the Indians disobey, but they are very careful to put the letter behind a wall so that it will not see them eating and therefore cannot say anything. When they hand over the cargo and the letter, they are discovered. The official says, "Why do you lie? This letter says you were given ten, and you have eaten two." The Indians can only confirm, "the Spaniards were rightly called gods . . . since they could penetrate such complete secrets" (Garcilaso, *Royal Commentaries of the Incas*, 604).

Significant on several levels, the "tale" again highlights the confrontation between orality and writing and their unequal insertion and use in the dynamic of social power. Though its tone is comic (or even ironic), it has a tragic resonance as well, since it repeats the story of the Indians' defeat, submission, and frailty in the face of the writs of the authorities, or, by the same token, the authority of writing.[25] I shall not pause to analyze this tale, which has been the subject of several noteworthy studies, but I would like to reiterate that its make-up—besides the struggle between what is oral and what is written—is definitely heterogeneous and subversive.[26] As Enrique Pupo-Walker points out, "In this tale . . . writing becomes the conflictive space of the narration and the measure of the interior distance between two cultural realities that suffered a mutual process of adjustment and painful rupture."[27]

We know that Garcilaso's "tale" is the direct source of one of Ricardo

Palma's *tradiciones*, "Carta canta," and that the same story appears in other chronicles, such those of Gómara and Mártir de Anglería as well as in the work of at least one more author in the *tradición* genre.[28] The liberty with which Palma employs his colonial sources indicates how seriously he assumes this tradición to be his own.[29] Although "Carta canta" refers not to the Inca, but to Father Acosta, it is obvious that what Palma has in mind, and perhaps even within sight, are the *Royal Commentaries*: the details of the plot are almost identical, perhaps the most important of which is changing the Indians' surprise at the Spaniards' supernatural powers into the punishment ("a good thrashing") that they receive.

Nevertheless, Palma's tradición includes a healthy number of linguistic asides, and in the end it is the author's intention to reveal the origin of the phrase "letters tattle." Indeed, he expounds upon sayings having to do with wealth, power, and happiness and explains the provenance of sayings and riddles commenting on the value of an item costing more than "Margarita Pareja's Blouse" or "Brother Gomez' Scorpion," and "How the Devil Lost His Poncho." He also gives the derivations of the terms *encomendero* and *mataserrano*, the latter being a fruit that causes highlanders gastric distress. Clearly these linguistic comments, all somehow having to do with Peru, underscore the tradición's most interesting point: the Peruvian origin of "letters tattle," as a variant of "letters read" and "paper speaks," the former "pure" Spanish and the latter "ultra-creole." "Letters tattle" is the form preferred by Palma, and he says, "I am going to petition the Royal Academy of the Spanish Language that it be called a 'Peruvianism.' In a certain sense the melon anecdote is a mere pretext within the tradición to expound upon Palma's predilection for the theme of Americanisms, and specifically the national origin of the saying that gives the tradición its title.[30]

In typical Palma style, the proposed "etymology" of "letters tattle" ("here follows the origin of said phrase") is based on a pleasant narration. The author notes that the first dialogue between the Indian bearers is realized in "indigenous dialect," a notation that disappears in the second (although the word *taitai* is used), obviously because the end of the story demands that the same Indians who began by speaking in Quechua now must do so in Spanish. One of them exclaims, "You see, brother, letters tattle!" There is thus an almost imperceptible displacement from Quechua to Spanish and the concomitant blotting out of the former. Ironically, with an improbability that does not seem to worry the author one whit, the Spanish saying is born from the words of the Quechuas.

Furthermore, the exclamation that gushes from the lips of the Indian in Spanish is heard by the official, who repeats it enthusiastically: "Yes, you scamps, and watch out next time, because now you know that letters tattle," which constitutes a second displacement. The Spanish official appropriates the word of the Indians and turns it into a threat against them. It is the official who tells his friends the anecdote, which allows the saying to pass into common usage and "cross the seas." So ends the oral leg of this curious journey whose basic stages go from Quechua to the Spanish spoken by the Indians, then to the Spanish of upper-class colonial society, and finally to the general (and later authorized) Spanish of both America and the Iberian peninsula.

Complex in its several layers of meaning, this process presents other surprises. Up to this point everything obviously happens within the confines of orality. Now the vessel becomes writing, indirectly at first, since the story that explains the origin of "letters tattle" is transmitted to Father Acosta, who then explicitly "wrote at length and frequently about the events of the conquest," proved in the very writing of the tradición. From there, it wins a place in the greatest authorized archive of the language, nothing less than the Dictionary of the Royal Academy, upon the its acceptance of Palma's proposal.[31] This sacred locus is the endpoint of a circuitous linguistic voyage, the curious story told in "Carta canta," where the question of orality and writing surfaces yet again.

In large part the tradición is registered in oral forms and is definitely governed by the spirit of valuing the grace, pertinence, and incisiveness of popular language, or (more generically) a presumed national language. At the same time, and probably unintentionally, it proposes a very defined linguistic hierarchy in which Quechua yields to Spanish, orality to writing, and all to the authority of the academy. From one point of view these appear to be steps in a just recovery of the Americanism, but an inverse reading reveals instead a gesture of compliance with the metropolitan insistence on authorizing (or not) what is spoken in America. This ambivalence is symptomatic: the recovery of one's own language is both the recognition of the outside authority that can either consecrate it or repress it and the celebration of oral creativity at the very moment of its loss, first inscribed in Palma's cultured writing and then installed in its niche in the academy's dictionary.

It would be overstated to consider Palma's linguistic process as a sign of a Hispanist or colonialist option, but one could understand it within the willful and globalizing strategy destined to modernize and standardize Spanish American social life at the end of the nineteenth century—a decisive part of the formation and consolidation of the new national states.[32] Andrés Bello's work alone proves that language plays an essential role as creator of the national community's socialized image and as the space in which the homogeneity that the nation requires to exist is realized.[33] Indeed, when Palma almost surreptitiously displaces Quechua and converts it into Spanish, he is producing an intact, homogenous space just where the national community runs the greatest risk of being broken. When he rearranges popular speech into cultured writing, he is generating a new and even firmer homogenous space just as he bridles the fickle and destructuring modifications of orality. And finally, when he hands over the whole process to the authority of the academy, he bestows exceptional power on a linguistic norm that governs—by model and rules—the "good" language. As he removes the conflict from Garcilaso's story, Palma creates an pleasant space into which he places a harmonious, new nation.

The politics of language in Palma and his immediate predecessors (*costumbristas* of liberal persuasion, some rather populist) is misguided: when they collect popular or generally colloquial usages in order to recycle them in their own style, they order, groom, and domesticate them, trimming away the excess that makes them unmanageable, and thus attempt to attain for their own language certain national stature as an adequate, overarching representation of artistic writing as well as common speech, now clearly stylized. Alberto Escobar demonstrates how the contradiction between the purity of Pardo and the plebeian language of Seguro seems to be dissolved in Palma's prose.[34] But in reality the tradición experiment goes further, because it not only resolves a literary controversy but proposes a model for a national language propped up, according to "Carta canta," on two pillars foreign to literature: Indian speech and the academy. This model extends itself to a whole genre (no coincidence that its name is "Peruvian Traditions") and finally is projected on the sense of the nation itself. Perhaps less explicitly than other nineteenth-century writers, Palma inscribes his production within the greater problematic of his age: producing an image and discourse that could dilute the contradictions that tended to undermine the very idea of nation by constructing homogeneous spaces on top of an overwhelmingly heterogeneous reality, with the intention of creating a national community in and through language. In sum, it was not the discourse's theme or content but the meaning of the linguistic process realized in the text that revealed the desired premonition that a common space where complete harmonic (but hierarchical) convergence could actually be constructed.

In one way it is a happy moment: Quechua is at peace with Spanish, the language of art with street talk, writing with orality, and all within a willed, conciliatory, and homogenizing order, which on the hard surface of the written page finds—or believes it finds—an encouraging social depiction. In another work I examine how Palma makes the colony an agreeable place and moment in the history of Peru, deemphasizing its problems with humor and subtlety.[35] On the level of language, something similar could be said: by carelessly diluting the tensions inherent in bilingualism, as if this act were totally natural, by erasing at the same time the boundaries between what is oral and written and what is cultured and popular, and by finally affirming the legitimacy of Peruvianisms by the authority of the Spanish academy, Palma produces a linguistic space that is agreeable, almost paradisiacal, where the nation can read itself—without conflicts—as it is. He was, of course, mistaken.

CONCERNING PATRIOTIC SPEECHES AND PROCLAMATIONS

For obvious reasons the most explicit homogenizing discourses were produced in the public, specifically political, sphere, in the form of several then-privileged literary genres that today lack artistic stature, namely the many variants of oratory. Neoclassic poetics were still in vogue and underscored in their Ciceronian bent the artistic and social importance of oratory. The convulsion of the times also generated conditions propitious for the cultivation of a genre especially geared for the most problematic and agitated areas of social life. Neither should the fact be overlooked that oratory was well adapted to a largely illiterate society.

Wartime speeches, sermons, civic orations, and parliamentary discourses form (along with no less assiduously practiced variants) a very full and complex corpus. This has not been well studied, partly because the genre itself soon inspired little interest among scholars of literature, and partly because portions of it were never published or were consigned to short-lived publications. In some exceptional cases, given the customs of the age, they could be considered oral discourses in the strictest sense of the word; that is, they were not read.

The oratory of the new republics was rooted in the colony, a period in which it was also carefully cultivated, although mostly in either its religious or courtly variants. It is in the latter where we best perceive the effect of this tradition. For example, there is not a great difference between the salutations offered to the new viceroys and those showered upon the liberators. One should note, however, that this link (which in some ways paradoxically prolongs some characteristics of baroque rhetoric) is the most obvious, but not the most significant. A large part of republican oratory comes from the "modernist" tradition, which had been able to partially displace the practices of the baroque.[36]

My point is that the oratory of the period is foundational with respect to the nascent republics. It is one of the most frequented *fora* in the debate over how and on the basis of which values the states that had just debuted their independence should be organized. (One has only to recall the oratorical tourneys of the first constitutional and parliamentary assemblies.) On a deeper level these discourses—for better or worse—must confront the most pressing social need of the time: imagining a sufficiently stable, comprehensive national community that could hide—or at least temper—the obvious heterogeneity of the respective country or, as a last resort, rationalize it quickly and easily as a reparable defect, mostly through education or technological progress.

I shall examine two texts, hovering somewhere between the categories of "proclamations" and "speeches," which are clearly foundational, not in the ideological sense of how to build a republic, but in a less explicit and more evocative way related to the nation's very image. As we shall see, both are almost literally foundational: the proclamation of Peruvian independence delivered by General José de San Martín on July 28, 1821, and the speech with which José Domingo Choquehuanca welcomed Simón Bolívar to Pucará on August 2, 1825.

With respect to the proclamation it is curious that, though it is a discourse that all Peruvians can repeat from memory, the unresolved contradiction that underlies San Martín's words has never, to my knowledge, been noted. The text follows: "Peru is, from this moment forward, free and independent by the common will of her peoples and by the justice of her cause, as defended by God. Long live the Fatherland! Long live Liberty! Long live Independence!"[37]

Obviously constructed with a bow to form (one has only to analyze the beauty of its rhythm), the proclamation also expresses a very subtle and meditated conceptual configuration, perhaps correlative to its commitment to loosen the internal tensions that threaten to undo it. Although clearly based on the historical experience of the partial, but effective, triumph of the patriot army, San Martín's discourse assumes the task of establishing that reality: "From this moment forward (that is, from the time of the proclamation) Peru is free and independent." At bottom, more than merely confirming a fact, the language of the proclamation seems to want to establish it and confer upon it a definitive solidity. This foundational linguistic act bridges the space between the juridical/notarial word, which is able to forge and consolidate realities, and the poetic word, which also functions, in its own way, as a producer of realities. Not magical, because underlying it seems to be the enlightened faith in the power of the word as bearer of reason, the proclamation resembles, just as it defines itself as a maker of history, that mysterious, primordial power.

From a different point of view, the Liberator's discourse tries to reconcile—also by way of language—two dissimilar consciences of history. Peru is independent on one hand, by the "common will of her peoples," but also, on the other, "by the justice of her cause, as defended by God." By using the conjunction "and" the proclamation stylistically brings together both reasons and gives no indication of perceiving any misalignment between the two. Being in a single sentence resoundingly contributes to producing this additive and relational effect. Conceptually, however, the matter is more complex. On this level the value of justice fulfills the conjunctive function, following a reasoning that has these general steps: Peru is independent (1) by the will of the people, (2) who incarnate a just cause, and (3) God defends this cause because it is just. Clearly the explicit appeal to justice constitutes a bridge between the will of the people and divine will, but this bridge reveals, on a second reading, that there is an empty or ambiguous space between one and the other. Resorting to justice, or any other value, implies at least that the (possibly unjust) sovereignty and voice of the people are not always the voice of God.

What is behind this reasoning? Political historians would probably not be wrong in finding hidden signs of the monarchic project in which San Martín was interested, but it seems undeniable that the unresolved problematic that shapes the proclamation is much more general and complex. It has to do with the uncontrolled emergence of modernity within a historically backward social body that had yet to enter into an even more radical process of rearchaizing itself.[38] As we know, modernity removes what is sacred in the world, the latter coming to be more and more firmly understood as a socially produced order beyond the reaches of any (even divine) design transcendent to it. It is a very long process of secularizing life and collective relationships, which leads along a twisting path to the privilege of political reason as the regulating force of the real order.[39] In one of its variants modernity finds in popular sovereignty the shaping and legitimizing principle of this order.

Clearly the first part of the proclamation ("by the common will of her peoples") calls upon a secularized awareness of history, now dependent on the decisions and actions of men, especially in their democratic version of the system of social relationships. It is possible to hear, in this fragment, overtones of the very concrete requirements of liberal patriots, some of which were very sure of being bearers and executors of a modernizing project for Peru, like, for example, the forgers of the first national constitution. In any case, in this deliberately placed first sequence, the proclamation obeys the call of an emerging ideology.[40]

The second segment of San Martín's discourse evokes, on the other hand, an older worldview, strictly premodern, which reconstructs the force of a transcendent and sacred principle as the legitimizing basis of the new social order. The breach between one worldview and the other is so pronounced (they are actually incompatible, in spite of the mediations of the Spanish enlightenment) that the first is obliged to deemphasize its inaugural presence: divine action appears as the final, forcible, and decisive stage of a history that—from this perspective—can no longer be perceived in lay terms.

One could say that this is not just a question of the struggle between two distinct worldviews concerning history and social life, but the contradictory simultaneity of two diverse times—with their differentiated rationalities—in the consciousness of a single subject. The drama of this breach is heightened and becomes more caustic because it is framed within the terse harmony of a discourse that is unaware of its own conflict. It is as if Peru had been founded in the split space of a great historical contradiction, the precipitous intersection of an archaic world, unable to imagine itself beyond the reaches of divine transcendence, and another, more modern world, decidedly assuming its production to be human; that is, between the sacred and the profane.

In this specific context the proclamation's premodern side repeats the rationale of the monarchic regime and the religious confirmation of its rule over conquered lands. It is, from this perspective, definitely colonial. The fact that at that moment its functioning was the inverse of colonial reasoning proves only that it is easy to cloak human interests in a pleasing divine will. Ironically the same God (or god) that sanctified conquest and all its horrors was now consecrating independence and all its promises.[41] The other side of San Martín's speech, with its modern appeal to popular will, appears to be halfheartedly inspired by both what was, in 1821, nothing more than a decision by the liberals, who were never able to consolidate their hegemony, and a vague dream for the nation's future: one that would overcome the backwardness and obscuration of the viceroys with secular and progressive reason. José Carlos Mariátegui and Jorge Basadre explain why this was only a dream, how the colony would not be ended with the advent of the republic, and in what ways the promises of emancipation were finally—and to this day—unfulfilled.[42]

This failure is prefigured in and by the contradictions revealed by San Martín's words and by the perturbing fact that they were neither perceived nor assumed to be such. Perhaps it was inevitable: appealing to the divine can be read as an attempt to place within the realm of the inscrutable the foundation of a social system that is rationally inexplicable and indefensible. A republic based on strict ethnic discrimination and an inflexible social hierarchy, Peru was able to neither secularize its historical rationale nor leave unbalanced an ideology sustained by popular will. Though much more metaphorical than real, the political proclamation that the legitimizing capacity of the "common will of her peoples" had to be inserted into a larger discourse capable on one hand of stopping and even suppressing its modern subversion and on the other of framing it within a transcendental design that could justify—like any coherent hierarchy—the dramatic inequalities among classes and ethnic groups. The caustic lack of balance between the proclamation's impeccable formal harmony, which establishes a homogeneous discursive space, and the conceptual and historical conflict unwittingly revealed prefigures the evasive ability of official discourse to hide the broken and belligerent reality from which it springs and which it pretends to represent faithfully and seamlessly, while all the while denying or distorting it in a zealous attempt at harmony.

There is also the case of the speech with which Choquehuanca welcomed Bolívar to Pucará on August 2, 1825, unanimously recognized as a masterpiece of republican oratory. Handwritten copies, some made by the author, were immediately distributed, and in 1860 it was transcribed by Francisco García Calderón in the *Diccionario de la legislación peruana*. The text of that version states,

> It was God's will to form a great empire out of savages: He created Manco Capac; his race sinned, and He flung forth Pizarro. After three centuries of expiation He has taken pity on America and has created Thee. Thou art, then, the man of providential design: nothing achieved before is similar to what Thou hast done; and for anyone to imitate Thee, there must be a world to liberate. . . . Thou hast founded five Republics, which in the vast development to which they are called, shall raise thy stature which none before has achieved. Thy glory shall increase with the centuries, as does the shadow when the sun sets.[43]

Descendants of Huayna Capac, the Choquehuancas belonged to the noble Inca class, but their affiliation with the royalist cause during the Tupac Amaru rebellion saved them from the downfall of the indigenous aristocracy resulting from the reprisals with which the Crown punished the group for its commitment to or sympathy for the revolution of 1780.[44] José Domingo Choquehuanca contradicted this family tradition, took on the cause for independence, and played an important but uneven public role in the first decades of the republic, all surely influenced by Enlightenment thought. This is borne out by his most important work, a statistical report on the province of Azángaro.[45]

Paradoxically this intellectual filiation does not appear in the speech, except—and it could not be otherwise—in its enthusiasm for independence. This fact is explained by the conditions of the genre employed, the evident attempt to use a rigorously spare style, and above all the limited objective of praising the hero. The contradiction in the background is, in fact, different: the speech's underlying rationale, which has little to do with enlightened thought.

I do not refer to the providentialism that runs through the entirety of Choquehuanca's discourse. This could be the result of heaping unbounded praise on Bolívar as nothing short of a personage chosen by God to fulfill his great plan for the lands of America, alongside abundant rhetoric surrounding the figure of the Liberator. But clearly providentialism has an even greater breadth in the speech's ideology. Bolívar here is "created" by God and the republics founded by him "are called" to partake in a history of progress.[46]

It is interesting to show the relationship between the speech, Garcilaso, and certain forms of Andean awareness of history. It is not instructive to discuss whether or not the phrase "[God] created Manco Capac" implies belief in the Adamitic state of the first Inca, but it is important that for Choquehuanca, pre-Inca times were "savage," repeating Garcilaso's idea that the empire was a great civilizing force on peoples that until then had lived in crudest barbarism.[47] Clearly Choquehuanca, as a member of the indigenous aristocracy, had to adhere to this interpretation of history. The phrase affirming that God "created Manco Capac" seems to be no more than hyperbole, but it fits well with Garcilaso's postulates relative to the providential function of the empire as preparation for the Christianization of the Indies.

Choquehuanca deviates from Garcilaso's path, however, when he alienates himself from his Indian heritage and says that "*his* [Manco Capac's] race sinned" (the Inca never stops vindicating his maternal ancestor), when he imagines that the empire was destroyed for having committed an undefined "sin," or when he interprets the conquest and colony as "three centuries of expiation," none of which corresponds to the Inca's thought as expressed in the *Royal Commentaries*. On this last point it is clear that Choquehuanca, within the context of the emancipation, criticizes a viceroyal regime in which there are paradoxical overtones of both indigenous thought (such as that of Guaman Poma) and Toledo's chroniclers, who carefully catalogued the "sins" of the Inca Empire and the reasons for its just punishment. It is also noteworthy that the indigenous heritage negated by this distancing "his" reappears at least indirectly in the mention of Pizarro: neither "created" nor "sent" by God, like Manco or Bolívar, but—like a whip or a plague—"flung forth" against the Indian people.

What is perhaps most unsettling about the speech is that its providentialist ideology seems to take shape within a cyclical and self-canceling concept of history that may be related to the Quechua consciousness of the time.[48] In fact, the speech takes into account four extended cycles: those of the "savages," the Incas, and the colony, and the one born with Bolívar (the omission of San Martín and his precursors is noteworthy). The transitions from one to another fluctuate between redemption and Messianism (Manco Capac and Bolívar) and apocalyptic catastrophe (Pizarro). I cannot confirm that this thought has a direct correlation to the indigenous interpretation of history, with its great cycles that conclude with a *pachacutec*, but it is worth considering.

In sum, Choquehuanca's speech interweaves several worldviews in a discourse again formally harmonious and internally heterogeneous and broken. Choquehuanca's voice seems to come from various times, as if it were transmitting a deeply heteroclite plurality, while his language dialogues with other languages. José Ratto-Ciarlo has noted that the reference to the sun, inevitable in the literature of the time, has a special significance in the proclamation and functions in a unique way compared to other treatments of this topic, whose most obvious manifestation is simply denominating Bolívar as "Sun" or—in the neoclassic spirit—"Febo."[49] But one must also note that in the speech the correlative descent of the sun and elevation of Bolívar goes beyond the author's rhetoric and the conscious motivations and can be read as a formulated substitution of the reign of the god of the Incas, the Sun, by the mythologized figure of Bolívar. From this perspective the breaking down of history into a series of closed cycles requires, once again, a certain homogenizing glue: Bolívar (and of course the republic) substitutes for but also continues the history of Manco and the Inca empire. This reading is enriched upon noting that Daniel Florencio O'Leary, Bolívar's aide-de-camp, a few weeks before Choquehuanca made his speech, had published in *El Sol del Cuzco* a tumultuous elegy to the Liberator signed by "Manco-Capac" employing Bolivarian rhetoric, and which ends by emphasizing the same idea of substitution-continuity: "The lamp of my glory is extinguished . . . in the shadow of your laurels," says "Manco Capac" (O'Leary) to Bolívar.[50] So underlying the speech's attempt to reconcile and unify Inca tradition and the Republic, several worldviews and symbols are expressed in a discourse that is profoundly syncretic, but hardly free of contradictions.[51]

These are two founding texts of republican Peru, to be sure, but also two texts whose homogenizing spirit does not and cannot obviate the fact that its internal contradictions not only presage the conflicts that the nation will have to face but also delineate the space from which the Republic speaks and determine the ambiguous nature of the subject at the edge of its radical multivalency. Perhaps both texts are signs that, as persistent in its intent as it may be, this literature cannot erase the contradictions that make it up, and that only now are we beginning to understand.

IN FICTION: THREE NOVELS

The novel is one of the clear signs of nineteenth-century Latin American modernity. One can argue ad infinitum about its origins in colonial accounts, since there are many with a certain novelistic bent, but it is obvious that as a more-or-less codified genre, our novel is a product of that century.[52] It also, from a complementary perspective, conforms to the worldview and certain social processes of that age. The link between the novel and modernity cannot be overstated. A genre just recently unveiled, it represents the coming of age of a literature that was ignorant of its existence and out-of-date and frames itself within a vast constellation of social needs. The first of these, of course, is modernization itself, but resting on the vehemence of a national definition. It is not merely a question of cataloguing and examining how literature treats social matters (though much of that can be found in the relationship between the novel and *costumbrista* genres), nor the proposals of explicit constitutional projects for nations worthy of such a title.[53] It is, on a deeper level, a question of the inevitable formulation, intentional or not, of what then—and for a long time thereafter—would be the nature of nationality: its overarching homogeneity. Frederic Jameson surely discovered and refined his concept of "national allegory" in the literatures of the Third World, but his postulates are exceptionally provocative when applied to the nineteenth-century Latin American novel.[54]

The first Latin American novelistic exercise obviously turns on the social obsession relative to the makeup of the new nations. In many cases the world of family relationships provides the plot through which is played out, consciously or not, the allegory of the desired founding of a nation. As a basic social nucleus with a strongly homogenizing content, the family was probably perceived to be in a metonymical (and sometimes metaphorical) relationship with the nation, or the social microinstitution that most lent itself to allegorizing the macroproblematic of the nation. It is not necessary to go into Freudian or Lacanian psychoanalytic concepts to see the significant network that ties the nation to the family. But the rhetoric of nascent nationalism, especially in the sense of filiation (citizens as "sons" of the homeland and "brothers" among themselves, for example), allows the reading that the desire to be a nation follows a familial pattern, including its possible perversions (from the stereotype of the "bad child" to the significant insistence on the theme of incest). This has to do with the problem of an identity crisis that probably cannot be resolved except by violating, at least indirectly, some dark taboo. This recalls Octavio Paz's philosophical, anthropological, and poetic reflections on the meaning of rape in Mexican culture.[55]

My question is simpler. Given that the novel implies an ironic distance between, through, or in relation to the inevitable frustration of the hero and the defectiveness of his world, or supposes the resemantization and refunctionalization of carnivalesque discourse, its semantic virtuality can easily harbor the cruelties of a history of frustration, although now the "true" protagonist is not an individual but the entire nation, disguised as a family. I am not proposing a conscious, metaphorical figure through which the author "prefers" to speak about private life so as not to treat a more complex and compromising public life, but rather a chance overlapping of national problems under the guise of family conflicts and interpersonal relationships. It is as if the same problems that weigh down nations were vented on a different scale and the nation enjoyed a consistency and problematic parallel to its less complex institutions. Speaking about the family was a way of speaking about those other, broader, more transcendent institutions, with the advantage of suspending explicitly political discourse, while developing implicit discourses about areas such as ethics and psychology. Language always carries a much more open and profound semantic charge than its specific referent. Perhaps the word that precedes all words and the one to which it responds form an unexpected arc: the one that says "family" answers the one seeking "nation."[56]

On the other hand, the novel—precisely because of its ties with modernity—lies definitively and exclusively on the side of writing; it is, in a manner of speaking, the genre least able to be oralized. Of course, as in Palma's *Tradiciones* or the language of *costumbrismo*, there is an attempt to include oral forms and formulae from popular speech. But this is clearly an artifice, where contrary to what one might imagine, the "citing" of oral language implies (by the use of quotation marks or italics) its exclusion from the linguistic norm that the very text proposes as correct and pertinent. It is no coincidence that one of the most significant scenes in *Torn from the Nest* describes one of Margarita's reading lessons, especially if one remembers that the same scene, with very similar connotations, reappears in *Doña Barbara* almost a century later.[57] It is as if the novel itself were theorizing the urgency of creating a *reading* public that needed to find its true meaning and, more vitally, exist within modernity's elevated social parameters, which obviously included literacy as an essential link.[58]

Cumandá

Reading Juan León Mera's Cumandá in the context I have just outlined leads to an examination of the importance of the author and his work to political and social life in Ecuador in the last third of the nineteenth century.[59] But I shall go in a different direction. I wish to examine just one problem: the oblique representation of the nation in the romantic adventures narrated in the novel. I realize the artifice that this analysis presupposes (but what reading does not?).

From the outset it is imperative to note that Mera is said to have written his novel to please the Spanish Royal Academy and to show himself worthy of the honor of having been made a member. At bottom he is proving his ability as a writer who credibly manipulates the codes of high metropolitan culture, as revealed by the dose of modesty present in the dedicatory letter. Clearly his explicit reader ("my little work goes directly to Y[our] E[xcellency] and I hope that, by such respectable means, it will be presented to the Royal Academy") has nothing to do with national matters, and the publication of the work narcissistically turns on the recognition of the author's personal prestige, all according to a ritual falling just short of courtly.

Also included in the dedicatory is the significant fact that the novel goes back, chronologically, to "the times when these lands belonged to Spain," and that its story is framed by the distant geographical space of the eastern jungles of Ecuador, immediately defined as being inhabited by savage tribes and almost completely unknown to civilized people, with the exception of missionaries. Outside of the Republic and its centralized space, *Cumandá* does not seem to speak at all to the formative problems of the Ecuadorian nation, although it does allude to these tangentially. For example, at the end of the first chapter, after describing the life of the "savages" quite briefly and then going to great lengths to extol the splendor and beauty of the jungle, it becomes apparent that the novel is offering an account of the unknown, strange, distant, and mysterious: "Dear reader, we have tried to present to you, though imperfectly, the theater into which we are placing you: allow yourself to be led and follow me patiently. We shall rarely turn our gaze upon civilized society; *forget* her if you wish to delve into the scenes of nature and the customs of the wayward and savage children of the jungle" (Mera, *Cumandá*, 10, Cornejo's emphasis).

As with all functions of memory, this is a selective operation, but in this case it is also profoundly symptomatic. Not only is "civilized society" not obviated, it presides over all the action through two of its most elevated representatives: the priest and the poet. And if the "children of the jungle" are "savages," it is because the expulsion of the Jesuits destroyed the achievements of their civilizing mission, begun again in the text by Father Orozco. His success with the Andoas is praised repeatedly (especially in chapter 5) and serves to compare these Christianized Indians with the savages of the other tribes. In this way the reader cannot "forget" that the primitive world presented in the novel is a strange archaism that endures as a result of the errors of a civilization that long ago could have integrated it. In fact, by trying to erase civilization from the reader's awareness, it is removed from the problematic space of the account. Or on an even more compromising level, we must "forget" civilization even if the author reminds us about it. The ideological effect of making others forget what the narrator knows is but one sign of the novel's authoritarian interpretation.

In addition it is evident that if the story takes place in another world, it is told completely from and for *this* world and from and for its memory and consciousness, even though its effect is the opposite. Consequently it is not wrong to subject the novel's referents, which are exotic in appearance only, to the necessities that notoriously—yet obliquely—govern its composition. From this perspective *Cumandá* relates the conflict between civilization, understood as Christian civilization, and savagery, which has several predictable meanings, all dependent upon its being pagan. At bottom, and always with broad strokes, Mera's novel constructs its strange world with the awareness that its true, significant space is not in the past nor in the jungle, but in the problematic of the Republic's formation. And he proposes for the latter, as Hernán Vidal has pointed out, a definitely theocratic system.[60]

I shall not detail the whole narration but would like to establish that its crux has to do with problems of parentage. In effect, in his secular life, directly condemned for obeying a desire for wealth that leads him to cruelly exploit "his" Indians, Orozco has formed a family (white, of course), which is at one point massacred by the savages. Apparently only he and his son, Carlos, are spared, although later it is made know that his daughter, Julia—kidnapped by the jungle dwellers—also survives. Repentant of his sins and now freed from matrimony by the death of his wife, Orozco becomes a priest and returns to the jungle to evangelize the Indians that killed his loved ones and thus redeems the sins of his previous life. He keeps Carlos, who has become a young, romantic poet, with him, so that he becomes a double father: both biologically and spiritually, as a priest. This double paternity is fundamental to the semantic economy of the text by overstating the virtues and sacred character of the patriarchal figure. It is only a small leap to say that *Cumandá* is a hymn to the patriarch.

As is predictable in Latin American romantic fiction of the nineteenth century, Carlos falls in love with a young Indian, Cumandá, who later discovers that she is his sister, Julia. The novel insists as often as possible on Cumandá's exceptional character, not only because of her (obviously white) outward appearance but also because of her evidently irreproachable moral virtues. It also takes every opportunity to say that the love between Carlos and Cumandá remains unpolluted and pure. So that this is even clearer, they frequently call each other "brother" and "sister" and make their courtship a filial one, so that even the least attentive reader assumes that Cumandá is Julia long before the narrator unveils the scantily concealed mystery of her origin.[61] As is common in this type of fiction, the girl's seeming father (who is the same one that abducted her, but has changed his name) and her supposed siblings, all clearly non-Christianized Indians, thrust an implacable hatred toward whites between Cumandá-Julia and Carlos. They not only try to kill Carlos on several occasions but also hand Cumandá over to the elderly chief of the most powerful tribe in the area. He dies before consummating the marriage, and according to the tribe's ritual, his young wife must die as well. She manages to escape but perishes in the attempt. Note the words with which (his) Father Orozco comforts Carlos: "If the course of providential events had not impeded your marriage to Cumandá, you would have been the husband of your own sister; by the sacramental blessing of a horrid incest, instead of domestic happiness, innumerable calamities would have befallen you. In order to avoid these evils, God chose to take our Julia away unto himself, adorned with her virginal purity and angelic candor" (Mera, *Cumandá*, 232). And even more so those of the offended suitor-brother: "Do you think, my father, that our love was an earthly and carnal passion? Oh, you could not imagine! It was an altruistic and totally pure love: it was, without our knowing it, brotherly love elevated to its greatest perfection. As brother and sister we would have been as united and happy as lovers or husband and wife" (Mera, *Cumandá*, 232–33).

Clearly the socioethnic group represented by the Orozco family in Mera's novel sees itself as self-sufficient in endogamic terms ("brother and sister . . . as happy as lovers or husband and wife"), and there is no doubt as to either the legitimacy of its position of dominance or the mechanisms for its indefinite reproduction.[62] On purely ideological grounds, as representatives of the Christian religion and Western civilization, they lose all credibility once the account has polarized their representation between the evangelizing priests (and poets) and the savage tribes, thereby slowly, but with systematic precision, diluting all intermediate strata. Thus it is easy to differentiate between Christianized savages, who are no longer bound by their old ways, and pagan savages, who are, and to an extreme degree. The author does not hide the fact that the former are radically inferior to their evangelizers (and masters) and that their natural function is to serve them materially and spiritually.

Among the many barriers that separate civilized whites from savage Indians, there is yet another: the one that separates writing from orality. Clearly orality is the realm of the savages, normally expressed not so much with words as screams and howls (and their zoomorphic meaning), or in some cases with the lugubrious beating of drums. Writing corresponds to the whites' side in two ways: as writing, disseminated orally by Father Orozco in his sermons, and poetry, rather hidden like some exotic jungle charm, by young Carlos. All we know of the latter is his love poem–message to Cumandá, written on the bark of a tree: an inscription cut into unbridled nature. The savages will burn this poem-message as an obvious manifestation not only of their barbarism but also of their irreconcilable struggle with the culture that expresses this writing as poetry, the highest art form of the cultivated West.[63]

It is not surprising, then, that the image of national society that emerges from Mera's text is arranged in a highly defined hierarchy: it functions vertically with religion as its justification and the high Western culture of the young poet clearly present on a second plane. There are historical-social explanations for this, but it is obvious that *Cumandá* is an anachronistic representation of the colonial system that split the continent in two, with the chronicles providing legal testimony. In effect, this novel proposes a model for a colonial nation (not an oxymoron, as we know) in which a "republic of Spaniards" is established above "a republic of Indians," where both Indians who were part of the high culture of the Tawantinsuyu and mestizos are left out in order to place them all under the "barbarism" of jungle tribes. These have only to accept their absolute dependency by adapting to the requirements of a socially powerful state religion, or be devoured by their own savagery or annihilated by a higher power.

Cumandá is the least conciliatory of the novels studied in this chapter. Marked by authoritarianism and underscored by the romanticism of its plot, it plainly defines a unique, vertical order. Thus the image of the national community is not constructed with the discourse of homogenizing integration, but under the protection of a transcendent mandate that permits the legitimization of that hierarchic verticality in its crudest and most aggressive form. The Republic should imitate the colony and establish its system according to the most basic of its dynamics: the all-encompassing superiority of one group, which is "obligated" to rule, and the inferiority of the other, the majority, which is in "natural need" of recognizing its subaltern state and, consequently, obeying.

Torn from the Nest

It is not my intention to examine in its entirety Clorinda Matto de Turner's first novel, *Torn from the Nest*, although a careful reading would lend itself to the matter at hand.[64] I wish to consider just one point. *Torn from the Nest* tells of life in Killac (a village that symbolizes the cruel workings and organization of Andean society) during a stay by the Maríns, a couple that obviously represents the values of the narrator: they are cultured, irreproachably moral, generous, and just. The Maríns, bearers of the ideology of an urban, liberal, and progressive bourgeoisie, are indignant over the exploitation suffered by the Indians at the hands of the political, judicial, and ecclesiastical authorities and the abuses committed against them by the wool merchants. They decide to defend the Indians, are attacked by those holding power in the town, and finally, having been "overthrown," decide to return to the city.

The Maríns' failure is somewhat mitigated by their decision to adopt the two daughters of the Indian couple Juan and Marcela Yupanqui, who died in the defense of their protectors' home. The bearers of civilization do not manage to change the implacable Andean social order, but at least they save Margarita and Rosalía, who are "torn from the nest" in the first part of the novel, from its ravages. In the second part, besides reiterating its accusations of exploitation, the novel narrates the ingenuous love between Margarita and Manuel Pancorbo and its unfortunate ending: they discover that they share paternity in Bishop Pedro Miranda y Claro, Killac's former priest, and the novel closes with these two now being even more tragically "torn from the nest."

The second part's clearly melodramatic plot is not unusual for the nineteenth-century Latin American novel, which incessantly criticizes the moral laxity of the clergy and in Matto's novel the celibacy of priests. But it goes far deeper than this. As I have said, in the nineteenth century our novel produced a complex allegory of the nation and its problems through the image of the family and the interpersonal relationships on which it is based and sustained. Obviously *Torn from the Nest* privileges the familial nuclei represented by the Maríns, Pancorbos, Yupanquis, and Champis to the point that there are hardly any characters in the novel outside of these circles. The major exception is the priest Pascual (and his predecessor Miranda, now bishop), but this exception only reinforces the importance of family ties as reiterated in the preface and other parts of the novel: clergy vice and the tragedies it engenders derive from the unnatural celibacy imposed on those taking religious vows. Paradoxically the families that appear in *Torn from the Nest* are either incomplete (the Maríns have no children) or harbor some terrible secret, like the hidden filiation between Manuel and Margarita and the violence suffered by their mothers.

The meaning incarnated by the family in Matto's novel links this theme to another that thoroughly intercrosses it: interracial relationships. In some ways, as presented in *Torn from the Nest*, the family is the privileged space in which ethnic alliances or conflicts can occur. The emphasis placed on the tie between family and race clearly justifies an interpretation on a social rather than ethical level, which in turn leads to considering the central issue of the nineteenth century: the formation of nations.

Matto's preoccupation with the future of indigenous people takes shape in the decision made by the Maríns (her narrative spokespersons) to adopt the Yupanquis' orphans. Since the novel relates the death or continued, inevitable suffering of the Indians, Margarita and Rosalía's adoption implies tangentially—but forcefully—that *Torn from the Nest* sees no effective solution for the indigenous race, though it is less skeptical when it comes to the fortune of isolated individuals.[65] Clearly the adoption, with its resulting change of name (Yupanqui to Marín), is an especially dynamic device underscoring the building of a new identity and the saving nature of this process. Of course the adoption is followed by an education meant to erase all traces of former identity: in *Herencia*, a novel that in part continues the story line of *Torn from the Nest*, one of the Maríns' adopted daughters is indistinguishable from other young women in Lima's high society.[66] A new identity is firmly established. The long process begins with the scene in which the tender and naïve Manuel teaches Margarita to read, continues through her education in the best schools in Lima, and ends with the triumph of the adopted girl at the apex of the capital's social order.[67]

Beyond Matto's intent and the stereotypes of romantic melodrama, in the radical transformation of the Yupanqui girls into Maríns there is underlying and disturbing meaning: the Indian's salvation depends on being changed into a different person, a creole, with the subsequent assimilation of different mores and customs, and the generosity of those who make this ethnic-social metamorphosis possible. In some ways, the adoption story is emblematic of that society's conviction that education was a powerfully transformative force. Manuel González Prada makes this explicit in his "Discurso en el Politeama": "Teach [the Indian] to read and you will see whether or not within a generation he rises to the dignity of a man."[68] In pedagogical terms, however, it consisted of merely Westernizing the pupil.

Within the framework of the "possible consciousness" of the time, education was considered to be nothing more than a process favoring the realization of European ideals. As an efficient resource for the homogenization of the country, education not only did not foresee pluralism and conflict but also—and on the contrary—openly opposed them. *Torn from the Nest* speaks of "true civilization" as a single system and education as a way of acceding to its ordaining principles. The "white" filiation of the Yupanqui children implies not only adoption then, but also education, although in the text the latter is intertwined with the experience of a stable home life. Thus *Torn from the Nest* proposes a totalizing category: adopting and renaming a child is a transcendent act because the name of the new parents carries with it the configuration of a new person. Motivated by mercy, the adoption of the Indian girls is a purely spiritual manifestation (and perhaps for that very reason more powerfully symbolic) of procreation.

As an integrative metaphor, the adoption of Margarita and Rosalía expresses the desire for a homogeneous nation by overcoming indigenous dissidence through the acculturating education of its obviously inferior citizens. But this eloquent allegory of an imaginary country integrated on a modern European model has, nonetheless, a surprising inverse. In a word, the Indian girls are the ones that allow the Marín family to be realized under its own ideology and fulfill its basic reproductive function. The novel emphasizes the sacred nature of paternity and maternity and insists that the family is the only realm where these can be sacredly realized. A complementary rationale purports that a family without children is not really a family and that infertility prevents a person from reaching the fullness of his or her human and sacred function.

Since *Torn from the Nest* is a clearly didactic, the reproductive function of the family is a device that extends well beyond procreation. The family is the great machine that reproduces socially accepted behaviors and values or, in other words, the ideological mortar that permits the smooth functioning of society within a determined order. Naturally, children are the gears in this mechanism. The transformation of the Yupanqui girls into Maríns demonstrates the efficiency of this process but has at the same time another meaning: it is thanks to them that the Maríns fulfill their function as a family and thereby acquire worth as reproducers of the social system. It is a notable paradox.[69] One wonders whether, if the adoption of the Indian girls can be read as an allegory of homogenizing the country, then the defects of the Maríns as a family had they not adopted might be interpreted in a like manner: as a symbolic representation of the need for the social sector they represent to take on certain commitments with other groups in order to realize its own social agenda.

As parents and educators of the Indians, the Maríns seem to recognize that on a social and national scale they must operate under the condition of absorbing others—in clearly dependent terms—as "children." From an inverse perspective, they do not seem to be able to reproduce themselves within their own social space, and much less make themselves part of the national "family" without a clearly asymmetrical alliance with other groups: a consensus earned through the assimilation of others, but to a subordinate position. Of course this obviously hypothetical reading in no way implies the presumption of authorial awareness. National allegories tend to be framed in literary discourse by using mechanisms that are much more complex than the intent and explicit ideology of the writer. They are representations of a vague social imaginary and tend to be forged in a language that assimilates collective impulses.

There are other notable dimensions to the allegorization of the family in *Torn from the Nest*. The characterization of Margarita makes her exceptional from the very beginning. Although Marcela, her mother, is presented as "striking for her typically Peruvian beauty" (Matto, *Torn from the Nest*, 9), the Maríns are taken aback when they meet Margarita and muse that "her loveliness reflected that mixture of the Spaniard and the Indian that has produced stunning beauties in Peru" (22) even when, at that point, they believe both her parents to be Indians. They are not yet planning on adoption but do wish to accept her as their goddaughter. The end of the story reveals that Margarita is the child of a Spanish or creole priest and that she is, as the Maríns intuited, a mestiza. This final revelation has a complex effect on the above reading: on one hand it distances the Maríns in their relationship to the Indians, since they adopted a young mestiza, not an Indian, whose origin contains echoes of the conquest's first mestizaje. On the other hand the fact that the adoption also includes little

Rosalía, child of Juan and Marcela Yupanqui, preserves that relationship. She is pure Indian.

The delayed confirmation that Margarita is indeed a mestiza has to do not only with openly ideological matters but also more indirectly with the system of verisimilitude present in the story. Since Margarita is a much more important character than Rosalía and only she is present in the continuation of the novel, it is natural that her absolute and sudden "whitening" would disturb the credibility of the story and thus create a potential conflict in the mind of the reader. One only has to remember that some years later in Enrique López Albújar's *Matalaché* something similar happens: the protagonist, a black slave, becomes a mulatto with direct descent from a white nobleman, shortly before consummating his love with his master's beautiful daughter.[70]

The two girls' different original parentage makes the homogenizing image of the family even stronger: the Maríns assume authority in a home that takes in both mestizo and Indian. But with respect to the latter the novel is somewhat elliptical. Rosalía is practically just a name in *Torn from the Nest*, and her story is not continued in *Herencia*. The novel clearly privileges Margarita's adoption, thus showing a definite, though not exclusive, predilection for the mestizo stratum. By slightly exaggerating Rosalía's invisibility, one might think that *Torn from the Nest* seeks first to generate an expectation of reconciliation between the extremes of the ethnic gamut (Marín-Yupanqui), then dilute its radical nature, and finally emphasize the importance of the intermediate, mestizo link (Marín-Miranda-Yupanqui), but saving to the last, like an evocative, almost imperceptible backdrop, the initial proposal.

Thus, the insistent problems that intercross in the familial space of *Torn from the Nest* seem to be representative of the contradictions that troubled Peruvian society at the end of the nineteenth century. At bottom the familial images offered by the novel often find their conflictive nexus in the problem of filiation: Margarita and Manuel are ignorant of their mutual paternity, and their discovery is tragic not only because it cuts off their love with the terrible pain of incest but also because the burden of a sacrilegious father is irresolvable and gives over the sanctity of parentage to violence and sin. The allegory seems to point to a deformed order that can only be transformed by the will and action of those, like the Maríns, who decide to extirpate it (by providing filiation and legitimacy) while they correct (through adoption) their own incompleteness and sterility. It is the allegory of a broken nation, of course, but one that is also hopeful: the family (the entire nation) can rebuild, protect, and strengthen itself by offering a home to those who have none.

Juan de la Rosa

I have left for last my comments on *Juan de la Rosa*, by Nataniel Aguirre, because it is the novel that most openly develops the theme of the formation of the Andean nations and provides a much broader and elaborate gamut of strategies, along with their inclusionary and exclusionary dynamics, than those that appear in *Cumandá* or *Torn from the Nest*.[71] As with the other two, I shall treat only certain aspects of the text, specifically those that have to do with recounting the forging of Bolivian independence (and identity), as well as the link between filiation and nationality. Obviously many other important aspects are left untouched, since this is a novel that—despite its apparent simplicity—conceals extraordinary complexity.[72]

Introduced by the subtitle "Memoirs of the Last Soldier of the Independence Movement," the text explicitly places itself at the intersection of personal experience as autobiography and experience of a social nature, related to the historical novel or history itself.[73] If the text of memory has a closed verification system in which the speaker is the same as the one being spoken of (a sort of self-referentiality), then history, whether fictionalized or not, transmits its truthful nature outside itself and demands that the one speaking have the "objective" authority to do so. The fact that the narrator/protagonist defines himself as a participant in the war of independence (with the addendum that he is the last survivor of that time) implies the use of a mechanism that allows him to transform his personal recollection into a collective text and guarantee the authenticity of his historical narration. In other words, the communicative contract presupposes that we have before us a privileged, highly credible testimony that contains the drama of its being the last one possible: no one can tell this story again. The "last soldier" also has the last word.

The link between memory and history as it appears in *Juan de la Rosa* also offers a complex temporal game that encompasses an extremely long period of time. The "memoir" is sent to the "Fourteenth of September Society" in 1884 (as told in the letter that serves as the novel's prologue), though its writing was begun in 1848; but the matters it specifically treats correspond to the period of time between 1810 and 1812, with some reports from other sources going back as far as the eighteenth century. The events occurring between 1810 and 1812 appear within a multiply-framed narration, each frame having a peculiar function: the sections that narrate what happened first chronologically merely establish a filiation between the eighteenth-century uprisings against the colonial regime and the one that is being related, while the later sections have no practical narrative formalization, but act as perspectives of conscience in judging what is being told (1810 to 1812) and not told (1813 to 1848 or even 1884) through the eyes of actualized experience.[74] Thus, the text constructs the story of a more-or-less distant past and the memories of childhood experience (Juanito's) through and with the much more complete and reliable awareness of the elder Colonel Juan de la Rosa, a patriarch who was formed alongside the nation, and, in some ways, sees himself as indistinguishable from it.

The selective filter employed in *Juan de la Rosa* in recounting the antecedents of the early Cochabamba independence rebellion has been sufficiently analyzed in comparison to the mestizo Calatayud's revolt of 1730 but lessens the importance of the indigenous ones led fifty years later by Tupac Amaru and Tupac Catari.[75] Clearly there is no direct lineage drawn between these great events and the Cochabamba exploits, while Calatayud's uprising, though much more modest historically, is justified enthusiastically. Friar Justo, who represents wisdom and the purest ideals of independence, explicitly contrasts both historical experiences when he says to Juanito, "I will not exhaust your attention with even the briefest account of any of the bloody revolts in which the indigenous race insanely attempted to recover its independence, proclaiming a war of the races—only inevitably to lose. But I will recount, at some length, a great event: a heroic, yet premature effort that matches my objectives and has special interest for us both. In November 1730 . . ." (Aguirre, *Juan de la Rosa*, 38).

There may be several reasons for establishing this opposition between the Indians' "bloody revolts," the remembrance of which is superfluous ("I will not exhaust your attention"), and the "great, heroic event" that is worthy of extensive recounting; but the main reason probably has to do with an effort to connect the Cochabamba rebellion with an exemplary historical event and not the gory "insanity" of the indigenous uprisings. The narrator insists on showing that both the Calatayud and Cochabamba insurrections were mestizo movements that brought together many classes and ethnic groups and that they were *national* from the novel's premonitory, but perfectly valid, point of view. Friar Justo's speech explaining the reasons justifying the struggle for independence can have no other meaning:

> [The Spaniards] consider themselves nothing more and nothing less than our masters and lords. Those of us who are their very children — the *criollos* — are looked upon with disdain; they think that we should never aspire to the honors and public positions that are reserved just for them. The mestizos, whose blood is half like their's, are scorned and condemned to suffer innumerable humiliations. The Indians, the poor, conquered race, find themselves reduced to being treated as beasts of labor — they are a flock that the *mita* decimates every year in the depths of the mines. These reasons alone would suffice for us to wish to have our own government. . . . (Aguirre, *Juan de la Rosa*, 35)

Here "our" clearly encompasses creoles (Friar Justo), mestizos (Juanito), and Indians, who have no personalized representation in the account, though they are mentioned several times as participants in the liberation movement. Since the child Juan is the protagonist of the story and Colonel Juan de la Rosa its narrator, it is not surprising that throughout the text this middle stratum, flanked asymmetrically by the other two with obvious preference for the creoles, is the one that functions as the principal axis of the social process leading to Bolivian independence under the tutelage of the irreproachable example of another heroic mestizo, the craftsman Alejo Calatayud. The idea of nationhood is, then, definitely framed by mestizaje functioning both as an emblem of internal synthesis, with the mestizo being living proof of this, and the intermediary position between creoles and Indians, which produces the same, convergent effect: it is the realm of homogeneity and harmony, the model for a nation that must unite its disparate factions into a coherent, compact, and representative whole. This zeal for inclusion can even — in its discourse's most Christian moments — take in Spaniards.

The account is at its most ambiguous in its characterization of the mestizo, for example, the introduction of Rosa, Juanito's mother and Calatayud's descendent, in the first pages of the novel: "Rosita . . . was a young *criolla* as beautiful as a perfect *Andalusian* woman, with a head full of long, plentiful curls . . . very white, small, tightly packed teeth, like those that are found only among *Indian* women, of whose blood *a few drops* must have flowed in her veins" (Aguirre, *Juan de la Rosa*, 8, Cornejo's emphasis).

This is manifestly a vacillating, even contradictory presentation, which defines the character first as belonging to the creole stratum and praised for her proximity to Spanish ancestry, and then made slightly mestizo with those few "drops" of Indian blood that "must" (in the dubative sense) flow through her veins. At a later point the author generalizes this indecision. For example, the narrator presents another female character, Mariquita, in these terms: "Few times have I seen such a beautiful model of a *chola*. Her wavy, chestnut hair; her large, brown eyes . . . everything about her was somehow better, finer, and more delicate than in the majority of the women of the robust Cochabambian race—[she was] much more Spanish than Indian" (Aguirre, *Juan de la Rosa*, 107).

Mestizaje, at least in Cochabamba, appears as an asymmetrical and unbalanced mixture of the two ancestries: more Spanish than Indian. Even then, only in exceptional cases ("few times") does it transcend material virtues ("robust") and reach the point of beauty. This and other, similar texts explain what is no more than a *lapsus*, when at the beginning of the novel the narrator remembers his childhood and points out that in spite of living in poverty, he and his mother were "a thousand times more fortunate than the masses, composed of Indians and *mestizos*." This marks a paradoxical distancing (we/them) from the stratum to which otherwise he says he belongs.

Clearly, the creole condition infiltrates a discourse that explicitly attempts to show its mestizo filiation. In my view, this has much to say about the fiction underlying the construction of the narrative voice as mestizo and the implicit ideology of speaking from this position. As we have seen, the mestizo identity of the character-narrator facilitates the representation of his biography as a symbol of a homogeneous nation made up of syncretic agreements, but it also permits the displacement of the indigenous component and the indirect preservation of creole hegemony. In a word, the emblematic mestizo is almost a creole and is largely indistinguishable from the latter. The representation of mestizo experience and voice as national categories is multifunctional, then, and responds to an inclusive movement that appears to unite everyone, while its involuntary fissures define a subtle system of exclusion or subordination.

At times excluded and always subordinated, the indigenous populace is a vague and mute presence throughout the novel. Nevertheless, it appears with symptomatic assiduousness through its mestizo characters. One portion is especially significant: after the first, contradictory description of Juanito's mother, we learn that Rosa used to sing tearfully in Quechua, "the most tender and affectionate language in the world, ... the *yaravi* of the farewell of the Inca Manco: the sorrowful lament ... addressed to his father—the sun—asking for death to take him so that he will not have to witness the eternal slavery of his race." This completes the report provided a few paragraphs earlier that in her modest house there was an illustration of the Virgin and one "depicting the death of Atahuallpa" (Aguirre, *Juan de la Rosa*, 8–9). These references to Quechua culture seem to diminish the emphasis placed on Rosa's creole and Spanish heritage, but it is significant that both musically and pictorially they refer to the defeat of the Incas and have as their basis imperial imagery.[76] What is rescued from the Indian world seems to be its glorious past; ending, however, in defeat: the pictorial representation of the death of the Inca and recounting the *yaravi* of his farewell are unequivocal signs of this awareness of closure and finality.

The narrator has a definite admiration for Quechua (in another section he qualifies it as "such an intimate and persuasive tongue"), but curiously the novel shows that it is employed by mestizos (Juan, Rosa, Alejo, and so on), creoles (Oquendo and the ultra-*fidelista* doña Teresa), and even foreigners (Cros), while the Indians do not speak in proper Quechua, but rather "that ugly dialect used by the brutalized descendents of the children of the sun." Thus one of the major attributes of the indigenous people, their language, merely subsists in its true form on the lips of others (especially the mestizos), while its native speakers have perverted, degraded, and vilified it. Perhaps this point best expresses the design and ideological function of the novel's mestizo protagonists: in effect the mestizos are the ones that take on the best of native tradition and preserve it in opposition to the Indians' own practices. If the former speak good Quechua and the latter degrade it, it is because in general the mestizos (and not the Indians) are the true heirs of Inca tradition and, consequently, the authentic bearers of a history with that splendid origin.[77] As alluded to above, the mestizo group has an unstable and porous representation: is it the mestizo who somehow wants to meld with the creole and thus gain prestige, or does the creole need to become more mestizo in order to better represent the all-encompassing nature of the state? In either case, the one into whom all history seems to have most naturally flowed seizes the moment and rises to the top. Since the Indians have lost their own history and language, it is the others, the ambiguous mestizo-creoles, who can successfully confront the task of producing a nation that in the end cannot help but be indistinguishable from their own self-image.

The novel provides another, more oblique dimension to the same problem. The social makeup of the nation has its correlate in the construction of a subject that evokes and narrates the story of his childhood, which is the story of the search for his filiation. Juanito appears as a "child of the wind," a "cast-off" who initially does not know who his parents are and is determined to "pull back the mysterious veil of [his] origin," although it seems clear to both him and the reader from the beginning that Rosita is his mother, as is later confirmed. She nevertheless refuses to reveal the identity of his father and expresses her will that this enigma not be unraveled for Juanito even after she dies ("Your dear mother never wanted you to know"). The mystery is melodramatically resolved only near the end of the novel: two creole brothers, sons of the rich Spaniard, fall in love with the mestiza Rosita. One of them decides to sacrifice his happiness for that of his brother and becomes a priest (Friar Justo, whom the reader met in the first chapter). The other brother goes mad because his father strongly opposes the marriage. By reading Friar Justo's papers, Juanito learns of his progenitor's identity and the close relationship that tied him to the priest, who has just died.[78] He immediately decides to go in search of his father, arrives as the latter is on his deathbed, and says, "I had no other mission than to close [his] eyes in pity." He then adds, "My life changed completely from that moment on."

This brief summary poses several questions. If his maternity is revealed early on and demonstrates that Juanito belongs to Calatayud's heroic, legendary, and highly praised lineage, his paternity is notably ambivalent. On one hand, the father is creole, and therefore very close to the Spanish stratum, which can be understood within the global strategy of the novel as not only offering a homogenizing and syncretic vision of Bolivian nationality but also belying the privilege that the narrator concedes to this ethnicity. On the other, the image of the father is negative in that he is absent, goes mad, and dies. In my opinion, and without resorting to any sort of psychoanalysis, the novel simultaneously affirms and negates the identity symbolized by the father. It fundamentally affirms the fact that Juanito is the grandson of a Spaniard and the son of a creole, but then reneges when the father fulfills none of his duties and the son recognizes his parentage only in the ceremonial closing of his dead father's eyes. All this seems to indicate that the authoritarianism of the Spanish grandfather and the correlative annihilation of the creole that obeys beyond reason (as opposed to his brother, Friar Justo, who disobeys and finds both religion and its underlying Enlightened reason) represent the demise of colonial power (precisely because of its irrational authoritarianism), and the decrepitude of a creole stratum incapable of rebelling against its alienating power. Nonetheless neither authoritarianism nor disintegration are sufficient to do away with such a lineage: it is necessary to feel a part of it, even though in the end the only prudent alternative is to "close its eyes," comfort it on its deathbed, and say a dignified farewell to a past and a tradition as prestigious as they are unacceptable. The most obvious contradiction underlying this shift in ideology (and there are many others) resides in the sure necessity of assuming a filiation and the urgency of negating it.

This significant and unresolved conflict leads to at least two no less problematic points. One has to do with the privileged role given to women: they are the more certain source of parentage, as well as the figures that often incarnate national values.[79] With respect to the latter, one need only remember that it is women who fight in the last defense of Cochabamba (chap. 20) under the command of the centenary, blind, and heroic grandmother, a witness to and major player in the war of independence (chap. 15), who rebukes the males by shouting, "There are no men left! They're running from the damned *guampos!*" On a different level there is the symptomatic and persistent presence of Marian figures at climactic points in the story, from the painting of the Divine Shepherdess who watches over Rosita's house to the image of Our Lady of Mercy, who blesses the women that will go out in defense of their city.

Just as women substitute for men in the last defense of Cochabamba, Rosita substitutes for the absent father and partially fulfills his function. There is, then, a strong matriarchal bent to the representation of a nation that is beginning to form and the profound (yet ambiguous) meaning expressed by its nascent identity. Clearly *Juan de la Rosa* does not develop this perspective, but compared to similar texts of the time in which patriarchy is supreme, this Bolivian novel offers a dissenting vision, even in its undefined, larval state.[80] Perhaps in the building of the foundational imaginary of a nation, the maternal figure is much more important than is usually conceded.[81]

The father's absence not only raises questions but also reveals the audacious inner workings of the text. The novel can be read as the recounting of the protagonist's self-construction as the father lacking both in his life and in the representative sphere.[82] This occurs in the narrative (and temporal) vacuum that goes from Juanito's childhood to the point at which the elder Juan writes his memoirs. In this span of time the boy Juanito has become a hero in the fight for independence; or more emphatically, the "child of the wind" has transmuted into the "father of the homeland." When a stunned Juanito says of his father's death, "My life changed completely from that moment on," he is insinuating a transformation that does not end in the realm of personal experience. He knows that his orphanhood is absolute and that he will have to build his life independently on the paradox of having discovered his parentage only in the silence of his father's death. On another level he knows that an entire society is beginning to live independently and that, in similar ways, this is happening with the death of the colonial tradition. This chance confluence of private and public spheres allows for the configuration of a person in corresponding relationship to society: by learning to live without parents, both the individual and society must function as their own parents. The colonel belongs to the generation of the homeland's founders and soldiers who see themselves as the fathers of the nation and express the most obvious fulfillment of that role in their recurrent—and at times dramatic—call to Bolivian youth of 1884. It is not necessary to note all the instances in which the text explicitly addresses this reader, beginning with the prologue: "I may now ask that the youth of my dear country gain some profitable lessons from the story of my life," a story that obviously becomes intertwined with that of the emancipation. One might say that Bolivian youth have in Colonel Juan de la Rosa the father that Juanito never had.

    Clearly the old soldier is proud of his work during the war of independence and the first days of the republic ("I am honored by the title of commandant and aide-de-camp of the Grand Marshal of Ayacucho"), has an unflagging esteem for his comrades in arms, and opines that independence did away with "fanaticism and ignorance" (because "they can no longer live under the sun of 1810") and that the "savages" that threatened Humboldt have disappeared in the face of civilization's advance. Nevertheless he expresses his disillusionment with the social process following independence, openly criticizes the morality of those who betrayed original ideals, and compares that heroic time with the unfortunate present. By referring to what he knows best, the army, he gives his opinion of the ragged and poorly armed combatants of yesteryear: "They seem to me a thousand times more beautiful and respectable than today's soldiers, who dress in elegant, French-styled materials, who wear white gloves and false beards, who break up congresses with the brute force of their weapons, who pitilessly murder the defenseless populace, who hand over Bolívar's blood-stained medal to a back-stabbing idiot, who laugh at the laws, mock the constitution, betray the country and sell themselves" (Aguirre, *Juan de la Rosa*, 126).

The author does not expound this topic, probably because the heroic image of the independence that he wishes to uphold would be destroyed by specific references to the calamities of the Republic.[83] It is no coincidence that after the impassioned critique cited above, the narrator interrupts his discourse ("No, I cannot go on! . . . I'm choking up!"), and has to regain his composure ("I am calm again") before continuing his account. He uses the same strategy later, when he again compares the two times: "Tell me, above all, if the men of today can compare with those of that time! Tell me . . . but no, for God's sake, don't say anything! Because the blood rushes to my head and the pen falls from my hand."

Other ellipses cast a shadow over the background that might explain his skepticism and ire. But even if independence has been betrayed, he still has faith in youth and its ability to take up the grand ideals of emancipation with vigor and authenticity. This is the source of his repeated demands that the history of those glorious years be written and its illustrious lessons of patriotism provide an example to new generations. The colonel fulfills, or desires to fulfill, his mission of being guide and teacher for them: a true father and generational link in the lineage that springs directly from the foundation of the homeland.

Behind all this is the idea that with independence the nation begins a new history, which clearly ordains the establishment of new codes of legitimacy and filiation. These are incarnate in those that heroically fought for independence, especially the last of their survivors, the one charged with writing the testimony and lessons that parents leave their children: a legacy and a memory that should not be lost. As Juanito did in Friar Justo's papers, Bolivian youth will find in the old colonel's memoirs their true origin and authentic filiation. Once again the written word is what reveals one's origins and honors them. It is the history of the nation in writing. Or, in plain and trenchant terms, the nation—in writing.

CELEBRATIONS

Though set upon and at times displaced by the Vanguardists, it was incumbent upon *modernista* poets, who preserved their hegemony in the realm of official literature, to be the literary voice of the festivities celebrating the first century of independence. Contrary to what happened in the nineteenth-century novel, which tangentially discussed the formation of nations, their long series of poems avoided this set of problems in order to celebrate calling, spirit, and valor.

It is not timely to discuss how *modernismo* represents society, an open topic in spite of the clarifications made in the debate between Ángel Rama and Françoise Pérus, mainly because in this case there is no ambiguity in the relationship: the authoritarian or dictatorial government in power "charges" the most renowned national poet with the creation of a work that will exalt the heroes and glories of the homeland on the occasion of the centennial.[84] These were normally remunerated tasks. The direct link between the government and a chosen writer has progressive overtones (the poet should be paid for this "task"), yet also retains characteristics of the archaic patronage system.[85] Though an individual case may be closer to one of these extremes than the other, these are poems made literally "to order," with little or no specification as to content, but with a peremptory delivery date.[86] These sometimes epic-lyric voices are raised in honor of the centennial of the independence, and shortly thereafter, the decisive battle of Ayacucho. I shall refer briefly to two samples: *Redención* by Gregorio Reynolds and *Ayacucho y los Andes* by José Santos Chocano.[87]

Reynolds constructs his extensive poem chronologically and dedicates cantos 2, 3, and 4 to the Inca empire, the discovery, and the conquest, respectively, while it can be surmised that the following sections, never written (or at least never published), would treat the periods leading up at least to independence, which was to have been the work's motivating theme. These three cantos are preceded by a prologue ("Isagoge") and canto 1 ("Geste"), which together provide a sort of cosmogony whose link, in spite of the confusing overlap between the two sections, is the laborious and repeated insistence on the idea that Atlantis is the origin of the *Antisuyo*, with visible proof of this being the ruins of Tihuanacu.[88] Since *Redención* is defined as a "cyclic poem," one supposes that its design included the utopian premonition of a return to the pristine grandeur of Atlantis' civilization, presumably understood in its future modality as universal synthesis. There are several indications of this in the first two parts, especially the prologue. Thus, for example, before dreaming of "the future . . . image of the Fatherland radiant in beauty," the poet associates "Tihuanacu of stone and silence" with the "divine conjunction of Zeus, Jehovah, and Pachacama" (10–11).[89] Clearly this erudite macrosynthesis, which echoes the extremes of homogenizing and harmonizing discourse, is no more than a utopian prefiguration relying much more on elitist rhetoric than on the vast and intense collective consciousness. The poem was to have ended with the apotheosis of the Fatherland, but probably, according to the clue offered by its title, by way of prior expiation of historical-moral culpability. As it was published, the title *Redención* (Redemption) has no correlation to the text.

In addition to this interpretation, it is important to remember that during the historical period that transpires in Reynolds's poem there is significant ambiguity in the treatment of the conquest. The two previous cantos do not reveal this uncertainty, since the first of these reiterates Garcilaso's version of the Inca empire (cast in culturalist references) and is a monotonous revisioning of each member of the royalty—as seen through the lens of traditional history or legend—whose purpose is to judge the deeds and virtues of some by contrasting them to the excesses and vices of others.[90] The second, dedicated to the discovery, is almost entirely a favorable rendering of the personage and actions of Columbus. The problem, then, lies in the poem's rendition of the conquest. Reynolds tests the weight of his historical balance by emphasizing the virtues of the conquistadors without forgetting to underscore, even in the same verse, their crimes: they are "rapacious, generous," capable of "abominable or . . . illustrious acts" (Reynolds, *Redención*, lines 181–82). At the same time the civilizing action of the conquest is never called into question, which gives way to a degrading view of the natives ("inhospitable tribes, savages . . . gurgling barbaric dialects"), thanks to which the poet can optimistically conclude that the Spanish race "by happy fate / is making its path around the world" (Reynolds, *Redención*, line 216). Thus, though he notes the insatiable avarice and limitless cruelty of the conquest, the overall process is assumed to be positive. Thanks to his words America, specifically Bolivia, is that syncretic realm in which the Iberian and native races converge and all of humanity's great cultural experiences are amassed. The proliferation of references to Oriental cultures, Christianity and its Hebraic roots, and Greco-Roman culture are rhetorical but also have two other functions: the perception of this history on one hand as being a porous entity that allows penetration from different sources, and on the other as lacking an internal referential and symbolic base capable of supplying the figurative needs of poetic discourse and allowing the consequent manipulation of often superlative, hyperbolic—and cosmopolitan—allusions. These are references that both legitimize and credit the history being narrated and provide authority, through their erudition, to the one who recounts it.

By privileging synthesis and finding in it the ultimate motive and meaning for national experience, the theme of mestizaje acquires great importance. Reynolds mentions it on several occasions but specifically dedicates two poems to this subject. They are numbers 5 and 6 of the last canto. In the first the protagonist is the conquistador who, "disquieted by abstinence," is so captivated by the virgin beauty of a "native of the earth" that, "erasing the limits of his caste . . . and with the earth's most ardent embrace, the despot submits to the slave at last." As is typical of Reynolds, the poem contains abundant classical references culminating in a transposition to the Hellenic world. The relationship between the Indian woman and the conquistador is rendered in these terms: "Dionysius is enraptured / by Aphrodite's adolescence," emphasizing the pagan sensuality of this first encounter. In the second poem, by contrast, it is the female protagonist who "awaits . . . the Promised One . . . beneath a canopy of splendid boughs." In their union "are consummated the loftiest nuptials / to ever purify two prodigious races," which transforms the "urgency of the flesh" into a love blessed by "the sacred bonds."

> Faith is changed in this graft of blood
> (marvelous mixture: Sun for Cross),
> Inca and Aztec infused with the blood
> of the Goth and his Castilian language.
>
> A die of steel gives its form
> to a new lineage that, deep-rooted,
> will impose its destiny as the norm
> for generations throughout the future.
>
> Virile race: prolific in love;
> a force that can move mountains.

Clearly this is a eulogy of mestizaje, although it is the "Goth" who imposes religion and language and only implicitly the Indian woman who provides fortitude. But the first stanza of poem 5 overbalances even this eulogy:

> The feudal lord with his gallows and dagger
> comes to the smiling western beach,
> where soon he will conquer the ruling chief
> and birth the creole, complete with a swagger.

The reader is left in doubt: is mestizaje the progenitor of this "swaggering creole" or the "virile race . . . that can move mountains"? Or perhaps both images come together and "swagger" has no negative connotations in this text. A closer reading may connect the first to the fact that the verses belong to a poem that emphasizes the "energy [of] instinct," while the second is part of the next poem, which flows into a celebration of the culture (in its primordial aspects of religion and language) offered by the conquistador in "the loftiest nuptials / to ever purify two prodigious races." In the final analysis mestizaje appears as the biological union of these "two prodigious races" (with all its allusions to nature) under the reign of a single, obviously Spanish, culture. This becomes even clearer when the image of the "crucible," implying admixture or blending, is associated with the opposing idea of substitution: "Sun for Cross." The native component appears to be thought of only in terms of nature, and in this sense nonhistorical, while on the Spanish side nature and culture are one and the same: the Goth infuses both his blood and "his Castilian language." Mestizaje, yes, but considered in terms of a union between solely the natural world of the Americas on one hand and Iberian nature, culture, and history on the other. Once more the rupture—and even mockery—of idyllic harmony, and again the hierarchical principle, in the midst of a defense of synthesis, raises its ugly head and makes of the marriage ceremony a tangential—but obvious—defense of the subjection of one of its members to the power of the other.

A similar analysis could be made of *Ayacucho y los Andes*.[91] José Santos Chocano's epic poem is also an unfinished poem, but in this case the author left clear indications as to his overall intent. The original project was the writing of a "pantheistic epic" in homage to Bolívar on the occasion of the one hundredth anniversary of the battle of Ayacucho. It was to have been entitled *El hombre-sol*, but Chocano finished and published only canto 4 ("Ayacucho y los Andes"). He first provides a prose "summary" of five more cantos, as well as an introduction and epilogue, all of which were to have been included in the finished work. It is not known whether the poet finished an additional segment, but the one he left is indeed extensive: sixty-six stanzas totaling more than fifteen hundred lines, with "footnotes" added at the end of each stanza.[92]

A reading of the project's "summary" emphasizes the fact that Chocano was struggling with many unresolved conflicts. If the introduction reveals Bolívar's plan to liberate the Sun god ("Inti" to the Incas) from Spanish domination and we witness the transfiguration of the hero into "Hombre-Sol" (in some ways the god of the Americas) under the protection of the great rebel Tupac Amaru,[93] the epilogue (after the hero's grandiose celebration of Bolívar's resurrection once his Americanist ideal is fulfilled) ends unexpectedly with the following: "The Four Elements of American Nature [elements of which the Liberator has taken possession and whose powers he has assumed as his own] break forth in a final Hymn to the glorification of Spain." It is difficult to reconcile the image of the liberation as the emancipation of the indigenous people and the breaking of the Spanish yoke with this final—and therefore significant—hymn to the glories of Spain.[94]

Clearly the shift from one position to another is quite abrupt in the summary, and one might think that this mitigates in the poem itself, but an examination of canto 5 reveals similar incongruities. For instance, elements of America's natural world—volcanoes, rivers, jungles, plateaus—"awaken" at Bolívar's arrival and offer him their powers in his quest for emancipation, and indigenous personages or representations (especially Tupac Amaru and the personified Andes mountains) welcome him and bestow him and his captains with indigenous attributes. But this Incaist Americanism does not obviate the explanation that both sides, the armies of the Liberator and those of Spain the colonizer, are of the same blood, alluding of course to the Iberian blood of those in charge and not the Indian blood of soldiers on either side.

> ... Do they fight? Their arms
> are enemies: but not the blood
> coursing through their veins;
> and before their swords can speak,
> the knights greet each other
> and speak in gentle terms.
> (Chocano, *Ayacucho y los Andes*, canto 7)

Hence the description of the captains of both armies and the account of their heroic actions clearly follow the stereotypical norms of the epic, but also those of the chivalric and courtly novel. After the battle, when Viceroy La Serna is taken prisoner and his wounded generals bemoan their defeat, the Andes intervene once again, but this time not in praise of Bolívar:

> The peaks of the Andes
> are moved by what they see,
> and thus break forth in a hymn
> where fused spirits are raised up:
> "Mother Spain! Much pride feel we
> that your blood has mixed with ours!"
> (Chocano, Ayacucho, canto 46)

But this new appeal to mestizaje, internally corroded by the subject and object of pride (the Americas feel proud to have received Spanish blood), soon faces a crisis. After the struggle ends, Pizarro's ghostly shadow appears:

> And like the father who delivers
> his son possession of the manor,
> he stretches out to him the Banner
> of the Conquest and gently gives it over.
> (Chocano, canto 49)[95]

The epic tradition, which would have sounded the trumpets of triumph upon the capture of the enemy's greatest trophy, yields to the chivalric code in all its gallantry, and the former enemy is transformed into the great legitimizer of the lineage and power of the liberators. This incredible scene clearly contradicts the poem's Americanist, or Incaist, rhetoric: although there are remnants of this rhetoric in the remainder of the text, even the most uninformed reader understands that the quest for liberation is an Iberian quest where power passes from one hand to another, but always along the same bloodlines.

Curiously this interpretation of the independence movement (excluding its mythical-historical extravagances) coincides with radical, contemporary perspectives, which assert that emancipation was nothing more than a superficial political change by which the power of the Crown passed to the creoles ("American Spaniards"), induced by the fear of a possible triumph of Spanish liberalism.[96] Clearly what appears to be a fatal historical flaw is for Chocano a means of satisfaction: this is precisely what drives his epic inspiration. But the question remains: if *Ayacucho y los Andes* is an epopee in honor of the creole stratum that effectively led the independence process, why the grand effort to incorporate indigenous references and construct the text around the idea of liberating the Sun, god of the Incas? Although the idea of mestizaje is behind this option, it is emphasized only in the few lines cited above.[97] Homogeneity, then, becomes an international project, according to Bolívar's dream of uniting the republics of this part of the continent and obviating their disintegration. Above all it becomes a unique historical vision that acrobatically links the grandeur of the Inca empire with the quest for emancipation, with the conquest understood as an act of grandiose heroism producing an America where all imaginable syntheses will be possible.[98] This adhesive history unites both the Inca Empire and the conquest with the Republic in the glorious whole of an America symbolizing a harmonious universe. On a temporal plane, the construction of this history as a peaceful rather than conflictive process is equivalent to the syncretic ideal contained in the image of mestizaje.

Both *Redención* and *Ayacucho y los Andes* strain to keep their narrative segments faithful to the view of history accepted at the time (the imperial Inca dynasty or the unfolding of the battle at Ayacucho are good examples). Nevertheless, in both cases there seems to be a driving need to tell the tale in mythological terms. Reynolds accomplishes this by using classical elements while Chocano, without discarding these, does so through the personification of the natural world of the Americas and the ghostly apparitions of personages from the past, from Manco Capac to Pizarro.[99] Beyond the conditions set by the genre, this excessive overlay raises the suspicion that literature is what guarantees the splendor of history in a reformulation of the adage of the poet as *dispensator gloriae*, except that in these texts fame comes not so much from the heroic quest that keeps the verse alive as from the global transformation of the event itself into a strongly rhetorized code that, in the end, takes its place. Through the lens of a eulogy to the fatherland and its heroes, one can discern a definite—but hidden—mistrust of a history burdened by an extreme, hyperbolic transfiguration whose ultimate motive may be its dilution into a space so stereotypical that it says very little about America and destabilizes its reality, its society, and its personages. In the final analysis the *Antis* are (in the accepted truth of poetic discourse) the *Atlantes*, and Bolívar is, also according to this truth, a divine being, sublime incarnation of the Sun and all the forces of nature.

If the above is a hermeneutic reading of these unfinished poems, it may be possible to risk a "reading" of their silences as well. Reynolds ends his homage to the centennial of Bolivia's independence with the canto dedicated to the conquest (which in itself is ironic), while Chocano, after celebrating the victory at Ayacucho in his lone canto planned to write three more: the founding of Bolivia; the hero's fruitless struggle against anarchy, his retreat from public life, and his death (all this very briefly); and, in the epilogue, his resurrection ("after three days lasting 100 years") when his Americanist ideal is accomplished.[100] If Reynolds silences the entire history of republican Bolivia and Chocano globalizes that period in continental terms under the abstract image of Anarchy (with a capital "A"), it is because, in more than one way, neither one seems to find a way to write the epic of the calamitous present, as if there were no rhetoric (and there is not) suitable to glorify a history of frustration and defeat. Consequently they both launch zealously into the future and imagine it as a period of splendid plenitude, in which each and every national and continental dream—and especially the ideals of peace, reconciliation, and harmony—reach their final fulfillment. The hyperbolic nature of the two epopees makes this possible not only in each nation, although this is the arena that generates the desire for integration and homogeneity, but in the American community, all countries, and ultimately the entire universe. This is the celebration of all Americans' syncretic destiny in Vasconcelos's "cosmic race," and the region that represents, through accumulation and synthesis, the culmination of universal history and culture. These excesses, almost purely rhetorical, should not obscure what is fundamental: the centennial commemoration of independence is critical in that national and continental failure and disintegration, in all their harsh reality, can only be cured in the representation of a glorious future constructed in the imagination of an elite unwilling to problematize either the present or the immediate past. There is nothing more explicit concerning the building up of nations and the continent as homogeneous entities than the dictator Augusto B. Leguía's critique of Chocano's poem: "If the *Iliad* led to the unity of Greece, if the *Divine Comedy* was the precursor of the unity of Italy, I have no doubt that the *Epic of the Liberator* will raise the continental spirit and determine in the days to come the unity of America."[101]

Leguía was wrong, since obviously Chocano's poem had no influence on the enterprise of continental unity, which of course was never achieved, but his words are especially lucid with regard to the building of the social imaginary by way of literary discourse. The poems commemorating the first centennial of the Latin American republics are the celebration of the homogeneity sought as the final solution for a history torn asunder. Here too the image of harmony belies in the very act of its discursive construction the deep-seated heterogeneity and the radical conflicts of a multiply contradictory America.

CHAPTER 3   Stone of Boiling Blood
The Challenges of Modernization

The linguistic course on which Palma and other writers of his time embarked was both efficient and convincing. At the very least its hegemony was lasting and allowed for the largely unquestioned supposition that the language of literature was both able to harbor national tongues and social dialects and in some way be representative of all these. As stated in the previous chapter, Palma's model presupposed the construction of an apparently homogeneous linguistic space in which all differences were smoothed over according to a high standard porous enough to absorb—as necessary— the other layers of its language's social usage. The result was a national literary language, although this was more a conciliatory act aimed at reining in sociolingual hierarchies than an aesthetic-linguistic one.

This model was accepted without question in literary circles, especially those dedicated to realist prose and having an underlying bent toward totalization and homogenization. Even the Modernists, antipathetic as they were to "unartistic" language, found themselves caught, not in Palma's rather archaic schematic, but in his verifiable presumption that the country and region as a whole could be "naturally" represented in literary language. It was no coincidence that their verses commemorated the Andean republics' independence and that José Santos Chocano prided himself on being the "Poet of America."[1] In any case there was no discussion for some time concerning a national legitimacy for the language of literature. The Modernists, however, sidelined the willful, overarching nature of Palma's project and overlaid it with a sense of hierarchy. Rather than subsuming other literary representations, the Modernists imagined their own artful language to be the one that could best represent the most enlightened sector of the nation, which was clearly also socially dominant. This was irrefutable proof that the nation was truly cultured.

Both versions became embroiled and lost hegemony with the intense renovation of literary codes that occurred during the first three or four decades of the twentieth century. This complex renovation includes the upsurge of the Vanguards, a new Indigenism, and a previously unobserved overlapping of the two. In the Andean region (with all its different national subtleties), literary and social Vanguards often became mixed and at times seemed practically of one voice, which makes the relationship between the Vanguard and Indigenist movements much more understandable. At this point it is not relevant to explore the social dynamics that underlie the appearance of these innovative movements, but to show how the upsurge of a new, culture-producing subject, grounded in clearly defined economic and social conditions, was so immediately important.[2] In broad terms one could say that this signals the emergence of a healthy, intellectual cast of characters from the well-read, middle, and provincial classes who were in most cases willing to resist the oligarchy and its cultural regime.[3] Clearly this new subject produced (and was somewhat configured by) a new language whose novelty implied not only other linguistic norms and customs, including literary ones, but also tangential, surreptitious, and even imperceptible forms of socialization in both public and private spheres.[4] Of course this is all intrinsically bound to the problem of modernity, though in this case we are dealing with a multiply peripheral Andean modernity.[5]

THE AMBIGUITIES OF A NEW LANGUAGE

Although it is clear that the essence of the social subject that produced the Vanguard and Indigenist movements was formed by the mesocratic and provincial intellectuals who were then bursting upon the national cultural scene (the most active of these nuclei were located in provincial cities such as Trujillo, Puno, Cusco, and Arequipa), there is insufficient research to prove a fact of much greater and transcendent value: the Modernists' norm was foreign to their social agenda. Of course, as Luis Monguió points out, the "abandonment of Modernism" was such a slow, confusing, and complex process that even the greatest proponents of literary renewal were unable to erase the imprint of this previous literary movement from their first—and even later—works.[6] Even so, there are testimonies to the perception that Modernist language was a language of the other, "on loan," so to speak, and without a valid, legitimate relationship to one's experience, beginning with the social and personal experience of the speaker. Following is a brief but significant example to prove my hypothesis: the two versions of lines 11 and 12 of César Vallejo's famous title poem of *Los heraldos negros*. The first of these, published not long before the definitive one, reads: "Those rude blows are the sudden explosions / of a golden cushion forged by an evil sun." The final version is changed to: "Those bloody blows are the crackling / of our bread just going into the oven and already burnt up."[7]

Clearly the initial version leans on the Modernist tradition in both the scale of the image that it creates (otherwise hardly convincing) and the sumptuousness of the language (with its inevitable reference to gold), while the definitive one opens the poem up to colloquial language under the socialized guise of a common saying. The drastic difference between the "golden cushion forged by an evil sun" and "our bread just going into the oven and already burnt up" would be interpreted insufficiently if it were owing merely to an esthetic or stylistic change. The true transformation is in the intricate network of statements forming the dialogue between the text and its interlocutors, tied to their habits of poetic decodification. In other words, the first version limits its system of resonance to the sociolinguistic space meticulously constructed by Modernist poets and formalized in an intertextual rhetoric that excludes the receptor unschooled in this literary norm. The definitive version, however, is based on a macrotextuality whose decodification demands only a certain competency in Spanish. The shift in the poem's implicit dialogue from the realm of a literary movement to one of a common, spoken language signals a new stance for the transmitter of the message and an unprecedented relationship between literature and its beneficiaries. Approaching this issue from a different critical perspective, Alberto Escobar affirms that it was only at that point that our writers felt that the language they were using was truly their own.[8]

In some ways, the reinsertion of literary language into common language, along with the breakdown of previously institutionalized linguistic and literary conventions that followed, is exactly what allowed literary experimentation to occur in an exceptionally open space. From then on we see various options exercised, from the reticence of one arm of the Vanguard to the "nonstyle" of certain Indigenists, though clearly the innovators themselves soon reconfigure different literary parameters according to their own conventions. The immersion in common speech, then, does not necessarily imply new, specific poetics, but it does make possible the appearance of several alternatives. This seems to be the basis for the extreme freedom and profound linguistic tension present in *Trilce* and, to a different degree, in certain constructs of the Indigenism of those years. In this regard one must remember the frequent overlays (including polemic ones) between Vanguardism and Indigenism in the Andean region. It is important to note that José Carlos Mariátegui not only encouraged both movements' production but also fostered their mutual interaction. He also offered an Indigenist reading of *The Black Heralds* (and less so, *Trilce*), without omitting references to their expressionist, dadaist, and surrealist elements.[9]

Of course, this is just one piece of a much wider phenomenon. Here we are witnessing a broad — but bewildered — questioning of language itself ("And if after so many words / the word doesn't survive!"), which naturally is more pronounced in the area of literary language and its conventions.[10] The intense, edgy experimentation of the Andean Vanguard and the incisive transformations of an Indigenism willing to seek new ways to confront the unavoidable aporias of its production show a certain dissatisfaction with not only literary language but language in general.[11] This largely unexplored dissatisfaction stems from two basic questions, representation and authenticity, as well as from the profound problematic accompanying both of these.

It is important to add here that this unease with codified language is correlative to the great care taken that the insistent calls for modernization, so strong among the Vanguardists, would not result in a false language that was new in appearance only. It is significant that Mariátegui and Vallejo shared this concern. One suspects that underlying this mistrust of pure "novelty" in form is a general criticism of "cosmopolitanism."[12] More important is the deliberate decision to create an essentially new and global literature that would go beyond any perceived superficiality or deception. This is Mariátegui's opinion: "This is not the case with Modernism.[13] Modernism is not only a question of form, but above all, of essence. No Modernist is happy with external audacity or arbitrariness in syntax or meter. In his cool, new suit he feels his old substance is intact. Why violate grammar if the spiritual ingredients of poetry are the same as twenty or fifty years ago? 'Il faut être absolument moderne,' as Rimbaud used to say; but one must be modern in spirit."[14]

And Vallejo's:

> The artistic material that modern life offers must be assimilated by the spirit and converted into sensibility. The wireless telegraph, for example, is destined, rather than to make us say "wireless telegraph," to awaken a new temperament and profoundly wise sentiments by broadening viewpoints and understandings and measuring out love: disquietude then grows to exasperation and the breath of life is enlivened. This is the true culture that progress renders; this is its only esthetic meaning—not filling our mouths with brilliant words. New voices can often fail. Often a poem does not say "cinema," yet it still possesses a cinematic feeling in a tacit, but effectively human way. This is the true new poetry.[15]

It is clear that Mariátegui's and Vallejo's shared fear is concerned with the question of authenticity. As the above quotes explicate, the problem rests on the possibility that what is "new," or "modern," or "Vanguardist," may be no more than a shell masking either a deep-rooted archaism or a spiritual vacuum. I propose that this fear is rooted in the knowledge that there was a large gap between the obvious social backwardness of the Andean nations (though there was some modernization due to their partial participation in international, especially North American, capitalism) and the manifestations of modern art. In other words, cultural modernism was not tied to an *authentic* social modernity and therefore produced tensions and contradictions of differing scope and depth, which in turn were capable of creating traps and aberrance. The problem is further complicated because modernity for Mariátegui and Vallejo was socialist modernity, and they both knew—despite their faith in the future—that in the Andean world this goal was distant and difficult. There were few options available, therefore, in the utterly conflicted space between the unacceptable extremes of backward, archaic reproduction and the configuration of a modern, but socially weightless art. Mariátegui and Vallejo resolved the problem by inserting their work into history, taking advantage of its transformative energy, and valorizing the renewing—or revolutionary—nature of cultural discourse. Thus, while collaborating in the demolition of the old order and the construction of a new one, they could simultaneously immerse themselves in the social modernity they were proposing and realize it in their own discourse. Neither one presupposed that art and ideology were secondary attributes of social history but, rather, considered them both to be dynamically and productively integrated into the social process and contributors to its source and meaning. In addition, Mariátegui and Vallejo both had had intense European experiences, which they chronicled vividly, and lived out in Peru fragmented processes of modernization.[16] The first of these was in Leguía's Lima, spectacularly renovated in those years, and the second took place on the northern coast at the time of the "Trujillian bohemia," one of the first and most profound manifestations of the power of modern capitalism: the absorption of dozens of sugar mills by large, foreign monopolies.[17] This explains how little thought is as modern as Mariátegui's and no poetry as modern as Vallejo's.

Writers were both attempting to struggle free from the hold of the Modernist canon in order to effect a free and authentic artistic change and feeling inhibited by the risk of producing a literature in which modernity was nothing more than a cosmetic, deceptive gesture. This situation forced them to pick their way through a veritable minefield of incoherence. Clearly the one who best dodged these dangers (although eventually some blew up in his face) was Vallejo. In large part his modus operandi consists of confronting an essentially primitive referential order with a visionary language that clarifies rather than avoids basic issues and articulates them in terms of a concrete, material transcendence. This places the past on a semantic plane that, without destroying it, converts it into contemporary words and experience. From the almost archeological depths of Santiago de Chuco's life, for example, Vallejo extracts texts imbued with an astounding modernity. There are also the poems centered on family life (the final ones in *The Black Heralds*, for example) or his traumatic experience in prison (in *Trilce*). Clearly Vallejo is unique (those who try to imitate him fail miserably), but the problem remains: how to modernize without creating a mere veneer to texts anchored in the past? Obviously there were many alternatives. Perhaps we can shed some light on this by examining the implicit contention between the Vanguardist prose of Pablo Palacio's "Un hombre muerto a puntapiés" and Jorge Icaza's Indigenist *Huasipungo*.[18]

Before contrasting the poetics of Icaza's Indigenist brand of social realism with those of Palacio's urban Vanguardism, we should first remind the reader that both are rooted in a common rejection of the hegemonic Ecuadorian (and Andean) linguistic norms of the day. Palacio's rebellion is explicit and violent, not easily borne by his contemporaries because of its obsessive and overarching condemnation of the abusive, detestable, degraded, and degrading reality that surrounded him. This condemnation is implicit in certain earmarks of Vanguardist writing: graphic-play, the use of unrelated images, the intentional garbling of sentences, and the configuration of inner thoughts reflected in dark pulsations rather than traceable conscious processes. Palacio subtitled his last novel "Novela subjetiva" with the obvious intention of placing its discourse and his previous work on a level where the exploration of explicitly social matters is wrathfully scorned. This reclusion into subjectivity explains why Palacio was not overly concerned with offering new alternatives to the literature of his country and his time, although he does do this, but was concerned rather with expelling the anguish produced by living in a world that was not only backward but poorly constructed. Hence his criticism of realism, its linguistic norms, and its pretense of true rendition, which is his major point of friction with Icaza's esthetics.

Here I offer a poetic reading of Palacio's short story "Un hombre muerto a puntapiés."[19] The account transcribes a police report of the death "of an individual named Ramírez . . . victim of an assault by individuals unknown to him" (Palacios, *Obras completas*, 17). Later, in first person, the narrator makes (gratuitous) efforts to reconstruct the crime and find its motive, which the newspaper report leaves ambiguous. In the end, returning to the use of the third person, the same narrator gives his version. Thus a "truthful" account from the newspaper and police report is juxtaposed with another, "fictitious" one proposed arbitrarily in the story, although the data from the former are carefully preserved. The fictitious narration covers the gaps and errors of the news article in order to add bits of data (for example the victim is given the name "Octavio") and reduce ambiguity. In this way the phrase "the depraved victim" (Palacios, *Obras completas*, 18) becomes, after a string of different hypotheses, an affirmation that the murdered man was homosexual. This also occurs with other information that the narrator obtains through pure fantasy, and in the end he draws a body onto the face in the police photographs: "Until finally I studied them so much that I had his most minute details memorized. . . . I grabbed the paper, drew the lines of the dead man's face. . . . Then when the drawing was done, I noticed that something was missing; that what I was looking at wasn't him; that I'd left out a complementary and indispensable detail. . . . There! I picked up the pen again and finished the torso, a magnificent torso . . . that looked vaguely like a woman's" (Palacios, *Obras completas*, 22–23).

Filling gaps and clarifying ambiguities help explain the events of the narration. This objective is reached only through the second, fictitious account that retells the original story in its own way. Or better, seen from the inside, the realistic narration is incapable of imbuing the action with meaning. This failing seems to be the most serious issue concerning the relationship between the language of realistic art and reality, especially when compared to its best model: photography. At bottom realism is tautological and, even worse, needlessly repetitive of an abject reality. This is why Palacio practices a fictional drawing from an intuitive process ("intuition reveals all"), which stands in opposition to the rationalist esthetic of realism and, above all, naturalism. In the end, however, the fiction's arbitrariness, which seems unstoppable (as in assigning a name to the character) and given over to ridicule and scandal (as in the Vanguardist humor used to describe the murder in graphs and onomatopoeias), is paradoxically bound to the need to semanticize reality. In effect Palacio's main objection to realism is that it is limited to repeating reality without finding its meaning, while in his poetics of fiction, that flight of imagination proposes to construct not a *different* reality but rather the meaning that realism mishears. It is not a question, then, of fictionalizing an autonomous world, but rather projecting fiction and its powers toward the revelation of the dark, human meaning immersed in reality and history. This is akin to what Mariátegui proposed in his 1926 article "Reality and Fiction."[20]

Like Palacio, Icaza had to make a considerable effort to break completely with the model of artistic prose in vogue in Ecuador at the time, such as Gonzalo Zaldumbide's *Egloga trágica*, which embodies classicism, *casticismo*, and the imperatives of a prose esthetic suffering from an incurable longing for poetry.[21] Above all Icaza needed to produce a prose discourse that at first glance exhibited a ground-zero style (strong, bare-boned images in the grammar of common language, interjections, cries or murmurs coming from no particular direction, interruptions into Quechua or its derivations, and so on) but also, as Agustín Cueva saw it, was non- or anti-oligarchic in nature.[22] He then shaped it according to a new rhetoric whose ideal was to reproduce—or rather, represent through the obvious fictionality of literary language—the dialect of the middle and popular strata as a new norm for the national dialect, including his notorious interruptions in Quechua. Clearly Icaza's linguistic work in *Huasipungo* (which Cueva describes as a process "of 'native accumulation' of cultural materials and [the creation of] an 'interior marketplace' of his own linguistic and other symbols") cannot be separated from the frontline efforts of the Grupo de Guayaquil and other Ecuadorian authors who shared the same disquietude.[23] Nor can one ignore the later contributions of Icaza himself, especially those relative to the configuration of a "mestizo" novel and a "*cholo*" language, which bravely assimilates words in Quechua and openly reproduces the plebeian Spanish of the city, as seen for example in *El chulla Romero y Flores*.[24]

The construction of this nonstyle, including its inevitable rhetoric, correlates to the conviction that indelibly marked the narrators of social realism and especially some Indigenists: language, through this or other means, should faithfully represent the profound nature of what is real. If Modernist tradition had put into place an artifice that separated language from its referent, the social realist narrators of the first decades of the twentieth century believed that they had reinstated an unbroken continuity between words and objects. Even José María Arguedas, who clearly is not cut from the same cloth, later used the phrase "as is" to refer to the image of reality in his texts.[25] It is symptomatic that few took exception to this faith in the representative validity of language, put forth either as the very nature of such language or by mediation of the author himself. So if on one hand there is the simplified use of the theory of "reflection," on the other there is a certain revival of the Romantic notion that places the burden of proof on the experience of the narrator. Although these two modalities seem to be contradictory, at bottom they work in harmony: language's transparency functions with respect both to the world referred to in the text and to the experience of its emitter and thus is converted into a guarantor of the "truth." Hence the multitude of paratexts verifying that the writer is capable of saying what he says.

Thus there is a fundamental change in the poetics of narration, whose main enemy was the ornateness of the prose esthetics of the day, but whose realization in writing is shaky and occasionally unsatisfactory (for instance the crude and convoluted allegory at the end of *Huasipungo*). Clearly we are not interested here in the success or failure of a narrative model, but in its novelty and how it challenges a different norm and, at bottom, a different notion of literature and language. This is a question of the social and esthetic legitimization of a "plebeian" manner of speech that glories in its own "imperfections" and grows to the point of becoming the new, more widely representative norm.[26] This representativity is doubled and even tripled, since it not only depends on common language, now given national prestige by being set in text, but also is assumed to be more faithful to the reality it evokes, since the author has knowledge of that world. Thus the new language is representative of a "real" and national speech and therefore more precisely reflects the nation's character and problems as they are known directly to an irrefutable writer. In other words, knowledge of the language and its usage codified by modernism's esthetic norms of excellence is substituted by knowledge of the world, whose profound nature is unveiled by clear, unrestrained language.

If Icaza's Indigenist tendencies presuppose that reality is eloquent and language does nothing more than make the world's mutterings more transparent, Palacio's Vanguardism affirms that fantasy and the language in which it is formalized are needed to overcome the silence of objects and human actions, uncover their meaning hidden from naively objective observation and the blunt, tautological language of realism, and express the exacerbated subjectivity of the author. One might suppose that Palacio's and Icaza's alternatives are the two extremes of the new linguistics of Andean literature after modernism, but, with all their obvious and significant differences, it is clear that they both affirm the link between literature and reality and coexist as divergent variants of a great movement opposed only by poetry and the self-referential works of the most radical Vanguardists. It could be said that one resolves the matter by way of re-presentation, in the sense that it presents again what reality has shown, while the other prefers the path of re-production, since it produces not an autonomous meaning but the one that hides in the world's silent hollows. Two different strategies, but the final goal of both is the direct or skewed, objective or subjective revelation of reality.

Moreover, both emphasize the link between literary writing and orality, most evident in Icaza's project and somewhat more diffuse (but traceable) in Palacio's "careless" prose. This is a question of opening up the language of art to the desires of speech, especially the popular speech of the lower-middle classes and even Quechua orality, in an attempt to tie esthetic norms to daily life and free artistic language for use by the majority. The project itself implied an effort to oralize writing, or at least allow it to be permeated by the inflections of effective voicing. This effort was more urgent (and complex), since it was realized within a context in which the mere act of writing marginalized the illiterate masses. Thus a serious and complex tension forms between the literary project and the social space surrounding it: the speech that writers attempt to show in their literary works is (at least in good measure) that of people who would not know how to transcribe it. This tension explains the ambiguities, pitfalls, and frequent failures of the writers' intent, especially with the incorporation of indigenous languages into the text, but it also reinforces a sense of representativity. In the end putting into writing the speech of those who cannot write can be—and was—interpreted as a way of representing the interests of the illiterate masses before the official, high culture, and a more generally lettered consciousness.[27] Clearly this is neither one of the intentions behind this project, nor does it give it legitimacy or authenticity. It is defined much more profoundly in the intricate relationship between voice and written word in a society split between pervasive illiteracy and the asymmetrical bilingualism of its linguistic map. Here the decision to transcribe common language should be seen not only as artistic efficiency or ideological pertinence, but, on a much more compromising level, as a visible sign of an extremely conflictive and contradictory sociocultural situation.

Linguistic-esthetic efforts tend to forge intersocial, intercultural, and interethnic bonds and, at best, a homogeneous space but in so doing reveal the magnitude of the problems that undo what language and literature desire but cannot achieve. The differences between these and similar efforts (analyzed in chapter 2) are that now the entire operation takes place on a lower social level, taking as its model discredited—yet majority—speech patterns, and that this homogenizing effort aligns itself with the populace, in open conflict with the "antinational" oligarchy. The irony continues in that this new exercise of cohesion results in making the existence of the bottom rung more evident. In broad terms, those who cannot write lend their voice to the lettered in an attempt to place it in a space that is radically foreign to the utterers of this discourse. Since they cannot write, they are written by others, the lettered intellectuals of the middle classes who, intentions aside, can hardly take on the role of representatives of what, in fact, they are not.

As for reception, this matter takes a different slant: those whose lives become the subject of literature find themselves completely outside this discourse's communicative circuit. Vallejo spoke to this in an only apparently enigmatic verse: "for the illiterate to whom I write."[28] This verse synthesizes the aporia of a project that legitimizes itself by, with, and in its links to those of the lower strata without the possibility of affecting them in their illiterate state or, if they can read, their having a real opportunity to do so. This does not invalidate the process (as some from ultraradical—even opposing—perspectives have done) but rather underscores the fact that the ethnic and social differences in the Andean area are so profound that even if literary practice takes place in the middle classes that proudly proclaim their plebeian state and try to align themselves with lower urban and rural strata, their lettered state alone displaces and threatens the entire project.[29] In terms of an overarching national-popular literature, there is always, at the bottom of the pyramid, a multitude for which writing—and even more so literary writing—is foreign and inexpressible.[30]

The drama of the problem comes not from the ethnic and social base that the written word cannot reach but most clearly from its magnitude and content. These masses exist everywhere, but in the Andean world of the first part of the twentieth century they are a majority and find meaning in building, as Manuel González Prada said, the "true nation."[31] Here we see the development of a curious ideological dynamic: all the Indigenists and many of the Vanguardists of the time, as part of their struggle against the former power of the oligarchy and aristocracy, chose to define their nations as bearers of an indigenous identity consistently denied them except in rhetorical celebrations of the grandeur of the Inca empire. Paradoxically this implied the marginalization of those who proclaimed it. They were not Indians and therefore could perform only a vicarious role with respect to their national identity and the language they remitted, authentically or not, to the lowest social strata as mere interpreters or translators. Many of the protagonists of this project were not aware of this contradiction, but it is clear that its urgency caused them to organize the vision of both their countries and themselves in terms of overarching contrasts and struggles. These intellectuals were partners in contradiction, and their literary agenda contained irreconcilable points of difference. Vallejo suggests several aspects of this problem in an early text, "Dead Idyll":

> What would my sweet Andean Rita of the rushes and wild fruit
> be doing right now;
> now when Byzantium suffocates me, and my blood
> dozes, like weak cognac, inside me.
>
> Where would her hands, that in the afternoons
> contritely ironed whitenesses yet to come,
> be now in this rain that washes away
> my desire to go on living.

What has become of her flannel skirt; her
toiling; her walk;
her taste of homemade May brandy.

She must be at her door watching some swift-moving clouds,
and finally she'll say, trembling: "It's so cold . . . Jesus!"
and a wild bird on the roof tiles will cry.[32]

It is important to note that this poem is the last in the section entitled "Imperial Nostalgias." Here Vallejo evokes the rural and village life of his former home of Santiago de Chuco in terms of a temporal distance that steeps this entire experience (which is really one of anticipation) in the past. By positioning the utterance of the text in the city, the poet transforms yesterday's world into a distant and irretrievable time. This displacement clarifies the opposition that frames the poem: a here, the urban world from which the text is written, and a spatial-temporal there, where Rita is located. This opposition is present on several levels but, as a whole, places nature in its simple, basic, and untouched state in the foreground, with the space fouled by the artifice of the modern city as its backdrop. Not only is Rita deliberately associated with nature ("rushes," "wild fruit"), but she becomes one with it: she is not slender like the rushes, nor as inviting in her dark sweetness as the wild fruit, but by way of absolute metaphor she is actually made of these natural, authentic, pure materials. In contrast the city (Byzantium) is a defective ambience where even breathing is no longer spontaneous ("[it] suffocates me") and life loses its meaning ("in this rain that washes away / my desire to go on living").[33] Clearly on the scale of values underlying this contrast, rural and village life are valorized, while over the city (which also represents modernity) dense storm clouds of hopeless negativity gather. This opposition reveals the unresolved contradiction inherent to the position of the cultured, modern, urban poet who can just as ably write pre-Vanguardist texts (sonnets as well as free verse) as yearn for the authentic time and culture of his origins. In other words, the basic experience that "Dead Idyll" takes as its theme is nothing less than schizophrenic: the modern act of writing it down only serves to hold up the natural—and archaic—values that would have been hidden, silenced, and unrecorded if they hadn't been abandoned in order to enter into a modernity that, though modest, both makes possible its expression in a contemporary code and sinks into the sweet nostalgia for lost plenitude. It is not coincidental that the final verses of the poem, which explain its title and underscore the bucolic connotations of "idyll," are tinged with a sense of tragedy. The formal devices in the original Spanish, from alliteration to the rather obvious symbol of the wild bird's cry to the multiple accentuation of the last verse, all point to a cultured, modern state of writing intent on evoking the permanent loss of elemental purity. It is also apparent that much of the formal strategy in the final tercet is aimed—by way of a twist in the text—at recreating sounds reminiscent of the orality that would have existed in that nostalgically remembered world. Again the tension between the technology of writing, which finds trust, delight, yet condemnation in modernity, and an ancient, simple world, distant in its backwardness, whose ultimate meaning is overshadowed by impending death. Perhaps the oscillation present in this poem quietly but significantly announces the arrival of the pronounced and destabilizing ambiguity of the new, cultural subject emerging onto the bristling Andean scene of the day.

THE EMERGENCE OF DUALISMS

Clearly the unresolved contradictions of the literary project outlined above are neither the only nor the main reason for sociocultural interpretations based on exclusive or contradictory binaries being the most visible way of understanding the Andean nations as split and unintegrated. Essayists of differing backgrounds, from Alcides Arguedas and José Carlos Mariátegui to Franz Tamayo, Pío Jaramillo, Luis E. Valcárcel, and Jaime Mendoza (to mention only the most important), took on the task of revealing the profound divisions present in Bolivia, Ecuador, and Peru and the resultant inconsistencies in their national statutes. With different emphases they all described geographies made up of a crazy quilt of internal regions that produced antagonistic social organizations and cultural systems. This common emphasis on the configurative power of geography is definitely positivist in nature, although it also displays philosophical underpinnings, from spiritualist vitalism to Marxism.

Each country is diverse in its territorial plurality, but the conclusion is always the same. If in Ecuador Jaramillo warns that a "deep regional division . . . seems truly to limit the organic functioning necessary for thought and action" and makes the building of an integrated and powerful nationality more difficult, Mariátegui in Peru echoes the theory of three internal regions, but insists that "the coast and the *sierra* . . . are the two regions in which it is actually possible to distinguish the differences in terrain and people [thereby generating] the duality of Peru's history and soul" (*Seven*

Essays 162–63).[34] Meanwhile Mendoza accepts the fact that in Bolivia "[national] integration has yet to become a reality" due to "incongruent elements and extravagant superpositions," in spite of his ingenuous faith in the power of "Bolivian solidity" that, despite individual failures, could on its own build the "true nation."[35] These are a few of the many examples of how geographic disparity is one of the links in a chain made unstable by (1) overtly or covertly racist biological reflection on the virtues or vices of the different races or the instability that results when they are mixed, (2) more modern, socioanthropological proposals that also result in bristling, irreconcilable binaries, or (3) opposing economic regimes (for example, feudal and capitalist), whose nature delays, hinders, or precludes the nation's formation.

The basis for these interpretations is the consciousness of a historic deformation that makes the Andean countries into tragically isolated archipelagos fraught with internal disparities. Hence the proliferation of dichotomies that describe these nations in terms of irreconcilable polar opposites: city-country, highlands-coast, province-capital, exploited-exploiters, nationalism-cosmopolitanism, tradition-modernity, and so on. Obviously one cannot help but first examine the dichotomous situation that confronts Indians and "whites" (and eventually is complicated by the inclusion of blacks), where the mestizo embodies the internalized conflict between both poles, although, as stated in the previous chapter, the persistent ideology of mestizaje often had conciliatory and even Messianic overtones.[36] Then there is the "indigenous question," concretized in the paradoxical situation of Indians who are both a majority and a minority that must endure perverse marginalization and discrimination. There is the explicit or implicit recognition that one cannot hope to examine national roots outside the historic tradition of this majority, even if, as Jaramillo points out, the despotism of the Inca Empire created degraded ways of being and behaving that have persisted over the centuries.[37] The crux, then, of the debate was the "indigenous question," which has normally led to considering all these authors (and others) as Indigenists, in spite of the fact that in many cases the Indians are viewed as unforgivably degraded beings either because they belong to an "inferior race," as argued outright by reactionary positivists, or because centuries of servitude and misery have damaged their authentic, human condition or have made them incapable of the development demanded by modern times.[38]

I shall not concentrate on these writers but on those that propose, despite their differences, that the recovery of Indian rights is a possible and urgent task, see it as the possible harbinger of social renewal, and verify the existence of a defective and intolerable reality. I am particularly interested in Luis E. Valcárcel and his *Tempestad en los Andes*, which enjoyed an exceptionally lively and fervent audience for many years.[39] Valcárcel was one of the leaders of the "Cusco School" and the "Resurgence Group" based in the capital of the Inca Empire and later expanded throughout his country and other Andean nations along with the revival promoted by that city's university. This provincial elite claimed to defend indigenous rights, proposed to reclaim the sociocultural attributes and values of these peoples and their history, and created—or consolidated—a national ideology based on an ironclad, forceful, and aggressive Indigenism.[40] In retrospect its practice was less effective than its promises, but it clearly put its mark on the ideological development of several generations, despite the fact that many of its intellectuals published in newspapers, journals, and books.

The most successful of these was *Tempestad en los Andes*, which soon became a veritable bible for Indigenists and was widely disseminated through teachers fond of citing it. Despite its brevity this is a highly complex treatise in which Andean nature descriptions (fashioned according to the telluric models of the day) are mixed with scenes of mountain life or characterizations of types (removed from *Costumbrismo* only by their social content) to form a seedbed for certain themes and symbols to be found in future Indigenist novels. Most fundamental to this process is the intense, passionate reflection on the past, present, and future of the Indian people. Its incisive, prophetic style is most memorable, while certain unresolved contradictions remain in the background.[41] Valcárcel begins with a description of the country in a bloody struggle between "invaders and invaded" (Valcárcel, *Tempestad en los Andes*, 23–25) that will end with the inevitable liquidation (except if love overcomes hate) of one of the factions ("Will a million white victims be sufficient?" he asks himself). In this struggle (love or hate aside) the mestizo is morally and physically excluded: if the "whites" are "strange, extravagant" entities (Valcárcel, *Tempestad en los Andes*, 111) who usurp power and construct society according to their interests, and Indians are "primitive" (Valcárcel, *Tempestad en los Andes*, 26) beings who nevertheless will avenge centuries of atrocities with revived, uncontainable strength and preside over a new cycle in history, then mestizos possess neither an identity nor a future. Valcárcel concludes that they are no more than "hybrid[s that] inherit not ancestral virtues but vices and defects" and that "the mixing of cultures only produces deformity" (Valcárcel, *Tempestad en los Andes*, 107). This is perhaps one of his gravest errors, since it negates this majority sector's participation in his national project. It is also one of his greatest incongruities, since in the final chapter he quotes a lecture he gave in Arequipa, which extols the virtues and the social role of those he so consistently denigrates in previous pages. As with González Prada, young Valcárcel's obvious predecesor, his social passion and inflamed rhetoric lead to dead ends such as this one. In addition the fact that Valcárcel was mestizo himself opens up the possibility of a (broadly ironic) psychological interpretation but does not change the basis of his thought in the least.

One should also note that the opposition between Indians and whites is repeated in a geographic dichotomy having psychosocial overtones: the highlands, symbol of masculine strength and asceticism, and the coast, representing feminine sensuality and fawning, resolved in the author's fervent adherence to the former. His conclusions are emphatic: "essential Peru, unchanging Peru was not, could never be anything other than Indian. . . . Peru is Indian!" and "the highlands *are* nationhood" (Valcárcel, *Tempestad en los Andes*, 112–116).[42] This explains Valcárcel's vacillation between the terms *Indigenism* and *Andeanism*.

The above is based on a crude, positivist concept of a "race" whose power and energy will overcome history: "it may be today an empire and tomorrow a herd of slaves. No matter. Race remains identical unto itself" (Valcárcel, *Tempestad en los Andes*, 21). In spite of this, it is in and through history that the "indigenous race" (a "dead Race whose very gods were killed by the invaders") can live out the "springtime miracle" of its resurrection (Valcárcel, *Tempestad en los Andes*, 20). This is the resurrection that Valcárcel predicts for the immediate future and that gives wings to his unmitigated optimism.[43] Curiously the utopian vision that lends credence to this almost religious fervor presupposes concrete and modernizing transformations in indigenous thought and behavior. Valcárcel thinks that the perpetuity of "race" is superior to that of "culture" (Valcárcel, *Tempestad en los Andes*, 21) and that history transforms only the latter without interfering in the identity and substance of the former. This is the tension that pulls at *Tempestad en los Andes*: the difficult coexistence of the fact of historic change with the principle of racial immutability. In the end we do not know what "race" preserves forever unto itself, why this is timeless, nor how such a concept of "eternity" is articulated according to the fluid categories of history that the book both relates and foretells. This confusion is further heightened when Valcárcel explicitly denies the restoration of the Inca Empire,[44] while on the same page implies that this very thing will one day happen: "The race, in the new cycle before us, will *reappear* resplendent, crowned with a halo of her *eternal* values, and striding firmly toward a surely glorious future" (Valcárcel, *Tempestad en los Andes*, 22, Cornejo's emphasis).

The conceptual ambiguity of *Tempestad en los Andes*, along with its rhetorical and apodictic tone, invited the reading of Valcárcel's project as a historical-mythic operation that inverts time in order to find the image of a desirable future in the splendid past. In this sense it is largely a project favoring the future restoration of what was destroyed by history while simultaneously denying the substance and value of what happened between these primordial beginnings and their imminent resurrection.[45] It was a question, then, of an inverse, regressive utopia setting out to reconquer lost paradise. As such it negates the concept of modernity as progress—or simply eliminates it altogether.

Valcárcel and other essayists who take up the "indigenous problem" find the construction of national identity for each of the Andean countries to be quite unsettling. Some are bitterly skeptical, such as Alcides Arguedas in *Pueblo enfermo*, whose examination of the nation's racial admixture leads to the disconsolate conclusion that the nation can never achieve the coherent, energetic "health" necessary to move toward progress.[46] But they all, each in a more voluntary than reflective way, try to configure a national identity as a promise to be fulfilled in the future but whose roots are indigenous or, as Uriel García would say, "neo-Indian." Thus arises a new and curious contradiction: if on one hand they continue to show Indians as prostrate (for Varcárcel they are "primitive" beings), on the other they make them the matrix of nationality and its future representation. It is curious, for example, that Franz Tamayo considers Indians as "the true repository of national energy," for their strength, efficiency, and will, but at the same time judges them to be naïve, primitive, and lacking in intelligence. (For this reason education, the true solution to national problems, should be concentrated on the formation of character rather than mind).[47] Likewise, the realist Jaramillo emphasizes the installation of a just economic and social order aimed at a positive and protagonistic integration of Indians into national life as a way of respecting their dignity, although he considers them ethnically and historically degraded beings.[48]

By proclaiming themselves defenders of the "indigenous race" and its interests, even the most skeptical of these essayists show how far they are from the very roots of the national image they are proposing and make themselves representatives of a social sector to which they obviously do not belong. The contradictions growing out of these texts are, nonetheless, highly significant. They reveal that in the complex and difficult process that leads to the definition of a national identity, the elite, either as its prophet or its "unnatural" representative, controls a political-intellectual operation producing an image of the Indian and itself within the context of a society that incarnates that identity. Identity would therefore presuppose the conversion of an exclusive "we," into which only that elite and its adherents (along with its self-image, interests, and desires) comfortably fit, to an expansively inclusive, almost ontological "we," in which the true—but unconsulted—protagonists are forced to amputate parts of their very being in order to be squeezed by the strict—even sacred—bounds set by its promoters' ideology. This all becomes more confusing when identity is tied to the past and considered to be the resurrection of pristine forces.

Not all were convinced by this retrograde image, especially those committed to concrete political projects. Although it was not his explicit intention, the concept of the "new Indian" that Uriel García proposes (even before his erratic embrace of Marxism) flies in the face of Varcárcel's ideas and underscores the importance of racially transforming the protagonists of national history, beginning with the Spanish invasion. This idea compels him to categorically reject any temptation to return to the past as pure Romanticism. The writings of Hildebrando Castro Pozo contain a similar negation of the idea of resurrection and speak to the possibility (or necessity) of affirming the ancient *ayllu* as the ancestor of a modern socialist cooperative.[49] It is Mariátegui who, without denying Valcárcel's importance (as shown in his being published in the journal *Amauta*), most clearly lays out the problem of how to join ancient indigenous tradition to the requirements of modernity as he understood it.

AN ANDEAN MODERNITY

In his foreword to Valcárcel's book, Mariátegui courteously warns against the archaisms contained in this work. In future writings—without necessarily referring to *Tempestad en los Andes*—he is much more assertive and blunt.[50] This in no way undermines the influence that Varcárcel, the Cusco School, and other Indigenist thinkers had on Mariátegui.[51] For him the main problem was to find a valid link between Indigenism and socialism, one that might raise questions about other relationships such as universalism and nationalism or tradition and modernity. Of course Mariátegui also believes that the national problem rests essentially on the persistence of a social order based on indigenous servitude and fervently affirms the need to end such an atrocious, unjust system.[52] But his openly Marxist analysis proposes an interpretation of history that assumes the simultaneous requirements of both tradition and modernity. This is not the time for an extended analysis, but it is interesting to trace Mariátegui's thoughts on this subject.[53] Following is a brief summary of his basic points:[54]

1. Contrary to conventional thought, only revolution can vindicate tradition and make it into living history rather than a museum piece.[55] In Peru the most ancient of traditions, which for Mariátegui is the Incas, has been recovered according to precisely that stance, which also establishes a dynamic that begins in the past and leads to the future: The propagation of socialist ideas in Peru has resulted in a strong indigenous movement aimed at recovering justice. The new Peruvian generation feels and knows that Peru's progress will be fictitious, or at least not Peruvian, as long as it does not incorporate the efforts or result in the well-being of the Peruvian masses, which are four-fifths indigenous and rural" (Mariátegui, *Seven Essays*, 48).[56]
2. Inca "Communism . . . cannot be negated or disparaged for having developed under [an] autocratic regime" (Mariátegui, *Seven Essays*, 35). Thus the recovery of ancient, pre-Hispanic tradition has both a historical and a political bias and confirms the classic Marxist view of the process of human development from a period of "primitive communism." Today the argument that the Inca Empire was a communist society is untenable, but one should remember that for decades there was little debate on this issue, despite differences among scholars. For instance, Jaramillo interpreted this fact as the origin of the Indians' submissive nature (without "personality" nor "initiative").
3. Although the conquest destroyed the indigenous social order, there is still a sense of "Inca communism" in some facets of indigenous community life, though clearly modified and weakened. Despite the fact that Mariátegui's writings treat this topic infrequently, "the survival of the Indian 'community' and elements of practical Socialism in indigenous agriculture and life" (Mariátegui, *Seven Essays*, 33) are key to tying the

modern socialist project to what survives of original national tradition. In other words, the affirmation of the existence of an "Inca communism" and its weak, but traceable, survival are the basis for the nationalization of socialism that Mariátegui proposed as a solution to the backwardness, chaos, and injustice of Peruvian society.

4. The conquest substituted the Inca social order with a feudal one, consolidated over centuries of colonialism and maintained after independence—and even into the Republic—with great rigor and consistency. For Mariátegui, the frailty and torpor of the Peruvian bourgeoisie and its compromise with the "Gamonalism" of the feudal regime made the realization of an authentic bourgeois revolution and the installation of a modern capitalist regime impossible, even in more developed areas. Imperialism barred the national bourgeoisie from its natural role of ushering in modernization.[57]

5. Thus it is socialism's task to modernize national society by realizing some of the goals that the bourgeoisie would not or could not achieve, through a process rooted in the remote, pre-Hispanic past and its survival in the contemporary Andean world. It is, then, a process that originates in national tradition. On this point Mariátegui is emphatic: in Peru socialism cannot be separated from Indigenism because the former represents and defends the interests of the working class and—as in other Andean countries—Indians make up its vast majority.[58]

Although it is clear that the idea of "Inca communism" is unsustainable in our day and the socialization of indigenous communities is cast very differently, Mariátegui's theoretical construct is exceptionally rich, provocative, and global. Based on the knowledge of his era, he was able to resolve many of the inconsistencies of his time. The "confluence and melding" of communism with Indigenism destroyed the opposition between the internationalism of the former and the nativism of the latter by chiseling out a unique riverbed in which both flowed more or less harmoniously, overcoming the polemic between "nativists" and "cosmopolitans," and giving a national and modern direction to his political project. It was the melding of socialism and Indigenism that would form the nation that neither feudalism nor the bourgeoisie was capable of consolidating. Likewise he overcame the heretofore irreconcilable opposition between tradition and modernity. In the end the most adequate modernity (which for him and many of his generation took shape not in a decrepit capitalism but in an emergent socialism) had its roots in pristine national tradition. Mariátegui countered the willful and improbable predictions of hard-line Indigenism, which foresaw indigenous development with the least possible interference from foreign contamination, and produced a convincing image in which the new was grafted onto the old trunk of national tradition and thus revitalized it.

The invalidation of some of Mariátegui's hypotheses does not detract one iota from the subtlety, originality, and coherence of his proposal, nor does it harm the validity of what continues to be a clearly transcendent problem: how to advocate a modernity that does not merely copies centralized countries, including the nascent socialist states of the time, but also develops its own set of social, historical, and cultural circumstances, in this case an Andean modernity. While today it has become more common to think that the modernity of Andean countries depends on their capacity to "deindigenize," Mariátegui proposes an antidogmatic alternative: there are many modernities—not just one—with various ways of arriving at that point, and it is senseless not to include among these the option of imagining and realizing a modernity rooted in and tempered by an Andean world view.[59] If today the option of Andean modernity is refuted from the heights of conservative ideology, in Mariátegui's lifetime his national (Andean) vision of socialism as a useful form of modernity was the object of misunderstanding and rejection by the Marxist orthodoxy of the time.[60]

The fact that Mariátegui does not define national identity as something finished nor as a univocal image of the future, but as the result of a historical process on its (own, national) way toward socialism, makes him perhaps the only thinker of his time who does not conceive of identity as merely historical. On one hand this implies that identity is not being but becoming, presupposing at the outset that it is fluid and changeable, and on the other that its bearing toward the future, though framed by socialism, is open to several alternatives. Thus Mariátegui insisted, using a phrase that unfortunately became commonplace, that socialism in the Americas would be neither "blueprint nor copy [but] heroic creation."[61] More politicized readings underscore what is secondary for Mariátegui in order to give a revolutionary bent to the construction of socialism, but what is more important here is that by invalidating all preexisting models ("neither blueprint nor copy") and placing national creativity in the forefront, Mariátegui opens up the space in which this future identity will take shape so that history itself can configure a new—but not immutable nor ultimate—national identity. Thus it is not the intellectual who defines the nation; it is the nation that, by way of its history, makes its way toward self-definition.

These briefly summarized proposals also appear (with obvious modifications) in the last chapter of *Seven Essays*.[62] In "Literature on Trial" Mariátegui states that the new periodization proposed in this essay is not social in nature—and much less Marxist—and calls it simply "literary" (Mariátegui, *Seven Essays*, 239). He establishes three long periods: the colonial, the cosmopolitan, and the national, immediately clarifying that the first two are not limited chronologically ("colonialist" texts appear after 1821, and there are cosmopolitan outcroppings in the national period) and that the final period is still in formation and therefore open to multiple possibilities. Moreover, and without explanation, Mariátegui tweaks each period, where diverse and conflictive currents coexist. For example, he places Melgar, who pertains chronologically to the colonial period, in the national and makes many contemporary writers direct descendents of the colony. All leads to the conclusion that Mariátegui sees the course of history as an overlapping and conflictive process in which there are long, alternating periods of hegemony and subordination. The correlation of these proposals to his general thesis is obvious at several points. For example, Mariátegui qualifies the relationship between the colonial and national periods as one of antagonistic contradiction, like the one between feudalism and socialism when capitalism is not full-blown, and finds that the cosmopolitan both opposes and paves the way for the emergence of the national period. Perhaps it is not going too far afield to say that cosmopolitanism, by merely shifting what it should change, is the literary equivalent of what did *not* happen in social life: the modernizing bourgeois revolution would propitiate the emergence of a social dynamic that, on the very strength of its internal contradictions, would lead to socialism. Cosmopolitanism presupposes an accumulation of symbolic and technological capital to international ends, from which a national literature will emerge as a transformative rechanneling of those and other energies toward new and unprecedented goals.[63] The opposition between the last two periods is not antagonistic, since the second simultaneously overcomes and feeds on the first, and Mariátegui did not feel uncomfortable in accepting the existence of a "Vanguardist Indigenism," which, in fact, he encouraged and stimulated. From a complementary perspective and by restating the necessary provisos, this "Vanguardist Indigenism" is to a certain degree the literary phraseology of the central thesis concerning the convergence of Indigenism and socialism.

If, for Mariátegui, the image of the nation and its future has indigenous roots, his interpretation of Peruvian literature, by contrast, is limited to what is written in Spanish, and its primordial origin is not "Inca communism" but the conquest. Putting this contradiction (which derives from the concept on which the great histories of national European literatures are based) to one side, it is important to establish that there are enough elements in Mariátegui's texts to invalidate what he expressed at the outset of "Literature on Trial." Fortunately Mariátegui's thought does not shield itself with hermetic dogmatism. Instead it opens itself up to discussion and permits—and even invites—debate. Here I would like to underscore (1) the idea that Quechua/Spanish duality is unresolved; and (2) the proposition that Peruvian literature is not "organically national" (Mariátegui, *Seven Essays*, 187–88) because of its dispersion and the fact that the integral country is still a "nationality in formation" (Mariátegui, *Peruanicemos al Perú*, 26); (3) the definition of what is national in literature as having an obvious and persistent content primarily indigenous in nature.[64] But if the referential framework outlined in the opening statements and based on writing in Spanish limits the reach of Mariátegui's proposal, the latter contains the seeds that allow boundaries—which today would be unacceptable—to be overcome, thereby producing more open interpretations. One of these is foundational: national literature, which by belonging to the last period is also modern literature, has its roots and ultimate meaning in the recovery of an indigenous worldview and the expression of the "indigenous soul," although this last point is discussed rather abstractly using the Indigenist rhetoric that Mariátegui had formerly rejected. In either case the national literary program that Mariátegui proposes joins two basic categories: a socialist version of modernity and an indigenous worldview. He will later intuit that it will be through either Indigenism itself or "Vanguardist Indigenism" that this project will achieve its artistic and social objectives.[65]

A HOBBLED HISTORY: THE INDIGENIST NOVEL

The problem that Mariátegui resolved by tying future socialist modernity to Andean tradition was basically the same one that Indigenist novelists faced, except that for them the emphasis was on the narrative representation of the Indian world and its recent history. And once again the issue of the opposition between tradition and modernity was quick to arise. These writers felt less urgency to treat the opposition between nationalism and cosmopolitanism, since there was an obvious preference for the former. Almost all denounced the anachronistic and ferocious "feudalism" that viciously oppressed the Indians and announced the imminence of the "storm in the Andes" in an attempt to chronicle an infamous present and presage its just punishment. Clearly one of their major problems was imagining the historical transit between the two.

We should begin by examining a paradox. For understandable reasons the Indigenist novel was constructed using the realist code (with a few naturalist shadings) and recounted a story that reproduced actual events, though the latter were fictionalized either through slight transformations or, more frequently, by abstracting a paradigmatic action with episodes occurring at different times and places. Using multiple strategies it tells a single story: the exploitation of the Indians. However, either out of the narrators' personal ethics or political convictions or because of the requirements of the realism they practiced, this story could not have the same ending that it had in reality: the persistence or worsening of the intolerable conditions in which the Indians found themselves. Thus the narrative resolution of the conflict often implies a violent change in code: in the final pages of the novel a naturalist realism becomes a type of allegorical idealism in order to symbolically foretell the Indians' triumphal rebellion. One need only recall the last paragraph of *Raza de bronce*: "A yellow ray scraped against the eastern side of the black dome. It was ashen at first, soon turned pink, and finally orange. Then the peaks of the mountain range were stenciled against the purple background; the snow spilled out the pure dawn of its dazzling whiteness. And upon the summits gold and diamonds rained down. The sun . . ."[66] Or *Huasipungo*: "At dawn, up from the demolished huts, from the rubble, from the ashes, from the still warm corpses, as if in a dream, a crop of thin arms sprouted like spikes of barley. Strummed by the icy winds of the paramos of all the Americas they emitted a piercing screeching cry: 'Ñucanchic huasipungo!'"[67] Or even *Todas las sangres*: "And he, like the other guards, felt the shaking of great torrents deep within the earth, as if the mountains were finding their feet. . . . As if an underground river were reaching its floodtide."[68]

Each of these paragraphs recounts the ignominious massacre of rural

Indians narrated under the norms of realism (or naturalism) by shifting the story line to nature to create a premonitory allegory of future justice. Alcides Arguedas does this through the dawn and sunlight that banish the darkness, Icaza through the "crop" and the "spikes" that announce the germinal force born out of the defeat and death of the Indians, and José María Arguedas through signs of a cosmic cataclysm that will destroy the old and forge a new, just order. Thus the desired image of future history imposes the need to transform narrative strategy by resorting to forms that have little to do with the modernity that would be realized by breaking with the feudal order. If the novel finds in the established code of realism an effective instrument that reflects the insufferable backwardness of the Andean region, it has few options—except for the allegory that makes the story into a natural phenomenon—for imagining the future. It is obviously difficult, then, for the Indigenist novel to imagine modernity, the same modernity that would begin to form with the hypothetical triumph of the indigenous rebellions over the ancient social order imposed on the Andes since the colony and rearchaized during the time of the Republic.[69]

This is linked to the difficulty of depicting the indigenous world. I have noted that most Indigenist novels begin with an unsettling action foreign to indigenous circumstances, whose essential function is to produce the tension necessary for a successful novel.[70] *Torn from the Nest* starts with the arrival in Killac of the foreigners Marín, who in their zeal to defend the Indians occasion all the action of the novel (which ends, symptomatically, when the Maríns abandon the tiny Andean village);[71] *Raza de bronce* pinpoints the beginning of the exploitation of Bolivian Indians through the laws and abuses of the tyrant Melgarejo, who strips hundreds of indigenous communities of their lands; *Huasipungo* does the same with the hacienda's change of ownership and its commercial relationship with a North American oil company; *Yawar fiesta* makes use of the ferocious plundering that the *mistis* commit against the *ayllus* of Puquio when they dispossess them of their best lands.[72] I would like to emphasize two points: from the perspective of the Indigenist narrator, who is both foreign to and in solidarity with the Indian world, the reality in which the Indians live stands on the fringes of history, solidified in repeated abuse and injustice, and only acquires dynamism (and thus the possibility of being novelized) with the appearance of someone or something, an "other," who for better or worse represents modernity and produces a commotion that dramatizes (novelizes) indigenous life.[73] In other words, this way of life seems to be imagined more in terms of nature than history, and history creeps in only with the intrusion of the "other." It would not be going too far afield to include in this intrusion and this otherness the novelist and—more precisely—the entire genre of the novel. After all, it is not inconsequential that such a modern genre is the preferred means of raising awareness about a society that possesses a rich and varied range of narrative forms but—for obvious reasons—has never produced a novel. The novel, then, is a sign that modernity is penetrating an archaic world. The fact that the Indigenist novel seeks to arbitrate between a solid, dependable state and a dynamic situation in which circumstances vary could well be a sort of metonymic displacement of the conflict between the pre-Hispanic world and the conquest, assuming that the former is a "natural society" (capable of its own myths, legends, fables, and elegies) and the latter a treacherous (but animated, fluid, and dramatic) realm of history from which emerges not only the novel but the very possibility of writing it.

It is evident—except for the more complicated case of José María Arguedas—that these characteristics are signs of the conflicts that remain unresolved in the Indigenist novel. It is symptomatic that the latter cannot begin until an element alien to the indigenous world transforms its ingrained passivity into dramatic conflict and cannot end without abandoning realist norms to imagine a just future through the allegorization of nature. Although the above should be sufficient to prove the depth of this conflict, the truth is that the difficulty of representing indigenous history as it is can also be interpreted in a wider scope. It is surprising that in several cases indigenous rebellion, which ought to signal modernity, tries to preserve regimes that the novel itself judges as primitive and unjust. This is the case in Icaza's novel, where the Indians defend the ignominious *huasipungo*, only to fall into an even more inhumane situation without suspecting that other, more just forms of social organization might exist. By this I mean that in the Indigenist novel, history is hobbled by a knot joining the allegorized utopia of the future, the radical, desperate condemnation of inconceivable, unbearable injustice, and the unimaginable defense of this regime when an even more dehumanizing situation threatens it. Each tries different ways of untangling this knot, including Alcides Arguedas's unexpected strategy in the definitive edition of *Raza de bronce* (1945) where he transforms a current text of denunciation into a sort of historical novel about a cancelled past, all in a final note in which one can read both naïveté and opportunism:

This book has had the dubious honor of working slowly on the national consciousness for over twenty years, because especially in recent years, the powers that be have been eager to write laws protecting the Indian, and many landholders have introduced agricultural machinery for working their fields, abolished the lending of free services, and built schools on their estates. A native conference held in May of this year and funded by the Government has adopted resolutions such that the pariah of yesterday is on its way to becoming the lord of tomorrow. . . . The scenes described herein, all taken from the true reality of yesterday, could hardly be reproduced in our day, except in details of minor importance. This should be said loud and clear.[74]

Rather than bemoan the irony of the text's direction changing from tragedy to optimism, one should emphasize the fact that the author again places the movement of history outside the indigenous world, since the Indians' improved living conditions result from the generosity of the landholders and government (that not only promulgates beneficent laws but "adopts" the Indians' own "native conference"), thereby repeating the old idea that indigenous salvation is in the hands of others. In the front lines is the novelist himself, who says his work can provide the moral incentive for a change in attitude among authorities and large estate holders. If this is an extreme case of the expropriation of indigenous history (no mention is made of the uprisings and rebellions that occurred between the publication of the first and definitive editions), one must remember that many Indigenist novels, even the more radical *Huasipungo*, offer up such a depressing image of the Indians that it is impossible to imagine them as protagonists of any transcendent action. If the unpardonable perfidy of landholders and agents of the church and state (for whom the reader feels nothing but contempt) is proved by the profound degradation to which the Indians have been so perversely subjected, the latter's irreversible dehumanization and incapacity to manage their own lives individually and socially is also brought to the fore. The reader feels pity toward them but can hardly harbor any hope that they will be saved through their own means: they are, in this version, destroyed both individually and collectively. Thus the rebellions recounted in these novels are, as Ariel Dorfman points out, "automatic, almost Pavlovian reactions," destined to inevitable failure and incapable of even minimally changing the painful and unbearable reality from which they spring.[75] Clearly this massive hobbling of historical thought is one of the problems that the Indigenists were unable to either perceive with clarity or confront in a productive manner. There is, however, one notable exception: *Broad and Alien Is the World* by Ciro Alegría.[76] It stands alone in making the problem of history and the ambiguous relationship between tradition and modernity into one of its major narrative and semantic threads, although this in no way implies that it either sheds light into all corners of this vast problem or resolves it.

Alegría's last great novel is exceptional in that it constructs from the outset an image of the indigenous community (Rumi) as a social organization that is only slightly less than perfect. Wisdom, kinship, and justice in interpersonal relationships and an almost religious respect for nature make this community a place where the Indian can live with dignity and realize the highest of human values.[77] This sustained praise of the community not only qualifies it as an ideal space for indigenous people but also defines it as the most complete, authentic, and perfect social order among the several that coexist in the Andean nations.[78] The narrator recounts, by way of numerous episodes interspersed with the main story line, the vicissitudes of the migratory *comuneros* and the deplorable suffering that the Indians are made to endure in each locale. It is no coincidence that all these stories end tragically. The author is obviously trying to prove that the community is the only legitimate space for the comuneros and the only system that allows them to carry out their existence with dignity, since on its fringes (the *latifundio*, the mines, the Amazon, the mountain villages, and the coastal cities) they can only contemplate their own unhappiness, yearn for their distant and lost community of origin, and conclude, tirelessly, that the "community is always better."[79] But these episodes carry with them a more far-reaching meaning: they allow a comparison between the indigenous community and the rest of national society, which leads to the affirmation of the great superiority of the communitarian system over any other form of social organization. This is not a question of a constrained valuation of the comunero perspective. Rather it is an exercise in social axiology handled by the narrator through the basic structure of the text. Thus the community becomes a paradigm for harmonious, just, and efficient human coexistence and a completely sensible and productive way of grafting society onto nature.[80]

Thus one could say that *Broad and Alien Is the World* is not only the story of a community, which is how it is generally interpreted, but also the story of the relationship between the indigenous community and national society as a whole.[81] If the first part of the novel is a eulogy to the community, what follows—up to its tragic ending—recounts the conflictiveness of its links to other aspects of national reality. At first the novelistic disposition is tenuous, but soon events enjamb in a dynamic plot. As in other Indigentist texts there is an external force (the ambition of a caudillo who wants all the communal lands for himself) that dramatizes the account and gives it the tension necessary to meet the demands of the genre. It is important to note, however, that the narrator is conscious of what the inclusion of the community in a broader social context means as he underscores both the great antithesis between former happiness and present misfortune and the paradox of the vigorous power of the community when it functions on its own terms and its extreme vulnerability when confronted by outside forces: "Thus the wind of October burst in and the villagers received it with their habitual calm. It would wear itself out in its attacks against the firm earth, a strong tree, in rain as dense as a wall. But there was another wind blowing, an invincible one, that threatened the community's very existence, and to whose challenge there was no answer of Nature. And, after all, that was the only answer the villagers knew.... Now, in the face of rampant sheaves of paper, that is to say, the new law, they were unarmed, and their hope could do nothing but affirm itself in the love of the land.... [They] had to go to town..."[82]

As the challenges of history arise, it is important that the communitarian order be understood in terms of "nature," especially since, from the very beginning, the comuneros are defenseless when faced with a new intrusion that obliges them to abandon their age-old customs and go trembling into town, the seat of central power. The community has to defend its lands, and it is at this point that the narrator develops the conflict between tradition and modernity. Rumi's wise old mayor, Rosendo Maqui, and other elderly comuneros choose a traditional strategy that combines the skeptical and inefficient use of law with offerings and magical rituals aimed at defeating the adversary. Both avenues fail, since the latter functions only within the bounds of communitarian life (where one divines through coca, for example) and the former implies subjection to foreign forces, from the sanctification of writing (the "property titles" that very few comuneros can read) to the compliance with a complex judicial procedure that is totally prejudicial and unintelligible to them. Thus Rumi's best lands remain in the hands of the landholders and the comuneros emigrate to the infertile highlands in order to continue their collective life, though with the fear of a new expropriation that will leave the community landless and annihilated.

These events coincide with the substitution of the former mayor, Rosendo, by a young mestizo whom he had adopted as a child. Benito Castro venerates his predecessor but does not share his devotion to tradition. It is significant that Castro has come to understand something of social dynamics in his pilgrimage through the enemy's universe (he has lived in the city, been educated, learned from the political radicals of the day, but has also been drafted as a soldier and participated in acts of repression) and that upon his return to the community has to confront the comuneros, who do not wish to change their ancestral customs and magical sense of the world.[83] In the end he succeeds in establishing the bases for a cautious modernization of the community: he insists on schooling, the need for literacy, the employment of new, but modest, technologies, the slight alteration of certain collective customs, and so on.[84] The conflict between tradition, which should be preserved because its qualities make Rumi a paradigm of social organization and human achievement, and the exigencies of modernization, which can be both an enrichment of the communal order and the last chance of survival for a community impoverished—or even dissolved—by the despoiling of its lands, remains at the forefront. Although the narrator's preference for the modernizing option is obvious, the text itself does not reveal what its results might be. There is a new assault, this time in order to obtain the labor of the landless comuneros, and Castro decides on force to start an indigenous uprising that is subsequently crushed. In the confrontation between farmers and soldiers the community is decimated and the few survivors must scatter into a world that is now truly "broad and alien."

Rumi's destruction is even more tragic because the narration points to this community as a model of social organization and functioning and a place where the individual can live with dignity; one of the last communities in the nation that has been able to survive the voracious expansion of the latifundio. The ending, echoing with the roar of the army's rifles, contravenes the norm of the allegorized Indigenist novel and leaves the reader utterly disillusioned. In fact Alegría had to explain his tragic culmination of events to the many readers accustomed to a curious type of happy ending. In the foreword to the tenth edition of this novel he says: "The reader may wonder how I believe this [he is referring to his affirmation that the indigenous problem will be solved in the latter's favor] when in my novel the Indians are shackled. The connection has presented itself to me many times. . . . Between Rosendo Maqui's resigned stoicism and mystic alliance with the earth and Benito Castro's decidedly modern and revolutionary attitude, all hope seems lost. This is the way it happens in the real world. But no reader will miss the fact that, in spite of apparent defeat, in these pages the Indian remains immovable, standing erect. The same thing happens in the real world as well."[85]

Apart from the importance of the realist poetics revealed in "This is the way it happens in the real world," one may ask what is behind the exacerbated mimesis that converts probability into truth, since these poetics are unachievable even in historic discourse, and taken literally can be deceptive.[86] The narrator uses a double and ambiguous strategy. On the one hand he attempts to be a transparent medium through which "reality" flows to the reader. On the other this same narrator maintains a stance of author/authority and configures a referential network of interpretations and valuations (either by way of explicit judgments or through placement, emphasis, or omission) that reflects the hermeneutic — or ideological — position of a monologic narrator.[87] Again, in the case of the Indigenist novel this matter is more complex, since the narrator is a foreigner in the indigenous world that he is attempting to represent.

If *Broad and Alien Is the World* is the novel that most profoundly problematizes the history of the indigenous people and reflects most openly on the difficult transition from tradition to modernity, it is also the one that allows an understanding of why this type of novel falters in its attempt to depict the situation of the Andean Indians. This has to do with the narrator's being an outsider to the narrated world, but also — and more decisively — the way in which he constructs a discourse that both emits from a subject with sole narrative authority and has a referent who is inescapably and copiously prevalued. That is, the narrator speaks with a single voice and imposes a single meaning on the universe of representation.[88] The protagonists' words, as eloquent as they may be, are never heard: somehow they are always "translated," just as their world is constrained within a solid referential framework.

Indigenist authors, whose mesocratic roots and social project oblige them to represent and speak for the indigenous masses, actually appropriate this social base in their discourse in order to mold it to their own needs.[89] These texts both serve as effective arms in the struggle against the historical enemies of the oligarchy and Andean *latifundismo* and move the very emitter of the discourse about the other, the Indian, to the center of the national scene. This does not imply that the denunciation found in Indigenist novels was not effective or that they contained ideological traps (although some did). Rather, by its heterogeneous straddling of two very different sociocultural worlds, the Indigenist novel of the time (even *Broad and Alien Is the World*) does not have the tools to effectively process the conflict from which it arises and on which it is built. It reproduces the internal conflict of divided and unintegrated nations that history cannot resolve. Although paradoxical, the great truth of Indigenism—and above all the Indigenist novel—rests not so much on what it says as on the real contradictions that it reproduces. Its incongruities, ambiguities, and aporias are, at bottom, those of a society that can neither understand itself nor produce convincing images of its problems, except when it reproduces them discursively. To read Indigenist literature is, above all, to read the extreme contradiction of nations that, upon trying to express their heteroclite nature and resolve the "national problem" (or rather, the "indigenous problem") by reflection and fiction, only repeat it. In the best cases this repetition is illuminating.

THE SUBJECT EXPLODES

The elegy that *Broad and Alien Is the World* becomes in the end was premature: in major areas of the highlands, communities survived the ferocious assault of Gamonalism in the first half of the twentieth century, some by preserving their age-old customs and others by modernization. All, however, were affected by the farming crisis in the Andes and subsequent waves of migration to the cities. Schematically speaking, one segment of Arguedas's literary and anthropological work explores their survival in terms of the anxiety caused by an unknown future and the other (smaller but no less important) examines migration, one of the most important phenomena of the century.[90] I will not study the thematics of these, but rather the way in which their creation depends on a recomposition of Indigenist—or neo-Indigenist—discourse, and the emergence of a new subject that may or may not pertain to these categories. Because of the extent of Arguedas's work, I shall first examine *Deep Rivers*.[91]

Like any writer, Arguedas constructs the identity through which he utters his discourse. It is senseless to ask whether it corresponds or not to his "real" biography, since the self-created subject (and which is not?) is the one that in the end speaks with its readers and persuades them—or not—of its legitimacy.[92] In his case, Arguedas was so convincing that he became a sort of "cultural hero" for a public that goes far beyond that of his readers.[93] Harking back to his childhood, Arguedas defined himself doubly—and at times ambivalently—as a "modern Quechua individual" that "like a cheerful demon proudly speaks in Christian and in Indian, in Spanish and in Quechua."[94] For Arguedas, having lived his first years under the care of the Indians and learned about their complex Quechua culture as well as their miserable living conditions was a paradoxical "happy trauma" that reappears both in his consciousness and his work. His misti origins (son of a lawyer and a landholder) and later roles, first in Lima's university life and then in the international literary and academic community, were never able to erase that literally foundational experience, which forms the matrix that produces a subject who cannot speak of the present moment without somehow referring to that pleasant, yet painful, past. I offer not a psychological nor psychoanalytical reading of Arguedas but an examination of the nature of a subject that utters its discourse based on an experience that is not strictly autobiographical, but that is indeed "real." It is by bestowing upon it this nature and by living it out that the subject configures itself, its utterance, and the manner and meaning of its representative framework.

This is globalized in Arguedas's experience (later shared by multitudes) as an early Andean migrant to the capital city. The feeling of uprootedness clearly has the paradoxical effect of both preserving the memory of the time and space left behind and making of these a sort of second life that constantly infiltrates and shapes later experiences.[95] While mestizos try to make a coherent—but unstable and precarious—whole of their double ancestry, the migrant population, also thoroughly mestizo, finds itself in two antagonistic worlds: the "here and now" and the "there and then," although each is marked by the ever-changing flow between them. Thus migrants speak from two or more loci and—even more compromisingly—duplicate (or multiply) their impact as subjects. It is likely that the configuration of plural subjects, discourse, and representation in Arguedas's work is related to his being a migrant. The broad socialization of this experience may be one of the reasons that a wide range of social groups indentifies with Arguedas's perspective and language.

To clarify, let us analyze one of the first episodes of *Deep Rivers*. Chapter 6 takes place in a boarding school where the narrator/protagonist, Ernesto, tries to defend himself against the physical, moral, and cultural aggression he suffers in this "world full of monsters and fire" by continually and vigorously resorting to the memory of his childhood, when the generous Indians of the community "protected me and imbued me with the unquenchable tenderness in which I live." In a rare, peaceful moment, Markask'a, one of his worst enemies at the school, asks him to write ("they tell me you write like a poet") a letter to a girl with whom he is in love. She belongs to the powerful group in Abancay, the small city where the school is located. Ernesto experiences these "*señoritas* as distant beings. . . . They weren't of my world. They sparkled in other heavens." But with little hesitation, he decides to write:

> I knew that, in spite of everything, I could cross that distance like an arrow, like a spark that flies upward. The letter I was to write for Markask'a's beloved would reach the gates of that world. . . . It did not matter that the letter was for someone else; perhaps it was better to begin that way. "Take flight, blind hawk, roving hawk!" I exclaimed.
>
> I burned with a new pride. And, like one who is about to go into combat, I began to write Markask'a's letter:
>
> "You are the mistress of my soul. . . . Dear nymph, you played among the mulberry trees like a butterfly. . . ."
>
> But a sudden discontent, an intense feeling of shame, made me interrupt the writing of the letter. I laid my arms and head down on the desk; with my face hidden, I paused to listen to those new feelings. "Where are you going, where are you going? Why don't you continue? What has frightened you; who has cut short your flight?" After asking these questions I went back to listening to myself eagerly.
>
> "And what if they knew how to read? What if I could write to them?"
>
> And they were Justina, or Jacinta, Malicacha, or Felisa, who had neither long hair nor bangs, nor wore tulle over their eyes. Only black braids, and wildflowers in the bands of their hats. . . . If I could write to them my love would flow like a clear river; my letter could be like a song that goes through the sky to reach its destination. Writing! Writing for them was useless, futile. "Go; wait for them on the roads and sing! But what if it were possible, if it could be started?" And I wrote:
>
> "*Uyariy chay k'atik'niki siwar k'entita . . .*
>
> "Listen to the emerald hummingbird who follows you; he shall speak to you of me. . . ."
>
> This time my own sobbing made me pause. . . . I wept from neither

sorrow nor despair. I left the classroom erect, with a certain pride; as proudly as I had swum across the rivers in January, when they are laden with the heaviest, most turbulent waters (Arguedas, *Deep Rivers*, 74–75).

The reappearance of the theme of writing for those who do not know how to read (and perhaps even speak) Spanish is important, as is the declaration that the natural way to communicate with the Indian girls would be through song. He decides to write in Quechua, however, after an ambiguous "what . . . if it could be started?" which could refer to either beginning to write in Quechua or initiating the process by which the girls would become literate.[96] Ironically the novel's readers inversely repeat the latter's limitations. The narrator shows this by leaving just one line of the letter in Quechua (that the "normal" reader does not understand) and translating the rest to Spanish. I shall not go into the problems that Arguedas's bilingualism created for him, nor why he opted for more Spanish during this period.[97] It is more important to emphasize the tension in the relationship between a modern and urban cultural tool, like the novel, and a referential modality that obeys different sociocultural norms. It is a sign of the conflicts inherent in an arrhythmic, unequal modernization that can only produce a new and more trenchant heterogeneity.[98] It is more trenchant, among other reasons, because, as the above quotation shows, heterogeneity introjects itself into the subject and destabilizes it. It is under these terms that one can read the substitution of the writer (Ernesto displaces Markask'a) and the other displacement (when Ernesto makes the letter his own and changes the addressee), which results in intermingling the very makeup of the subject. It is no coincidence that the letter is imagined first as "an arrow, like a spark that flies upward" that "would reach the gates of [the *señoritas'*] world" and that in order to get up the courage to realize this flight the writer calls up a figure of Andean song, the sparrow hawk. More telling is the fact that at the critical moment when he feels ashamed to be writing another's letter in Spanish, the Quechua song is also nostalgically evoked as a flight "through the sky [that reaches] its destination," and that this series of images concludes with the memory of crossing the river in triumph.[99] There is a mix of several possible meanings here. The shift occurs between both Ernesto's self-image as an "Indian" and the space inhabited by the "*señoritas*" and his position as a misti adolescent, educated and capable of exercising the modernity of writing, and the "archaism" of the illiterate Indian girls. Thus we are left with an allegory of the distance that separates two coetaneous times and the possibility of a coming and going between them that is both painful and exhilarating. Additionally, these same shifts reveal an unstable, divided subject built more on a complex set of variable positions and relationships than on a stable, tidy identity.

This unsettled and changeable subject utters a decentered, multiple, and scattered discourse. In short, the overarching discourse is novelistic in nature, with an epistolary subgenre unfolding in the form of two letters: one in Spanish and another in Quechua, with the latter, even in its Spanish translation, holding up Indian song as its impossible, yet desired, model. These are the first few lines: "Listen to the emerald hummingbird who follows you; he shall speak to you of me; do not be cruel, hear him. His little wings are tired, he can fly no farther; pause a moment. The white stone where the travelers rest is nearby; wait there and listen to him; hear his sobs; he is only the messenger of my young heart; he shall speak to you of me" (Arguedas, *Deep Rivers*, 75).

The letter in Quechua (which, except for the first line, the reader sees only in its Spanish translation) rearticulates themes from both ancient and modern indigenous songs.[100] This implies that the discourse is submerged in a broad and disparate intertext, with the significant peculiarity that the letter written in Quechua goes back, via this intertextuality, to traditional Andean song, which is its impossible model. In this sense then, both the discourse and the subject that produces it are plural. Their multiplicity extends far beyond the substitution of Markask'a by Ernesto and romantic Spanish rhetoric by indigenous song to the complex participation of the speaker in another tradition and genre, thereby blurring his individuality and language and collectivizing them in the expression of a socialized consciousness. Thus there is a joint utterance between the cultured narrator who translates the letter for the readers, the protagonist who writes it in Quechua but can only do so by resorting to the songs he knew as a child, and the originators of the latter who express an age-old consciousness in collective rather than individual language. Thus the identity of the subject founders in words shared among many. Caught between the oral and the written, novel and song, the modern and the ancient, the urban and the rural, Spanish and Quechua, the subject has no other alternative than to intermingle with a heteroclite people.

The same can be said with respect to the splendid opening of the novel, which recounts Ernesto's discovery of Cusco and his astonishment when he first sees the ancient Inca walls surrounding the former capital of the Tawantinsuyu:

> The stones of the Inca wall were bigger and stranger than I'd ever imagined.... Then I remembered the Quechua songs that keep on repeating pathetic phrases like "*yawar mayu*," river of blood; "*yawar unu*," bloody water; "*puk'tik' yawar k'ocha*," lake of blood that boils; "*yawar wek'e*," tears of blood. Couldn't you also say "*yawar rumi*," stone of blood, or "*puk'tik yawar rumi*," stone of boiling blood? The wall was still, but it was boiling out of its joints and the surface changed as you looked at it, like the rivers in summer, that have a crest this high, towards the center of the flow, which is the most powerful, terrifying part. The Indians call these muddy rivers "*yawar mayu*" because when they move in the sunlight, they shine like blood.... "*Puk'tik yawar rumi!*" I shouted, facing the wall. (Jentsch's translation)

Although the subjectivity of the protagonist/narrator is pervasive in this excerpt (song and foreign words are interjected into the intimate space of memory), it can only exist in dialogue with another, collective voice that defines its alterity in language. The evocation of the Quechua songs allows an understanding of the millenary stones' mute message, but without socializing it in its immediate decantation into the Spanish of the modern novel. The protagonist's rumination accentuates the instability of a text configured by a deeper and more extensive bilingualism than that of the previous excerpt. The translation of the Quechua disappears at the end when Ernesto's exultant exclamation that the stones are truly "*puk'tik yawar rumi*" rises from the depths of his own being and not from the memory of songs heard long ago. Thus personal memory persuades the text's "objective" narrator, binds him to the subject of each idiomatic song and draws him into its worldview.[101] The Quechua songs are translated in order to create a bilingual discourse, and in the end a Quechua phrase becomes the final word. Thus the text's bilingualism is apparently resolved in a phrase that, because of its position, is transidiomatic. In a sense it is both Quechua and Spanish. Clearly this unstable combinatorial of subjects and languages reveals a complex operation that shifts original orality to writing, although in the fiction of the text the written conclusion is imaged orally: "I shouted," we read, which again establishes an ambiguous, uncertain, but effective convergent space.

Once again we have the construction of a plural subject experiencing discontinuous times and disparate cultures. And it operates in several languages: the oral Spanish of the astonished adolescent and the experienced narrator who recreates him in novelistic writing and the Quechua of traditional songs harking back to a previous, unchronicled time and another anonymous, collective subject generically identified with the Quechua people. Who, then, is speaking in this text? The only answer would have to underscore its multiple, dispersed, intermingled nature, capable of offering a broad polyphony that includes the subtle interweaving of two languages.[102] The strong, almost authoritarian subject attempts to preserve its seamless identity as a guarantee of its very existence and thus, along with its monologic discourse, begins to break down. Now we have, in effect, the inverse. Subject and discourse become pluralized and the novel becomes a space where both lose their safe, defined identities and share a conflictive, vacillating, and socialized semiosis.

The complicated and intelligent construction of the plural subject is intertwined with its mimetic exercise. The excerpt unveils an analogic framework through which the Inca wall (the specific referent) is displaced by remembered and feely associated utterances of river-water-lake-tear, all of which contain blood. It is telling that this sort of comparative epistemology, which has existed since the earliest chronicles, is apparent here in objects that are not only dissimilar but, in more than one sense, contradictory. Through the transmutation of the immutable solidity of stone into the boundless fluidity of water and the latter into blood, which preserves its liquid character but profoundly transforms its cultural and artistic nature and meaning, what is usually a symbol of life and purity becomes tied to aggression, violence, and death.

There is no explanation of why the sight of stone would turn memory toward water and blood. But there are reasons, ranging from the extreme of Vanguardism, which occasionally infiltrates Indigenism, to Andean binarism and the Quechua worldview, which hold with the uniformity of the world's materiality. I sense, however, that all these vacillations between the stone that is stone but also water and blood are rehearsals for the splendid, final vision (or version) that begins in doubt ("Couldn't you also say?") and then explodes in the joyful yet tragic affirmation "stone of boiling blood," which, despite deriving from Quechua song, does not quote from it. Its origin is in "lake of blood that boils," but its daring creativity comes in, converting the water into stone and imagining this material in an impossible—but semantically complete—boil. There are many possible readings here, but I prefer one that carves in the stone the primordial Andean order, represents in the blood the history of its destruction, and discerns in the boiling the evanescence of that sorrowful time and its substitution by another. This corresponds to the Andean worldview that affirms the end of one time and its substitution by another, different one rising out of a cosmic catastrophe.[103] Here the solid rock is substituted first by a liquid (blood) and then by a vapor, which, by its nature, opens the text up to a multitude of interpretations, although it is impossible not to make an association with the wrath that boils over after centuries of unresolved, injurious treatment.

The same text offers yet another reading: if the constitution of the subject and its language allows for shifts between the individual and the collective, the ancient songs and the modern novel, Quechua and Spanish, orality and writing, to conclude with an indecisive coupling of different subjectivities, worldviews, languages, and cultural codes, then the complex mimesis begun in the Inca wall could represent the utopia that boils away all the mythic-historical, collective-personal contradictions between stone and blood and inaugurates the image of a cosmos that is as disquieting as it is integrated and inclusive. Still more disquieting is the fact that, according to Jorge Lira, the Quechua word *nina* means both "fire" and "word" (or that which "can be said").[104] This astonishing synonymy allows us to investigate the function of a polyform and multivalent language (Quechua and Spanish, song and writing, ancient and modern) with an igneous force that makes the "stone of blood" glow and boil in order to change a world and time depleted by the age-old, daily suffering of an entire people.

Perhaps in this case subject and mimesis are two sides of a discursive operation that reveals the disunity and violence present in the world and, out of want, nostalgia, and desire, erects the great utopia of perfect harmony between man and the world, with both being modalities of a single, living cosmos.[105] Since the subject is figured in a thousand and one ephemeral ways and the object of mimesis appears, vanishes, and reappears in the ebb and flow of time, it is possible to read Arguedas's utopia not as a conciliatory synthesis but as a multiple, even contradictory, plurality that does not abdicate before the disturbing desire to be many beings, live many lives, speak many tongues, and inhabit many worlds. In *Deep Rivers* the discourse is a space disputed among several voices in a dialogue that is not always dialectic (as Bakhtin points out), since it can function without synthesis and take up an interrelated but not totalizing coexistence in a space that either lacks limits or has — even in its center — an open, unstable, and porous border.[106] From this perspective the problematic of "national integration" or the nation as a uniformly homogeneous social body loses its meaning and can be imagined in terms of a just, joint coexistence between plurality and distinctiveness. In one of the moving farewells written shortly before his suicide, Arguedas said, "And that country in which there are all kinds of men and natural environments—I am leaving it while it is boiling with the strengths of so many different essences that are swirling to become transformed at the end of a bloody centuries-old struggle; that struggle has truly begun to break through the shackles and gloomy darkness that have been used to keep them separated and restraining themselves. In me bid farewell to an era of Peru, whose roots will always be sucking juice from the soil to nourish those who live in our homeland, where any man no longer shackled and brutalized by selfishness can joyfully experience all of the homelands."[107]

If this text contains the idea of unity, its main idea is the celebration of a homeland capable of joyfully taking in all homelands. That is, a social space open to the peculiarities and dissentions of the human groups coexisting within it that have wished to preserve the idiosyncratic ways of their cultures, not in order to repeat their fate, but as a result of more symmetrical and nonhegemonizing interactions with their collective neighbors. As in *Deep Rivers*, these interactions are again symptomatically imaged in the action of "boiling." It is not a question, then, of establishing a "linguistic model" that "by overcoming the contradictions between two peoples and two cultures" throws itself premonitorily into the constitution of a new and presumably homogeneous society.[108] Rather, as my analyses and the above quotation show, it is one of recognizing the inviability (and even illegitimacy) of a model that makes what is disparate, diverse, and contradictory into a single unit. This tangled, boiling material demands the cancellation of monologic discourse and the strong subject that resolves it in order to give way to a radical hetereogenization of each and the complex language (including subtexts) that comes with the realization that one's identity has many diverse and powerful sources. It was perhaps Arguedas who risked the most along this daring, difficult, and unpredictable path, and it is in *Deep Rivers* (but also in "La agonía de Rasu-Ñiti (1962)" and *The Fox from Up Above and the Fox from Down Below*) where he most audaciously experimented with the construction of an intrinsically multiple and decentered subject, discourse, and representation.[109] Herein lies the perturbing, disquieting beauty of *Deep Rivers*.

UNDERGROUND VOICES

Clearly Arguedas is not the only Andean writer who realizes an authentic discourse like the one examined above. Vallejo came before him and several neo-Indigenists followed, as well as others from the virtually unexplored Afro-Andean sphere where deep ethnic tensions also exist, still others nurtured by the mysterious Amazon, and one or two cases of urban-based literature. This discourse, by and large, comes out of the tradition of "enlightened" literature, although this institution begins to break down when its cultural producers no longer come from the middle classes, as in the first half of the century, but from the *populus*. These were generally first-generation writers for whose families not only literature but also the practice of reading and writing had been foreign for centuries. It is, however, somewhat uncomfortable that in Arguedas and others, the heterodoxical subject, discourse, and representation (even when they compete and win out over hegemony) reproduce—and even celebrate—subalternity. One of the other voices, precisely the one pressing for vindication, associates itself with nature (instead of civilization), social archaism (rather than progress), and myth (not history), or, in short, feeling (as opposed to reason). What happens when the one uttering the word is the subaltern?

I shall not go into the elegant sophism of Gayatri Spivak, for whom subalterns as such cannot speak, first because they obviously do speak—and most eloquently—to those in their sphere, and second because we non-subalterns do not have the ears to hear them, except when we attempt to listen and decode at the same time.[110] I recognize that we critics, like the redactor-translators of testimonies or "other," native, discourse, are parodying King Midas: all we touch turns not to gold but to literature. No matter how uncomfortable it is, this suspicious alchemy is irresistible for those of us who were brought up (and those that we continue to bring up) as interpreters of written texts. The subaltern voice is present in our daily lives, but we make it part of our academic activity only when it has fulfilled certain requirements: it should be selected and adapted (and frequently translated) by prestigious colleagues, or transposed and transformed (by other colleagues) into "testimony." Faced with the overwhelming quantity of subaltern texts, we literary critics should understand the anguished irritation of young anthropologists and ethnographers and find a way for our academic goals to not make subaltern discourse little more than the raw material of a product made in our very image and likeness.[111] Rather than invalidate the fruitful work of those redactor-translators of marginal literatures or subaltern testimony, I wish to place these texts not in the world that is their source (under the extreme idealism that pretends to value them as the "authentic voice" of the dominated) but where they are literally realized and received. Though this may lack certain refinement, for the moment I see no other alternative.

This perspective invalidates the fact that reading their voice in testimonies is equivalent to listening directly to the other and at the same time recognizes the buried resonance of the subaltern word in these texts. I would like to look briefly at the testimonies of Domitila Barrios de Chungara and Gregorio Condori Mamani, which have perhaps the widest audience in the Andean world, and then offer a partial analysis of another that seems to have been overlooked by literary criticism.[112] Originally published in 1977, the first two are surprisingly more dissimilar than they are alike. Barrios's is a classic testimony in which the original narrator represents an oppressed group and is thereby obliged to be a strong, stable subject who is both political (vindicating the mining proletariat) and redemptive (the suffering of the individual and the group will bear fruits of justice in the end). Condori's, on the other hand, contains much less political pretension and is framed as an individual's life story (the subtitle in Spanish calls it an "Autobiography"). One could say, then, that the former deals broadly with social liberation while the latter focuses on the difficulties of personal survival.

As Moema Viezzer's foreword establishes, *Let Me Speak!* is a montage of discourses, from interviews done specifically for the book to written texts taken from recordings of Barrios's speeches. But if this makes for certain stylistic and sociodialectical variety (Barrios changes register according to the circumstance), these variations clearly have no bearing on the configuration of the subject that utters the discourse. When Barrios made the conscious decision to embark upon the complex task of recounting her life as testimony, she had just returned from her polemical leadership role in the United Nations' 1975 conference on the International Year of the Woman, where she aggressively represented classist radicalism with minor concessions to the feminist agenda.[113] Obviously her participation in this forum internationalized and reinforced her long-standing stature and prestige as a political leader in Bolivia.[114] It is from this vantage point that she utters her testimony and other texts woven into the book. It is clear to the average reader that even the memories of her childhood and the period prior to her precarious ascent to popular leadership are reorganized and projected as formative experiences that inevitably lead to (and legitimize) her role as a leader. This role implies full representation of others (who share the same ideals and have suffered as she has), an invulnerable ethic (she will never betray them), and a vocation as heroine or even martyr. The legitimacy and authority that come out of revolutionary practice and its risks imbue the author of such material: "Some of us have to suffer, play the role of martyr, others have to write our history. And that's how all of us have to work together" (Barrios, *Let Me Speak!* 44).

Thus there is a rift between the one who struggles and suffers and the one who writes (a division of labor), as well as a blurring of this line through a "whole" that becomes a vast and vigorous representation of the subject. The mining proletariat (and its history) is faithfully represented in this leader, just as her consciousness and voice are faithfully represented in the writing of the testimony. The climax occurs when the miners acquire the representation of all the people and point them toward the inevitable socialist revolution that will put an end to shame, poverty, and discrimination. Thus the main agenda of *Let Me Speak!* is to transform an individual subject (Barrios) into a broadly collective one, growing first from miners' wives to the mining proletariat, then to the working class, and finally to the socialist nation of the future. In this process each has a place and function (including the writer), with the exception of other collective subjects defined as the oppressors of the Bolivian people, whose antinational demeanor is repeatedly denounced. This broadening and strengthening of the subject to the point of doubtful subalternity keeps Barrios's testimony from entering the private sphere (or, if it does, only as part of a larger strategy) and valorizing the multiplicity of cultural manifestations open to the mining proletariat, including song, dance, and myth. Thus through constant and overarching synecdoche, the part (the individual and her biography) becomes the whole (the people and their history).

This is Barrios's and Viezzer's intention. The collectivization of the subject signals something very different here than in Arguedas's work. In the latter the socialization of the subject splits and pluralizes it dramatically, while in testimony the subject is an inclusive and synthesizing construct that follows the tune of proletariat hymnody. It is a modern subject disposed not to problematize its identity but reinforce it with an overarching and equally deproblematized "we." A crude form of Marxism identifies it as a social class seen as a harmonious and consistent whole at war with other, equally coherent classes. *Let Me Speak!* takes on this battle boldly, with a furor that allows no dissidence, polyformism, or multivalence. This is its strength, but also its weakness.

The tenor of the testimonies of Condori and Asunta Quispe Huamán, his wife, could not be more different.[115] As I have suggested above, these are essentially accounts taking place in a private sphere whose theme is mere—and splintered—survival. Condori recounts his life when he is elderly, unable to continue his arduous work as a porter in Cusco, and awaiting the unbecoming death suffered by so many of his fellow workers: "We porters are always walking around begging when we die. Who knows, maybe that'll happen to me, too. I'll get run over by a car, they'll take me to the hospital, do an autopsy on me, and then they'll just toss me in the graveyard" (Condori, *Andean Lives*, 101).[116] Quispe similarly narrates her experiences when she is old, tired, and sick and also awaiting her imminent death: "I wake up exhausted . . . as if I'd been walking for miles and miles throughout the night. No doubt my soul's spirit has already begun walking, because it's said that eight years before we die, our souls begin their journey, tracking our footsteps back to all the places we've gone while living in this world" (Condori, *Andean Lives*, 136). Both the sense that death is near and the stories these witnesses relate lend a tragic note to their accounts.[117]

In Condori's case tragedy is associated with a fate that interweaves his whole existence with the experience of death. Having lost both father and mother at a young age, Condori witnessed the deaths of all the women who shared their lives with him (except, of course, Asunta) as well as the many children that he had by them. If being an orphan has marked his life (by having no family he can participate only marginally in the Andean system of reciprocity), the deaths of his children reaffirm this marginality (in the *ayni* he can neither offer nor receive conscripted labor). To make matters worse, he has no one to turn to in his old age. Referring to the death of the last of his children he says, "If he had lived, right now at this very moment he'd be a young man, and I wouldn't be in the state I'm in—my son would always be saying to me: No, that's all right, Papa. If you can't haul goods anymore, your son's arms are here for you" (Condori, *Andean Lives*, 73).

His first experience with marginality may explain why, in the many jobs Condori has (shepherd, mason, soldier, factory janitor, porter), he does not attempt socialization and instead repeats his primary state as a solitary orphan.[118] The image of him as a porter, trudging alone down the streets of Cusco under a backbreaking load, is a sign of the isolation suffered by this marginalized person. Thus it is a personalized subject that utters the testimony because of the tragic nature of his life marked by the deaths of his parents, partners, and children. At the same time it is obvious that this is not a strong subject, comfortable with his identity, but rather one that is extremely vulnerable to the circumstances that surround him and somehow—by chance—define him. Two things, however, seem to palliate this isolation and certain weakness. First, it is hardly less than astonishing that he knows simplified but true facts concerning official political life (he can name the presidents in succession and uses this information to date some of his experiences) and certain important happenings (the construction of the railroad, the landing of the first plane in Sicuani, and the first man on the moon, though he dismisses the latter as hearsay).[119] Thus, although he appears marginalized in his immediate surroundings, he is relatively familiar with some aspects of the national and regional ambit in which he lives, thereby widening—albeit superficially—his referential sphere and weakening his dependency when facing the tragic destiny that marks his individual existence.

Of greater import is Condori's enormous capacity to actively integrate this existence into the vast realm of Quechua culture. He makes constant reference to ancient, colonial, and modern indigenous myths, ritualized customs of the Andean world (or interpretations of the same), when speaking about the events of his life. One would have to be a specialist in this field to know which accounts Condori repeats in their traditional or modernized versions and which he modifies by inserting them into his life and/or narrative. Wherever this path may lead, the fact is that Condori has at his disposal a copious mythic archive that allows him to reflect on a wide variety of circumstances. Thus when he decides to travel to Cusco he narrates the mythic founding of the city. And when he sees an airplane for the first time he immediately remembers an uncle telling him "that a few days before the end of this world, a messenger eagle with a condor's head and llama feet will come and forewarn us runas, we the Inka's kinfolk, to be waiting ready for the end of this world" (Condori, *Andean Lives*, 35). Even more significantly, when he is asked about his and other Indians' poverty, he taps into a wide repertory of equally mythic answers. For example, he recounts that "our God" had asked Inkarrey, "What kind of work would you like me to give you?" and that Inkarrey had answered, "We don't want any. . . . We know how to make stones walk, and with a single throw of a sling, we can build mountains and valleys. We don't need anything at all; we know everything there is to know." For that reason "this two-faced" God went to Spain and there "they asked him for everything. . . . That's why today we runas don't know how to run engines, cars, or those machines that travel high above like birds, the helicopters and planes . . . but those Spaniards are clever and know how to do everything" (Condori, *Andean Lives*, 56).

It is startling that in Condori's mind, the primary opposition (and the cause of indigenous poverty) is between "*españas*" and *runas*, that he can trace his history from the conquest ("those greedy Spaniards were hungry for power, so they killed our Inka") through Tupac Amaru's rebellion and death ("Túpac Amaru was from Tungasuca; he was one of our people, son of Inkas, but one day those Spanish enemies killed him. They ripped his tongue and eyes out by their roots"), and that he asserts his belonging to this saga of defeats: "We are Peruvians, native people, and they were Inka runa; but we're their children, and that's why those Spaniards also killed Túpac Amaru" (Condori, *Andean Lives*, 56–57). His anger spurs him to reiterate as a question ("What would the Spaniards say if our Inka were to return?") the messianic message of salvation he had proclaimed earlier in the text: "*Inkaríy* has been living in the underworld ever since Pizarro the priest killed him. And the day this world ends, he'll emerge and join all the runas" (Condori, *Andean Lives*, 35).

This solitary and vulnerable subject makes a narrative of daily life, thereby entering into a spontaneous and fruitful dialogue with an age-old culture that provides multiple meanings and references for their interdiscourse. The narrative voice becomes the bearer of other, numerous voices that lack a definite chronology (some going back to antiquity) but are present as a semiotic and hermeneutic repertory, ready for employment at any relevant moment. Through these other discourses Condori at once identifies with the history and culture of an entire people and participates personally in the configuration of a far-ranging, collective subject. His word flows into the bubbling torrent of Quechua consciousness, becomes part of it, and simultaneously transforms it with his idiosyncratic contributions, even when he does not see them as such. From this perspective one might proffer that Condori acts and speaks within this interdiscourse and, by offering it his own intonation and energy, actualizes it. This is evident in three excerpts that I have linked. In the first, as cited above, Condori tells that the Spaniards had "ripped [Tupac Amaru's] tongue and eyes out by their roots." The second is the evocation of Atahuallpa's death, which Condori relates as follows: "And he flung the paper [the Bible] to the ground. The Inka didn't know anything about writing. And how could the paper talk if he didn't know how to read? And so they had our Inka killed" (Condori, *Andean Lives*, 57). The third refers to the failed attempt to teach him to read during his imprisonment: "So it was. You'd enter the army sightless, and sightless you'd leave because you'd never really get the alphabet right. And just the same, you'd be unable to speak when you entered and unable to speak when you left, Spanish barely dribbling off your tongue" (Condori, *Andean Lives*, 52). Is it too farfetched to draw an oblique line from Condori's blind-mute experience to the inability of the Inca to learn to write due to his blindness and deafness and then, more directly, to the torture of Tupac Amaru, with his eyes and tongue (mouth) "ripped out by their roots"? I think not and propose that Condori subconsciously associates his failings in speaking and writing Spanish with those of Atahuallpa and Tupac Amaru. Runas like him are deprived of both mouth and eyes, which seems to explain a series of defeats whose tragedy (though it is born of not speaking or writing the language of the dominant culture) results in the mutilation of one's own body. In Condori's case this is not metaphoric in the least: bent over with the excessive weight of his burdens, he is a paradigmatic figure of this expropriation of the body, which is also the expropriation (and negation) of a language and a culture.

The text itself follows much the same pattern: Condori speaks his oral Quechua, but that voice first has to be transcribed, then translated and written down. In the final analysis, who and how many could have listened to or read it in Quechua? We cautiously congratulate ourselves for entering—surreptitiously and through the back door—into a consciousness that on one hand seems to be dissolving, but on the other is socialized in a complex and ambiguous interdiscourse that, even while speaking of defeat, paradoxically and irrefutably proves the fortitude, persistence, and vitality of the collective subject that utters it. He also speaks, via the mediations to which he has been subjected, to the disunity of the Andean world and the displacement and conflicts heaped upon intellectuals and critics when they try to reflect the sociocultural configuration that continues to show evidence of a deep-rooted heterogeneity.

I cannot close without reference to the exceptional testimony *Nosotros los humanos*.[120] Included here are two testimonies given to the same anthropologists who redacted the testimonies of Condori and Quispe, this time venturing into the communities and *ayllus* of the most remote areas of the Apurimac Department in the southern mountains of Peru. Here there has developed—no one knows since when—a culture of theft: the rustlers who steal cattle, crops, and personal property are just as frequently despoiled, sometimes by their victims of the night before. It is a curious case in which the stubborn persistence in ownership (all are monolingual Quechuas, for example) combines with other processes of such strong trans- or aculturation that these ayllus offer a reinterpretation of their own indigenous myths. It is significant, for example, that the messianic figure of Inkarri, who in the rest of the Andean world promises the triumphal return of Inca rule upon his resurrection, is interpreted here as a weak, alien figure. Victoriano Tarapaki, one of the two rustlers who offer their testimonies, says, "When their [the gentiles'] time ended, *Inkariy* was divested of power" (Escalante and Valderrama, *Nosotros los humanos*, 5), clearly assuming that he and his kind live in the time that Christ created and that, consequently, they are Christian.[121] However the narration of their adventures and misadventures, which would be picaresque if they did not contain terrifying violence, underscores an opposing dynamic: various categories of Hispanic—or generically Western—origin are interpreted according to Quechua models. Thus, for example, they undertake official juridical practices by grossly "Quechuacizing" legal terminology, including Latinisms, all within systems, procedures, and values that have more to do with daily life and age-old customs than national law.[122] Relationships with Catholicism are even tenser.

For example, Tarapaki tells how, during one of his innumerable incarcerations, he heard the accounts of *tayta* Melcho, an old, indigenous storyteller renowned for his masterful tales and a veritable living archive of the community's oral tradition. Tarapaki says, "His are the words I put in my head" (Escalante and Valderrama, *Nosotros los humanos*, 114). His first story is a version of the life, passion, and death of Jesus Christ. Its major points reproduce the New Testament, but with glaring changes. The Holy Spirit does not appear, for example, and Mary's impregnation is the result—surely with divine intervention—of the quiet and unfulfilled desire of Saint Joseph: "'Hell, I'd marry that lady' . . . [and] with nothing more than a glance from *Taytacha* Saint Joseph, God had put Christ our father in the virgin." Mary expresses her dismay in common language that humanizes the Biblical account: "How did I end up like this [pregnant], dammit? . . . And now, dammit, what will become of me? The only thing I did was walk by that carpenter guy." As time went by, in effect, "the Virgin's belly got big, just like our ladies' bellies do when they get pregnant" (Escalante and Valderrama, *Nosotros los humanos*, 115). Clearly the community has appropriated the Biblical tradition according to the needs and norms of its daily life. According to Melcho's story as reproduced by Tarapaki, Christ came to the world in order to "steal" the time of the gentiles, was persecuted and killed by the mistis in power, rose again with the help of the "good thief," and fled to the "world above," taking with him as booty the old time in order to put in place a new, Christian one: the time of thieves, that is, the time of the Apurimac rustlers (Escalante and Valderrama, *Nosotros los humanos*, 114–19). It is significant that the entire account, from its first utterance, is meant to legitimize the practice of rustling: "In those days [the thief] was most beloved by God; in the same way our God was persecuted as a thief and suffered greatly" (Escalante and Valderrama, *Nosotros los humanos*, 114). Even more telling is that the reformulation of the Biblical narrative is changed into something akin to the myth of the Apurimac ayllus' origin.

Ambiguities and contradictions of another sort besiege this link between the community and the Catholic God. Several are present in the narration's final paragraph: "[One] says that our God is sitting up there [in heaven]. That's why we can't make ourselves heard even by suffering or crying. Surely he only listens to us from time to time, at midnight, when all the world's runas are silent" (Escalante and Valderrama, *Nosotros los humanos*, 119).

Clearly God's inattention to the suffering of the Indian rustlers does not fit with the account's global meaning, which instead emphasizes the relationship and identification of the community with a divine being who is both creator and protector. Here I am not concerned with the problems inherent in all testimonial discourse, which in this case are complicated by the fact that we are dealing with not only transcription and translation but a narration heard from the lips of tayta Melcho and relayed by Tarapaki. In this way, not counting the transcriber/translator, there are two narrators of the story, the first making use of an extensive social memory. Clearly the word "one" that begins the citation could be the grammatical translation of the impersonally assertive Quechua validator, but it could also be the discourse's reference to a remote, collective agent, which in the end socially and semantically legitimizes the account.

We are not dealing merely with the socialization of the many voices that emit oral literature, but rather the intricate social interweaving that reveals a discourse in which we hear the sermons of colonial evangelization, the ancient and modern Andean voice, and of course the crepitations of this brittle intercrossing. Here, then, the word "one" is emitted by two more voices: those of the evangelizer and the Quechua narrator, both cultural figures that have accumulated centuries of experience, making history in reality two — or more — superimposed histories. The first affirms the resurrection of Christ and his ascension into heaven as great signs of his divine power, while the other, without denying these precepts, paints a picture of an insensitive God who is hardly kind to his children and does not listen to their laments. This culminates in the tragic final irony that God "only listens to us from time to time, at midnight, when all the world's runas are silent." Through connotation we see here the silent servitude of the colony's Indians, but also an unexpected strength, which provides a spokesperson for "all the world's runas" and a universalizing of their plight and experience. Thus, history comes to us through the redactors of the testimony, two recognizable narrators who dissolve into an extended plural subject from a time of uncertain chronology, and "the evangelizer," who, again from an imprecise time, proposes his own plot and meaning from a disturbing and subversive perspective. In the end the intersection of the evangelical discourse and the Quechua discourse becomes a multiethnic supradiscourse that joins, but does not synthesize, their deep and extensive contradictions.

It makes no sense to wonder about the identity of the subject that utters such a text and finds it necessary to palpate the undulations of a linguistic space in which the fluid worldviews of many unsynchronized and disparate cultures unsuccessfully compete for the semantic hegemony of the discourse. The text becomes a battleground, and though alliances and negotiation are possible, all recourse to an individualized subjectivity based on solid and coherent identities fails irremediably, creating impediments for literary criticism and interpretation.

OVERTURE

This book began to take shape when, in the first draft of chapter 1 on the "dialogue" between Atahuallpa and Valverde in Cajamarca, I included a rather abrupt reference to the poem "Pedro Rojas" by César Vallejo. I suspected then that the bristling conflict between voice and writing displayed dramatically in 1532 was somehow still alive in written Andean culture, and that it was expressed in the profound and impossible nostalgia that our writers feel for lost orality. With apologies to Derrida, this assumes that the authenticity of language resides in the spoken word.[1] I later discovered that under literature's ever-mysterious spell that certain dreamers have tried to reduce to an iron-clad grid, there were other symptomatic correlations between the Andean representations of the Inca's death and Vallejo's poem: the many deaths of the Inca and those of Pedro Rojas, or the Messianic signs in some of the former and the resurrection image at the end of Vallejo's poem, for instance.[2] I also suspected that José María Arguedas's "stone of boiling blood" had something to do with Pedro-piedra (stone) and blood-Rojas (red). I took the title of this book from a verse of Vallejo's poem when I finally realized that this text, although present throughout my research, had received only tangential mention in this study. I have no idea along which twists or turns "Pedro Rojas" evaporated temporarily from my consciousness. Then it dawned on me that, instead of a classic "conclusion," I could explicate Vallejo's incredible poem. So, happily, little is concluded and much is left open.[3] The complete text follows:

He took to writing in the air with his best finger:
"Lib long, komrads! Pedro Rojas,"
from Miranda de Ebro, father and man,
husband and man, railroad worker and man,
father and more man. Pedro and his two deaths.

Wind paper, they killed him: Pass it on!
Flesh quill, they killed him: Pass it on!
Tell all the komrads, quick!
Trunk where they strung up his beam,
they killed him;
they killed him at the root of his best finger!
They killed both Pedro and Rojas!

Lib long, komrads
on the front lines of his written air!
Lib with this b for the buzzard disemboweling
Pedro and Rojas, hero and martyr!
As they searched his body, they discovered
in it a body big enough for
the soul of the world,
and in his jacket a dead spoon.

Pedro was used to eating
among his own flesh and blood, washing up, painting
the table and living sweetly,
championing all people.
And this spoon traveled in his jacket
awake or even as he slept, always,
a dead spoon alive with its symbols.
Tell all the komrads, quick!
Lib at the foot of his spoon forever!

They killed him, forcing him to die.
Pedro and Rojas and the worker and the man and that
tiny baby, looking up at the sky,
who grew up, turned red
and fought with every cell, refusal, dream, hunger and piece
of his body.

They killed him quietly,
wrapped in the hair of his wife, Juana Vázquez,
in the hour of fire, the year of the bullet,
and when he was on the verge of everything.

So Pedro Rojas, after dying,
rose, kissed his bloody coffin,
wept for Spain
and once again wrote in the air with his finger:
"Lib long, komrads! Pedro Rojas."
His corpse was full of world.[4]

Clearly "Pedro Rojas" (also known as poem III of *Spain, Let This Cup Pass from Me*), is one of the great moments in Vallejo's poetry because of how the poet brilliantly and movingly transmutes vibrant tension into equally intense language.[5] It has, in addition, a most unusual and profoundly tragic source. Some years ago Julio Vélez and Antonio Merino found that it comes from another, nonliterary text, but one that is chillingly authentic: a scrap of paper containing the anguished scrawl of a Republican militant who was soon to be shot.[6] Antonio Ruiz Vilapana (a friend of Vallejo who wrote one of the reports) transcribes the following:[7] "Next to the cemetery in Burgos [was] found the cadaver of a poor farmer. . . . No one dared identify him, but in one of his pockets we found a wrinkled and dirty piece of paper where he had crudely written in pencil, with misspellings:"

Tell all the komrads and march soon
they beatin us like animals and killin us
since all is los' they
gone wild.[8]

Ruiz adds facts about the case that speak directly to Vallejo's poem: some of the condemned were railroad workers; sixty-six were from Miranda de Ebro and had been jailed because on their "bodies they carried . . . the prison's fork, spoon, and metal plate." Even more explicitly the body of one worker "was handcuffed and badly . . . bruised and [the man's] pockets still carried the aluminum fork and spoon of the Prison" where he was being held and would be executed.

This testimonial "first version" of "Pedro Rojas," one of the few manuscripts that remain of Vallejo's work, begins with the transcription of the agonizing message of the Republican militant, although the fact that it is a transcription is not noted.[9] It includes, as does the definitive version, several references ("Miranda de Ebro," "railroad worker," "spoon"), which obviously come from the testimony cited above. Juan Larrea deciphered part of the photographic copy of this manuscript and offered the following version:

> Tell all the komrads . . .
> soon; they beatin us like animals
> And killin us, since all is lost, they . . ."[10]

Larrea considered this the first version of "Pedro Rojas," but he had not seen—nor forgotten—the text that Ruiz Vilpana had transcribed. In either case it is obvious that Vallejo initially wanted to include it as it stood. The final version of the poem is different, but the original text holds sway and, as we shall see, is more faithful. Although he does not copy it word-for-word, he socializes its utterance. Despite the fact that Vallejo transcribed only the first line ("Tell all the komrads") and the aforementioned references, it is absolutely clear that "Pedro Rojas" is born out of the testimony recorded in *Doy fe*. It is easy to imagine how the pathos of the condemned man's message shook Vallejo to the core and inspired him to build a poem around it. But it is not as simple to explain why he first tried to transcribe it literally and later used just part of the message and certain characteristics of its language and circumstances in forging a new text. Vallejo often used "quotes" in his poetic discourse: from the cry of the lottery vendor in "Win a Thousand" to Biblical texts, as in the title *Spain, Let This Cup Pass from Me*, but in this case there are other reasons.[11]

The first is circumstantial and has to do with the spoons found in the pockets of the men who had been shot. This must have moved Vallejo because, beginning with *The Black Heralds*, he had worked intensely with the symbolic options that this most humble of utensils offers. It appears in neither the Romantic-Modernist dictionary nor the Vanguards,' though it may be vaguely related to the Nativists' fascination with simple words.[12] In short, with "Pedro Rojas" Vallejo clearly solidifies his symbolic use of the spoon, which had heretofore been ambiguous. Its inherent contradiction is deepened by being present in death's waiting room, but also in the fraternal gesture of sharing a meal among fellow sufferers: "a dead spoon alive," then, that Vallejo found once again in the real, irreversible tragedy of a comrade's execution. The strength of the exclamation "Lib at the foot

168   Overture

of this spoon forever!" comes as much from the incredible turn of history as the internal process of Vallejo's poetry. The Vanguardists' dream of reintegrating art and life had suddenly been fulfilled, along with one of their most consistent fears: modern life was closer to death than it was to itself. On this point Vallejo was an exceptional witness.

The second reason refers to Vallejo's Vanguardist experiments with the writing of the words (for example "Vusco volvvver," "Busco volvver," and "Fallo bolver" from *Trilce*'s poem IX) and the erratic spelling in the desperate message from the defender of the Republic, whom the poet intentionally names Pedro Rojas in the definitive version of the text.[13] Although a relationship to Vanguardist experimentation exists, in this context it takes on rich and complex meaning. For example, the message's most obvious deviation from spelling norms (the labialization of the labio-dental "v" as in "lib") is not only repeated in the poem ("Lib long, komrads") and reiterated twice but acquires substance in the verse that functions as the refrain "Lib long, komrads" (repeated five times) and yields one of the most forceful utterances of the life/death dialectic that underlies the text: "Lib long, komrads. . . . Lib with this b for . . . buzzard." Thus Vallejo takes the word of his dead comrade as his own and revives it in his discourse. This appropriation and revival are much more evident upon remembering that "Lib long, komrads," a verse written by Vallejo and not a copy of the message, appears twice with quotation marks and another three times without. It is a word clearly shared and socialized by a subject that has opened himself up to the other (in fact, to a whole people) and his writing to popular orality. Vallejo is careful to characterize this language as uttered by more than one voice. Following are several significant excerpts:

He took to writing in the air with his best finger.

Wind paper . . .
Flesh quill . . .

Lib long, komrads
lifted up on his written air!
And once again [he] wrote in the air with his finger:
"Lib long, komrads! Pedro Rojas."

Especially evocative is the intentional instability of a language that straddles the space between writing and orality: Rojas "writes" it, clearly, but "in the air," on "wind paper" and with a bodily instrument—like the voice—where a "finger" becomes a "flesh quill."[14] It is well known that Vallejo experimented with the oralization of his poetic discourse starting with "To My Brother Miguel" in *The Black Heralds*, explored this theme in "Intensity and Height" from *Human Poems* (whose first line is "I want to write, but it comes out spume"), and frequently linked written language with voice in *Spain, Let This Cup Pass from Me*.[15] The very title of this book harks back to the great Biblical exclamation, while some texts are titled with terms that allude more to voice and song than to writing ("Hymn," "Drumroll," "Response"); there is almost no poem that does not include words such as "say," "speak," "shout," "sing," "pray," or "exclaim."

To be more exact, one should remember that in poem I there are phrases such as "shouting at the top of my lungs" and "I keep on saying"; in the final poem there is the famous refrain "I mean, as they say"; in number IX, whose central image is a book, there is an unresolved tension between the latter and the spoken word: "his mouth entered our breath." Clearly this language, uttered to itself as voice, occurs within *Spain, Let This Cup Pass from Me*'s overarching organization and utilizes mechanisms typical of orality, including the virtually physical intervention of the poet in his discourse, as if he were relating it "directly and immediately" to his audience.[16] One should remember that in the "Hymn to the Volunteers for the Republic," Vallejo refers specifically to the "illiterate to whom I write," thereby shifting the urgency of spoken language from the point of utterance to the consignee and completing the circuit of poetic communication.

It is not difficult to understand why Vallejo feels this call to orality so strongly. At least in *Spain, Let This Cup Pass from Me* there is the natural receiver of a word dramatically fraught with historical urgency calling to the Spanish people (and its representatives) and the realization that we are dealing more with a hearer than a reader. Vallejo exacts tension through contradiction in his poetry, which is written primarily for (and because of) those who cannot read, and builds imaginary bridges in order to reconvert the written word to voice.[17] This is the nostalgia for orality that imbues a large and distinguished part of the literature of Latin America.[18] This unconscious nostalgia has its roots in the sudden appearance of writing and the book as enigmatic instruments of conquest with no immediate ties to language or communication, as seen in the "dialogue" between Father Valverde and the Inca Atahuallpa in Cajamarca and the resultant manipulation of all writing through the antonomasia of the Bible.[19]

Returning to "Pedro Rojas," it is clear that the language of this text is lodged in an ambiguous space where writing attempts an impossible return to orality, as expressed in the repeated imagery of "writing in the air." One might even conclude that the consistent deviations in spelling are either images of this ambiguous space between orality and writing where the poem is produced or those unstable (and impossible) bridges across which the written word flows in search of its primordial sound. To be forthright, "bad writing" seems to be a middle ground, though clearly a figurative one, between the written word and voice, between "cultured poetry" and popular culture. Paradoxically the source of "Pedro Rojas" is a manuscript, but Vallejo wastes no time in placing the text within the sonorous dynamics of speech by seeing it not only as an anguished call to attention and cry for help but also an ardent proclamation of life. It is as if the dramatic charge of the poem cannot fit within the confines of writing and tries to expand into the realm of limitless sound. These lines from *Human Poems* come to mind: "What does it matter that I whip myself with the line / and believe I'm pursued, at a trot, by the period?" They speak to the concept of the linearity and finitude of the written word—the line pursued by the period that will end the utterance. If a pragmatic approach tells us that all linguistic-literary acts arise out of the fiction of language, "Pedro Rojas" contains a second fiction: the "fiction of orality," an essential element in a discourse that expresses an intense vocation for the spoken word.

Thus, although it may be part of a Vanguardist experiment, the "b" in "Lib long," is an oblique sign of this nostalgia going back to the conflictive insertion of the cultured poet into a society whose culture—in terms of its people—is the culture of the spoken and heard word. Clearly Pedro Rojas, the railroad worker who writes aerial graffiti, is a symbol of those people just as he assumes the ethical representation of all worthy people's values. From this perspective one understands why the poet, who neither can nor wants to renege on writing, construes it both as a constrictive barrier that should—if only in the imagination—be surpassed and, contradictorily, as an option of permanence, modernity, and universality. In this sense the leap over the written word is a metaphorical desire: that of the reintegration of the poet into a people capable of performing miracles, as in "Masses." Clearly, upon assuming the word of his protagonist (a very *real* word), Vallejo is subtly but vigorously linking himself to the popular world. As we shall see, he is shifting a neat, chronological, snippet of writing toward an expansive voice that in and because of its own fugacity seems able to overcome time (and death), both inherent to the written word, especially when it attempts to recount history.[20]

Pedro Rojas is the image of the popular, dying, and triumphant hero. If the ominous buzzard infiltrates his proclamation of life, his corpse—"full of world"—resists life's stubborn design, which throughout the poem is the same as that of people who fight to defend the rights of all, even the enemy's. His name is clearly emblematic: Pedro = stone (piedra) is vigor, consistency, and firmness as well as indestructible foundation; Rojas (red) contains ideological overtones, Republican and Marxist in this case, as well as references to blood, a fountain of infinite connotations. As stated above, there is a mysterious connection to the image of the vigorous and illuminating "stone of boiling blood" that arises from among the ageless stones of Cusco before the eyes of Arguedas's endearing Ernesto. In *Deep Rivers* as well, Quechua *song* is mixed with the novel's *writing*. I would venture to say that Pedro Rojas is, like the mythic wall of Cusco, a "stone of boiling blood."[21]

I would even go so far as to ask if the poem does not reproduce the same mythic transmutation, the same alchemy, in which the written word, symbolized by the persistence of stone, recovers its primordial sense of voice, which in belonging to the body is associated with blood. This happens through poetry that boils them together, creating a full and complete language. The utopia that this total language suggests is, perhaps, an echo of another, more profound utopia: one that ridicules the ominous rule of death and overcomes it with the everlasting song of authentic poetry that humans "write in the [indelible] air" of this world.

Now I know why Vallejo's verses kept haunting me during the years it took me to birth this book. These beautifully intense utopias are only possible through the many intercrossings of deeply heterogeneous subjects, discourses, representations, and worlds.

NOTES

Introduction

All translations are Jentsch's.
1. See Jean Franco, "Tendencias y prioridades de los estudios literarios latinoamericanos," *Escritura* 6.11 (1981); Saul Sosnowski, "Spanish-American Literary Criticism," in *Changing Perspectives in Latin American Studies*, ed. Christopher Mitchell (Stanford: Stanford University Press, 1988); and *Revista de crítica literaria latinoamericana* 16.31-32 (1990), especially articles on Bolivia (Sanjinés), Ecuador (Handelsman), and Peru (Díaz, Fernández, García-Bedoya, Huamán).
2. See Roberto Fernández Retamar, *Para una teoría literaria hispanoamericana y otras aproximaciones* (Havana: Casa de las Américas, 1975). The survey published by *Texto crítico* 3.6 (1977) indicates that debate ensued. See also Raúl Bueno, *Escribir en Hispanoamérica* (Lima: Latinoamericana Editores, 1992).
3. Ángel Rama, *Transculturación narrativa en América Latina* (Mexico City: Siglo XXI, 1982); see also Carina Blixen and Alvaro Barro-Lémez, *Cronología y bibliografía de Ángel Rama* (Montevideo: Fundación Ángel Rama, 1986); Edmundo Bendezú, *La otra literatura peruana* (Mexico City: Fondo de Cultura Económica, 1986); Enrique Ballón, "Las diglosias literarias peruanas (deslindes y conceptos)," in *Diglosia linguo-literaria y educación en el Perú: Homenaje a Alberto Escobar*, ed. Enrique Ballón and Rodolfo Cerrón (Lima: CONCYTEC, 1990); Martin Lienhard, *La voz y su huella* (Hanover, NH: Norte, 1991); other editions: Havana: Casa de las Américas, 1990; Lima: Universo, 1992; see Antonio Cornejo Polar, *Sobre literatura y crítica latinoamericanas* (Caracas: Universidad Central de Venezuela, 1982); Néstor García Canclini, *Culturas híbridas: Estrategias para entrar y salir de la modernidad* (Mexico City: Grijalvo, 1989); René Zavaleta Mercado, *Lo nacional-popular en Bolivia* (Mexico City: Siglo XXI, 1986); and Carlos Rincón, *El cambio actual de la noción de literatura* (Bogotá: Colcultura, 1978).
4. See Antonio Cornejo Polar, *La formación de la tradición literaria en el Perú* (Lima: CEP, 1989).

5. See Beatriz González Stephan's *Contribución al estudio de la historiografía literaria hispanoamericana* (Caracas: Academia de Historia, 1985); and *La historiografía literaria del liberalismo hispanoamericano del siglo XIX* (Havana: Casa de las Américas, 1987).
6. See Miguel León Portilla for Mesoamerica and Jesús Lara for the Andean area.
7. See Carlos Rincón, "Modernidad periférica y el desafío de lo postmoderno: Perspectivas del arte narrativo latinoamericano" and George Yúdice, "¿Puede hablarse de postmodernidad en América Latina?" both in *Revista de crítica literaria latinoamericana* 15.29 (1989). See also *Nuevo texto crítico* 3.6 and 4.7.
8. See Ana Pizarro, ed., *La literatura latinoamericana como proceso* (Buenos Aires: Centro Editor de América Latina, 1985); and *Hacia una historia de la literatura latinoamericana* (Mexico City: Colegio de México y Universidad Simón Bolívar, 1987). See also Cornejo, *Sobre literature y crítica latinoamiericanas*.
9. See José Morales Saravia, "Alejandro Losada (1936–1985): Bibliografía comentada," *Revista de crítica literaria latinoamericana*, 11.24 (1986).
10. Ángel Rama, *The Lettered City*, trans. John Chasteen (Durham, NC: Duke University Press, 1996).
11. Carlos Pacheco, *La comarca oral* (Caracas: Casa de Bello, 1992).
12. See M. H. Abrams, *El espejo y la lámpara. Teoría romántica y tradición crítica acerca del hecho literario* (Buenos Aires: Nova, 1962).
13. Walter Benjamin, *The Concept of Art Criticism in German Romanticism* (Bern: Francke, 1920).
14. See José Vasconcelos, *The Cosmic Race* (Baltimore: Johns Hopkins University Press, 1997) (the first edition in Spanish was published in 1925); and Uriel García, *El nuevo indio* (Lima: Universo, 1973) (the first edition was published in 1930). See also chapter 3.
15. See Luiz Costa Lima, *O Controle do Imaginário: Razão e Imaginação nos Tempos Modernos* (São Paulo: Forense Universitária, 1989); and Erich Auerbach, *Mimesis: The Representation of Reality in Western Literature*, trans. Willard R. Trask (Princeton, NJ: Princeton University Press, 1953).
16. A reference to the quotation "any man no longer shackled and brutalized by selfishness can joyfully experience all . . . homelands." José María Arguedas, *The Fox from Up Above and the Fox from Down Below*, trans. Frances Horning Barraclough (Pittsburgh: University of Pittsburgh Press, 2000), 260. See chapter 3.

Chapter 1: Voice and the Written Word in the Cajamarca "Dialogue"

1. See Walter G. Ong, *Orality and Literacy: The Technologizing of the Word* (London: Routledge, 1982); Martin Lienhard, "Arte verbal quechua e historiografía literaria en el Perú," [Bulletin of the] *Société Suisse des Américanistes* 52 (1988), 47; and see Eric Havelock, *The Muse Learns to Write* (New Haven: Yale University Press, 1986), 45. See also Paul Zumthor, *La letra y la voz* (Madrid:

Cátedra, 1989); Jan Vansina, *Oral Tradition: A Study in Historical Methodology*, trans. H. M. Wright (Harmondsworth, UK: Penguin, 1973); and Carlo Ginzburg, *El queso y los gusanos: El cosmos según un molinero del siglo XVI* (Barcelona: Muchnik, 1981).

2. See Serge Gruzinski, *La colonisation de l'imaginaire: Sociétés indigènes et occidentalisation dans le Mexique espagnol. XVI–XVIII siècle* (Paris: Gallimard, 1988); and Mercedes López Baralt, *Icono y conquista: Guamán Poma de Ayala* (Madrid: Hiperión, 1988).

3. See G. S. Kirk, *The Songs of Homer* (Cambridge: Cambridge University Press, 1962).

4. See Edmundo Bendezú, *La otra literatura peruana* (Mexico City: Fondo de Cultura Económico, 1986) and Lore Terracini, *I codici del silenzio* (Turin: Dell'Orso, 1988), 14.

5. See Antonio Cornejo Polar, *La formación de la tradición literaria en el Perú* (Lima: CEP, 1989). In a wider sense heterogeneity precedes the European conquest in that within a single area such as the Andes, distinct and diverse cultures were already interacting.

6. See Walter Mignolo, "Cartas, crónicas y realciones del descubrimineto y la conquista," in *Historia de la literatura Hispanoamericana*, vol. 1, *Epoca colonial*, ed. Luis Iñigo Madrigal (Madrid: Cátedra, 1982); and Beatriz Pastor, *Discursos narrativos de la conquista: Mitificación y emergencia*, 2nd ed. (Hanover, NH: Norte, 1988).

7. Walter Mignolo and Rolena Adorno's proposal to substitute "colonial literature" with "colonial discourse" is based in part on the need for a construct that includes oral manifestations and those originating in nonalphabetic writing, which would otherwise be omitted from the field bounded by the concept of "literature." For them "literature" refers to a late European or Eurocentric cultural experience that cannot be separated from writing, so that applying this term to another space in another time, especially in the case of oral manifestations, would be to distort the specificity of that particular construct. Without entering into this debate, I opt for preserving the use of the category "literature" in its broadest sense. See Rolena Adorno, "Nuevas perspectivas en los estudios literarios coloniales Hispanoamericanos," *Revista de crítica literaria latinoamericana* 14.28 (1988); and Walter Mignolo, "La lengua, la letra, el territorio (o la crisis de los estudios literarios coloniales)," *Dispositio* 15.28–29 (1986); "La historia de la escritura y la escritura de la historia," in *De la crónica a la nueva narrativa mexicana*, ed. Merlin Forster and Julio Ortega (Mexico City: Oasis, 1986); "Anahuac y sus otros: La cuestión de la letra en el Nuevo Mundo," *Revista de crítica literaria latinoamericana* 14.28 (1988); "Literacy and Colonization: The New World Experience," in *1492–1992: Re-discovering Colonial Writing*, ed. René Jara and Nicholas Spadachini (Minneapolis: Prisma Institute, 1989); "Teorías renacentistas de la escritura y la colonización de las lenguas nativas," reprint of the *Simposio de Filología Iberoamericana*, Seville,

1990; "La semiosis colonial: La dialéctica entre representaciones fracturadas y hermenéuticas pluritópicas," *Crítica y descolonización: El sujeto colonial en la cultura latinoamericana*, ed. Beatriz González and Lúcia Costigan (Caracas: Academia Nacional de Historia, 1992). See also Neil Larsen, "Contra la desestetización del 'discurso' colonial"; and Ricardo J. Kaliman, "Sobre la construcción del objeto en la crítica literaria latinoamericana," *Revista de crítica literaria latinoamericana*, 19.37 (1993).

8. Clements R. Markham, ed. and trans., *Reports of the Discovery of Peru* (New York: Lenox Hill, 1970), 118. From the "Letter of Hernando Pizarro to the Royal Audience of Santo Domingo," written in 1533.

9. Pedro Pizarro, *Relación del descubrimiento y conquista del Perú*, ed. Guillermo Lohman Villena (Lima: Universidad Católica, 1978), 37–38 (Jentsch's translation). The original text dates from 1571.

10. Alexander Pogo, "The Anonymous *La conquista del Perú* and the *Libro ultimo del sumario delle Indie occidentali*," *Proceedings of the American Academy of Arts and Sciences* 64 (1928–1930); and Cristóbal de Mena, *La conquista del Perú, llamado la Nueva Castilla*, first edition 1534 (Jentsch's translation). The authorship of this chronicle is now in doubt. See Franklin Pease, "La conquista española y la percepción andina del otro," *Histórica* 13.2 (1989): 174n.

11. Markham 53–54. From Francisco de Xerez, *Verdadera relación de la conquista de la Nueva Castilla*, first edition 1534.

12. Miguel Estete, *El descubrimiento y la conquista del Perú*, in *Los cronistas del Perú*, by Raúl Porras Barrenchea (Lima: San Marti, n.d.), 76 (Jentsch's translation). Written 1533.

13. Franklin Pease, "Las crónicas y los Andes," *Revista de crítica literaria latinoamericana*, 14.28 (1988): 124–25; and *Del Tawantinsuyo a la historia del Perú*, 2nd ed. (Lima: Universidad Católica, 1989).

14. See Hayden White, *Tropics of Discourse: Essays in Cultural Criticism* (Baltimore: Johns Hopkins University Press, 1978).

15. Porras, *Los cronistas del Perú*. There is a second edition (Lima: Banco de Crédito, 1986), 76.

16. See Tzvetan Todorov, *The Conquest of America*, trans. Richard Howard (New York: Harper and Row, 1984), 146–49; and Silvio Zavala, "Introducción," in *Juan López de Palcios Rubios: De las islas del mar océano*; and Matías de Paz, *Del dominio de los reyes de España sobre los Indios* (Mexico City: Fondo de Cultura Económica, 1954), 124–27.

17. J. M. Cohen, ed. and trans., *The Discovery and Conquest of Peru* (Baltimore: Penguin, 1968), 101. From *Historia del descubrimiento y conquista del Perú*. The first edition dates from 1555.

18. Francisco López de Gómara, *Historia general de las Indias y vida de Hernán Cortés*, vol. 1 (Caracas: Bibioteca Ayacucho, 1979), 171 (Jentsch's translation). First published in 1552. See also Garcilaso de la Vega, El Inca, *Royal Commen-*

taries of the Incas and General History of Peru, pt. 2, bk. 1, trans. Harold Livermore (Austin: University of Texas Press, 1966), chaps. 21–24.
19. Jerónimo Benzoni, *History of the New World*, trans. and ed. W. H. Smyth (New York: Lenox Hill, 1970), 179 (Cornejo's emphasis).
20. Also annotated in Porras, *Los cronistas del Perú*, 216.
21. Pedro Cieza de León, *Crónica del Perú: Tercera parte*, ed. Francesca Cantú (Lima: Universidad Católica, 1987), 132. The first part was edited in 1553; the third was discovered more recently and probably written between 1548 and 1553.
22. Miguel Cabello de Balboa, *Miscelánea antártica: Una historia del Perú antiguo* (Lima: Universidad de San Marcos, 1951), 470. The manuscript was finished in 1586.
23. Martín de Murúa, *Historia general del Perú y descendencia de los Incas*, vol. 1, ed. Manuel Ballesteros (Madrid: Instituto Gonzalo Fernández de Oviedo, 1962), 175–76. The manuscript was finished in 1590.
24. Sabine G. MacCormack, "Atahualpa and the Book," *Dispositio* 14.36–38 (1988): 159.
25. Sara Castro-Klarén in *Escritura, transgresión y sujeto en la literatura latinoamericana* (Mexico City: Premiá, 1989), 165.
26. Cieza, *Crónica del Perú*, 132.
27. López de Gómara, *Historia General de las Indias*, 171.
28. Agustín de Zárate, *Historia del descubrimiento y conquista del Perú*, ed. J. M. Kermenik (Lima: D. Miranda, n.d.), 59 (Jentsch's translation, Cornejo's emphasis).
29. Qtd. in MacCormack, 149. One should read this passage noting the use of the verb "to stare" (*ojear*, not *hojear*), and its relationship to the verb "to hear." There seems to be a link between simple faculties (looking-staring-hearing) that both leaves in suspense and tacitly evokes the cultural act of "leafing through" (*hojear*). This happens similarly in other versions.
30. Gruzinski's comments about the recitative of Mesoamerican pictographs are especially interesting. Although this topic has barely been treated in the Andean area, it is probable that a similar system was at work with the less developed signs of this region's cultures. The relationship between writing and orality in medieval sermons as studied by Zumthor has special relevance for early colonial literature.
31. MacCormack, "Atahualpa and the Book," 157.
32. See Patricia Seed, "'Failing to Marvel': Atahualpa's Encounter with the Word," *Latin American Research Review* 20.1 (1991).
33. MacCormack, "Atahualpa and the Book," 157.
34. MacCormack, "Atahualpa and the Book," 159; Seed, "Failing to Marvel," 17, 32.
35. Garcilaso, *Royal Comentaries of the Incas*, bk. 2, chaps. 24–25.

36. *Relación por don Joan de Santa Cruz Pachacuti*, in *Tres relaciones de antigüedades Peruanas*, ed. Marcos Jiménez de la Espada (Buenos Aires: Guarania, 1950), 278–79. The text was probably written around 1613.
37. Qtd. in Seed, "Failing to Marvel," 20–21. From Titu Cussi, *Yntruçion del Ynga don Diego de Castro Titu Cussi Yupangui para el muy ilustre señor el Licenciado Lope García de Castro*, ed. Luis Millones (Lima: El Virrey, 1985). The original manuscript is from 1570.
38. See Raquel Chang-Rodríguez, *La apropiación del signo: Tres cronistas indígenas del Perú* (Tempe: University of Arizona Press, 1988); Rolena Adorno, ed. *From Oral to Written Expression: Native Andean Chronicles of the Early Colonial Period* (Syracuse: University of Syracuse Press, 1982); and Martin Lienhard, "La crónica mestiza en México y el Perú hasta 1620: Apuntes para su estudio histórico-literario," *Revista de crítica literaria latinoamericana* 9.17 (1983); and *La voz y su huella* (Hanover, NH: Norte, 1991).
39. See *Relación de los Quipucamayos* in *Relación de la descendencia, gobierno y conquista de los Incas*, ed. Collapiña, Supno, et al. (Lima: Biblioteca Universitaria, 1974). The first testimonies date from about 1542. It was first published in 1892.
40. Felipe Huaman Poma de Ayala, *Letter to a King: A Peruvian Chief's Account of Life under the Incas and under Spanish Rule*, trans. and ed. Christopher Dilke (New York: E. P. Dutton, 1978), 109. See also MacCormack, "Altahualpa and the Book," 148–65; Rolena Adorno, *Cronista y príncipe: La obra de don Felipe Guamán Poma de Ayala* (Lima: Universidad Católica, 1989), 151; and Seed, "Failing to Marvel," 27–29.
41. Garcilaso, *Royal Commentaries of the Incas*, 688, chap. 22. See also MacCormack, "Atahualpa and the Book," 160–63.
42. See José Durand, *El Inca Garcilaso, clásico de América* (Mexico City: Sepsetentas, 1976); Enrique Pupo-Walker, *Historia, creación y profecía en los textos del Inca Garcilaso de la Vega* (Madrid: Porrúa Turanzas, 1982); Susana Jákfalvi-Leiva, *Traducción, escritura y violencia colonizadora: Un estudio sobre la obra del Inca Garcilaso* (Syracuse: Maxwell School, 1984); Margarita Zamora, *Language, Authority and Indigenous History in the Comentarios Reales de los Incas* (Cambridge: Cambridge University Press, 1988); Nicolás Wey-Gómez, "¿Dónde está Garcilaso? La oscilación del sujeto colonial en la formación de un discurso transcultural," *Revista de crítica literaria latinoamericana* 17.34 (1991); and María Rostworowski de Diez Canseco, *Historia del Tahuantinsuyu* (Lima: Instituto de Estudios Peruanos, 1988).
43. Seed, "Failing to Marvel," 23.
44. Garcilaso, *Historia general del Perú: Segunda parte de los Comentarios Reales*, ed. José Durand (Lima: Universidad de San Marcos, 1962), 128 (Jentsch's translation).
45. Alberto Escobar, "Historia y lenguaje en los *Comentarios Reales*," in *Patio de Letras* (Lima: Caballo de Troya, 1965). See also José Luis Rivarola, *Lengua, co-*

municación e historia del Perú (Lima: Lumen, 1986); "Contactos y conflictos de lenguas en el Perú colonial," in *Essays on Cultural Identity in Colonial Latin America*, ed. J. Lechner (Leiden: Rijksuniversiteit, 1988); Regina Harrison, "Translation and the Problematics of Cultural Categories," in *Signs, Songs, and Memory in the Andes: Translating Quechua Language and Culture* (Austin: University of Texas Press, 1989); and Garcilaso, *General History of Peru*, 127–130, specifically treats the problems inherent in translation.

46. Juan de Betanzos, *Narrative of the Incas*, trans. and ed. Roland Hamilton and Dana Buchanan (Austin: University of Texas Press, 1996), 263. Palma de Mallorca manuscript.
47. Rivarola, *Lengua, comunicación e historia del Perú*, 10, 18–20.
48. See *La conquista del Perú* (Lima: Universidad Nacional de Educación, 1969), 32–33, 40.
49. See Garcilaso, *General History of Peru*, chap. 38; and Huaman Poma, *Letter to a King*, 359. Ong means by "primary orality" that which belongs to a culture "untouched by writing." Ong, *Orality and Literacy: The Technologizing of the Word* (New York: Routledge, 1982), 11.
50. Ernest Robert Curtius, *European Literature and the Latin Middle Ages*, trans. Willard Trask (New York: Pantheon, 1953), vol. 1, chap. 14.
51. Coinciding with the "discovery" of America was Antonio de Nebrija's *Gramática de la lengua castellana*, ed. Antonio Quilis (Madrid: Nacional, 1981), whose prologue says: "that after your highness placed beneath your yoke many barbarous peoples and nations of strange languages and with being vanquished they had need of receiving the laws that the victor puts on the vanquished and with them our tongue." See Walter Mignolo, "Teorías renacentistas."
52. Let us not dismiss the possibility of an inverse reading that emphasizes the failure of the book. Is there not horrific historical sarcasm in Valverde's terrible death, as he was devoured (mouth-voice) by the Puná Indians in 1541?
53. See Franklin Pease, *Inka y kuraka: Relaciones de poder y representación histórica* (College Park: University of Maryland Press, 1990).
54. Titu Cussi, *Ynstruçion del Inga*, 4 (Jentsch's translation).
55. Huaman Poma, *Letter to a King*, 108. See also MacCormack, "Atahualpa and the Book."
56. Castro-Klarén, 163. See Manuel Marzal cited in Alberto Flores Galindo, *Buscando un Inca: Identidad y utopía en los Andes* (Havana: Casa de las Américas, 1986), 85–86.
57. Max Hernández, "Prólogo," in Luis Millones, *El Inca por la Coya* (Lima: Fundación Ebert, 1988), 23.
58. For the Andean, the exercise of writing meant managing a complex process closely tied to self-image. This is not a question of a mere change in linguistic "technology," but a basic reformulation of one's own identity, now implicated in a discursive process entirely different from orality, and without taking into

account what the act of writing (the formulation of a world consciousness) in a second language implies. Regrettably for the Andean region there is no global study like Gruzinski's that analyzes the traumatic transformations of a mindset subjected to both another language and writing.

59. Titu Cussi, *Instruçion del Inga*, 1 (Cornejo's emphasis). It is curious that this praise of writing is based on a tacit rejection of orality and the memory that supports it, precisely when Titu Cussi is orally narrating his remembrances. This is another manifestation of the triumph of the written word over voice.

60. See Rolena Adorno, *Guamán Poma: Writing and Resistance in Colonial Peru* (Austin: University of Texas Press, 1986); and Adorno, *Cronista y príncipe*. See also López Baralt, *Icono y conquista*.

61. This is the "emitting subject" of what Martin Lienhard defines as "alternative literature," a basic concept in his *La voz y su huella*.

62. Gregorio Condori recalls it in his testimony. See Ricardo Valderrama and Carmen Escalante, *Gregorio Condori Mamani: Autobiografía* (Cusco: Barlotomé de las Casas, 1979), 42.

63. Hernández, "Prólogo," 23.

64. Michel de Certeau's *La escritura de la historia* (Mexico City: Universidad Iberoamericana, 1985), 19, 127.

65. Manuel Burga, *Nacimiento de una utopía: Muerte y resurrección de los Incas* (Lima: Instituto de Apoyo Agrario, 1988).

66. Some informants affirm that in certain towns, the dance concludes with the Inca's execution. These must be exceptional cases and probably have to do with the eventual incorporation of the dance into "theatrical" representations of the death of Atahuallpa.

67. Burga, *Nacimiento de una utopía*, 49.

68. Flores Galindo, *Buscando un Inca*, 79.

69. In another version, the Inca and Pizarro's chorus members come together in the end to pay homage to not Atahuallpa, but Huascar, while they sing, "Our powerful Inca, let us dance; / let us dance, Sir Don Juan Pizarro. / And all together let us do it around them." If it were not for the description of the festival and the commentaries of the author, the Quechua text could reflect a conciliatory act in which both sides dance in a circle. See Adolfo Vienrich, *Azucenas quechuas* (Huancayo: Casa de la Cultura de Junín, n.d.). The first edition dates from 1905. Vienrich's edition includes both Spanish and Quechua texts (Jentsch's note).

70. We have access only to texts that have been edited and must depend on these transcriptions. These texts have been taken out of the context in which they function, when, in reality, they are part of a complex ritual in which verbal language is one of many components. The corpus treated is the following: *Tragedia del fin de Atawallpa*, trans. Jesús Lara (Cochabamba: Imprenta Universitaria, 1957); Teodoro Meneses Morales, *La muerte de Atahualpa: Drama quechua de autor anónimo* (Lima: Universidad de San Marcos, 1987); Cle-

mente Hernando Balmori, "Drama indígena bilingüe quechua-castellano," in *La conquista de los españoles y el teatro indígena americano* (Tucumán: Universidad de Tucumán, 1955); Roger Ravines, Mily Olguín de Iriarte, and Francisco Iriarte Brenner, *Dramas coloniales en el Perú actual* (Lima: Universidad Garcilaso de la Vega, 1985); Wilfredo Kapsoli, "La muerte del rey Inca en las danzas populares y la relación de Pomabamba," *Tierra adentro* 3.3 (1985): 139–76; Luis Millones, *El Inca por la Coya: Historia de un drama popular en los Andes peruanos* (Lima: Fundación Ebert, 1988); Herminio Ricaldi and Pío Campos, *Prisión, rescate y muerte del Inca Atahualpa*; and Emilio Mendizábal Losack, "La fiesta en Pachitea andina," *Folklore Americano* 13.13 (1965). All translations are Jentsch's.

71. Cited in Lara, *Tragedia del fin de Atawallpa*, 10. Arzanz wrote his chronicle between 1702 and 1735, centuries after the festivals occurred. See also Betty Osorio de Negret, "La sintaxis básica del relato: Ensayo comparativo de dos tradiciones dramáticas sobre la prisión y muerte de Atahuallpa," *Lexis* 8.1 (1984): 115–17; and Teresa Gisbert, "Art and Resistance in the Andean World," trans. Laura Giefer, in *Amerindian Images and the Legacy of Columbus*, ed. Rene Jara and Nicholas Spadaccini (Minneapolis: University of Minnesota Press, 1992), 663–64 (Jentsch's note).

72. Lara, *Tragedia del fin de Atawallpa*, 58–59. See also that Adolfo Cáceres Romero agrees in "El teatro quechua," *Runayay* 1.1 (1988): 21.

73. Burga, *Nacimiento de una utopía*, 378–82.

74. Lara, *Tragedia del fin de Atawallpa*, 16, 22–23.

75. See Millones, Francisco Huamantinco, and Edgar Sulca, "Los Incas en el recuerdo poético andino," *Nuevo texto crítico* 1.1 (1988).

76. Lara, *La tragedia del fin de Atawallpa*, 49–57; Balmori, *La conquista de los y el teatro indígena americano*, 52; and Terracini, *I codici del silenzio*, 127.

77. See Meneses, *La muerte de Atahualpa*; Kapsoli, "La muerte del rey Inca en las danzas populares y la relación de Pomabamba," 140; and Osorio, "La sintaxsis básica del relato," 116.

78. See Marcel Bataillon, "Por un inventario de las fiestas de Moros y Cristianos," *Mar del Sur* 3.8 (1949): 1–8; and Kapsoli, 140.

79. Burga, *Nacimiento de una utopía*, 399–400. See also Pease, *Inka y kuraka*, 15; and Osorio, "La sintaxis básica del relato."

80. Meneses, *La muerte de Atahualpa*, 4.

81. See *Teatro Quechua Colonial: Antología*, ed. Teodoro L. Meneses (Lima: Edubanco, 1983), especially the prologue, 8.

82. Balmori, *La conquista de los españoles y el teatro indígena americano*, 48–55. See also José Pol, *Atahuallpa* (Cochabamba: Imprenta de El heraldo, 1887), 21; and Christoval María Cortés, *Atahualpa* (Madrid: Por don Antonio de Sancha, 1784). Through the generosity of Dr. Guillermo Ugarte Chamorro I was able to consult the originals of his 1957 article "Atahualpa en el teatro peruano y universal." This includes *La conquista del Perú* from "El ciego de la Merced,"

performed in Lima in 1748. See also Concepción Reverte Bernal, *El teatro de Fr. Francisco del Castillo: "El ciego de la Merced"* (Barcelona: EDT Micropublicaciones, 1988); and *Aproximación crítica a un dramaturgo virreinal peruano: Fr. Francisco del Castillo* (Cadiz: Universidad de Cadiz, 1985), esp. 179. See also two unusual works: Nicanor della Rocca, *La mort d'Atahoualpa* (Lima: Imp. La Sociedad, 1871); and Antonio Ghislanzoni, *Atahualpa: Lyric Drama in Four Acts*. Music by Carlos Enrique Pasta (Lima: Imp. La Patria, 1877). Pasta was the first to incorporate mestizo and Indian music and songs in "cultured" musical works. The librettist of *Aida* wrote the words. See Guillermo Ugarte Chamorro, *Centenario del estreno en Lima de la ópera "Atahualpa"* (Lima: Servicio de Publicaciones del Teatro Universitario de San Marcos, 1979).

83. This refers to the questions, answers, and requests, all identical, that the Inca makes of no less than six characters or groups of characters.
84. See Osorio, "La sintaxis básica del relato."
85. Meneses's *Teatro Quechua colonial* is the most complete compilation.
86. This is most visible in the vocatives and the participation of the ñustas.
87. Balmori, "Drama indígena bilingüe quechua-castellano," lines 253–54.
88. Balmori, "Drama indígena bilingüe quechua-castellano," lines 365, 471.
89. Balmori's text is the one used by a "folkloric group" that since 1950 has been called "La comparsa de los Incas." See also Richard Shaedel, "La representación de la muerte del Inca Atahualpa en la fiesta de la Virgen de la Puerta en Otuzco," *Escena* 4.8 (1956): 23.
90. Nathan Wachtel, "La visión de los vencidos: La conquista española en el folklore indígena," *Ideología mesiánica en el mundo andino*, ed. Juan Ossio (Lima: Ignacio Prado Editor, 1973), 37–81. See also Flores Galindo, *Buscando un Inca*, 74.
91. See Burga, *Nacimiento de una utopía*, chap. 1.
92. Meneses, *Teatro Quechua Colonial*, 165–67 (Jentsch's translation).
93. See Mikhail Bakhtin, *Rabelais and His World* (Bloomington: Indiana University Press, 1984).
94. Balmori gives a short version: "King of Spain: What are you telling me? You were not ordered to take the life of a great King, perhaps stronger than I. Sit down here. Destroying a great King of the New World must have tired you.... This envoy committed incredible excesses by murdering and taking the head of a great king of the new world. This Pizarro should have the same death, and once dead take him to burn with all his lineage." It should be noted that this death sentence appears mixed with a long discourse that synthesizes the history of the conquest and does not once criticize Pizarro (lines 475–549).
95. Lara, *Tragedia del fin de Atawallpa*, 188–89. "This visage that you have brought me [the head of the Inca] is the same as my visage," the King tells Pizarro. The problem of regicide is treated in Cortés, *Atahualpa*, 121.
96. Lara, *Tragedia del fin de Atawallpa*, 191–95.
97. See Garcilaso, *General History of Peru*, bk. 8, chap. 20. Here the king harshly

reprimands Toledo for having killed Tupac Amaru I with words very similar to those in some of the versions of this wanka, emphasizing the fact that the Viceroy died shortly thereafter of melancholy. In addition, Professor Macedonio Villafán opines that this episode might have parallels with classical Spanish drama (like *Fuenteovejuna* or *El mejor alcalde, el Rey*). See Terracini, *I codici del silenzio*, chap. 12.

98. See Lara, *Tragedia del fin de Atawallpa*, 147–48; and Balmori, "Drama indígena bilingüe quechua-castellano," lines 432–44.
99. Balmori, "Drama indígena bilingüe quechua-castellano," lines 427–28.
100. Balmori, *La conquista de los españoles y el teatro indígena americano*, 46–47.
101. See José María Arguedas and Josafat Roel Pineda, "Tres versiones del mito de Inkarrí," in *Ideología mesiánica en el mundo andino*, ed. Juan Ossio (Lima: Prado Pastor, Ignacio, 1973).
102. Wachtel, "La visión de los vencidos," 37–81.
103. Kapsoli, "La muerte del rey Inca en las danzas populares y la relación de Pomabamba," 174.
104. Kapsoli, "La muerte del rey Inca en las danzas populares y la relación de Pomabamba," 144.
105. Although this is an extrapolation, the episode in question recalls chap. 1, pt. 8 of *The Kingdom of This World* by Alejo Carpentier, in which the black slaves intuit that Mackandal has been saved from the stake by being changed into a bird.
106. See Ravines, Olguín, and Iriarte, *Dramas coloniales en el Perú actual*.
107. See Ong, *Orality and Literacy*, chap. 3.
108. Zumthor, *La letra y la voz*, 5.
109. Ravines, Olguín, and Iriarte, *Dramas coloniales en el Perú actual*, 101–2.
110. Ravines, Olguín, and Iriarte, *Dramas coloniales en el Perú actual*, 18.
111. In some cases this interference seems to have a comic effect, especially in translations made by Felipillo. See Rivarola, "Contacto y conflicto," 101.
112. Ravines, Olguín, and Iriarte, *Dramas coloniales en el Perú actual*, 31.
113. See "Un documento para la historia del español peruano (siglo XVI)," *Diglosia linguo-literaria y educación en el Perú*, ed. Enrique Ballón Aguirre and Rodolfo Cerrón-Palomino (Lima: CONCYTEC, 1989), 131 ff.; and Rivarola, *Lengua, comunicación e historia del Perú*, 34–39. See also José Luis Rivarola, *Anuario de lingüística hispánica* 1 (1985).
114. Millones, *El Inca por la Coya*, 58.
115. See also Osorio, "La sintaxis básica del relato," 115; and Max Hernández in Millones, *El Inca por la Coya*, 23–28.
116. Ravines, Olguín, and Iriarte, *Dramas coloniales en el Perú actual*, 22.
117. César Vallejo, "Mass," in *César Vallejo: The Complete Posthumous Poetry*, trans. Clayton Eshleman and José Rubia Barcia (Berkeley: University of California Press, 1978), 261.
118. Balmori, "Drama indígena bilingüe quechua-castellano," lines 25, 52, 165. It is

worth noting that "writing" and "book" are not always culturally homologous. See also Zumthor, *La letra y la voz*, chap. 1, pt. 5.

119. Lara, *Tragedia del fin de Atawallpa*, 103–5.
120. Lara, *Tragedia del fin de Atawallpa*, 107–9.
121. Balmori, "Drama indígena bilingüe quechua-castellano," lines 165–67 (Cornejo's emphasis, Jentsch's addition).
122. Margot Beyersdorff, "La adoración de los Reyes Magos," in *Vigencia del teatro religioso español en el Perú andino* (Cusco: Centro Bartolomé de las Casas, 1988).
123. Balmori, *La conquista de los españoles y el teatro indígena americano*, 43.
124. Beyersdorff, "La adoración de los Reyes Magos," 58.
125. See Lara, *Tragedia del fin de Atawallpa*, 52; Balmori, *La conquista de los españoles y el teatro indígena americano*, 109; and Meneses, *Teatro Quechua Colonial*, 588.
126. Lara, *Tragedia del fin de Atawallpa*, 101. See also Marta Bermúdez-Gallegos, "Atahuallpa Inca: Axial Figure in the Encounter of Two Worlds," in *Amerindian Images and the Legacy of Columbus* (Minneapolis: University of Minnesota Press), 620–21; and Gisbert, "Art and Resistance in the Andean World," 666–67 (Jentsch's note).
127. Balmori, "Drama indígena bilingüe quechua-castellano," lines 170–222.
128. Ravines, Olguín, and Iriarte, *Dramas coloniales en el Perú actual*, 49.
129. Kapsoli, "La muerte del rey Inca en las danzas populares y la relación de Pomabamba," 170.
130. Even if the wanka is very early, primary orality is part of the representation and therefore supposes a fictitious re-creation of an experience that by then had been thoroughly treated.
131. Balmori, *La conquista de los españoles y el teatro indígena americano*, 45–46.
132. In the Spanish tradition at least since *The Book of Good Love*.
133. Huaman Poma, *Letter to a King*, 796.
134. See Terracini, *I codici del silenzio*, 197–229. "Drama for the vanquished, comedy for the victors."
135. Meneses, *Teatro Quechua Colonial* 106–7. In the preceding Quechua text Felipillo uses the word "letter" [*karta*] and associates it with deceit. In Meneses's Spanish translation it is obvious that Felipillo is playing with double meanings for communication and a card game, as if trying to warn the Inca: "the card [*carta*] for playing and the deceit of the wager," which Atahualpa obviously cannot take in.
136. Kapsoli, "La muerte del rey Inca en las danzas populares y la relación de Pomabamba," 170.
137. Ravines, Olguín, and Iriarte, *Dramas coloniales en el Perú actual*, 31 (Cornejo's emphasis).
138. Ravines, Olguín, and Iriarte, *Dramas coloniales en el Perú actual*, 49 (Jentsch's translation). This speech is very similar to one in the Pomabamba version.

139. Millones, *El Inca por la Coya*, 59, 87.
140. Ravines, Olguín, and Iriarte, *Dramas coloniales en el Perú actual*, 110.
141. Ong, *Orality and Literacy*, 43–45.
142. Terracini, *I codici del silenzio*, 17.
143. Terracini, *I codici del silenzio*, 7.
144. See Osorio, "La sintaxis básica del relato," 128; see Balmori, *La conquista de los españoles y el teatro indígena americano*, 43–44; and Ravines, Olguín, and Iriarte, *Dramas coloniales en el Perú actual*, 76–78. These descriptions largely match the photographs mentioned below.
145. See Mercedes López-Baralt, "La crónica de Indias como texto cultural: Articulación de los códigos icónico y lingüístico en los dibujos de la *Nueva corónica* de Guamán Poma," *Revista iberoamericana* 48.48 (1982). See also her *Icono y conquista*; and Adorno, *Cronista y príncipe*; *Guamán Poma*; *From Oral to Written Expression*.
146. Lara has noted the almost complete absence of Spanish interference to the point that "we have searched for a good way of expressing the Bible: *Qhíspiy Simi* (Word of salvation)" (32). Rather than speaking to the "authenticity" of this version, this seems to indicate the intervention of a highly cultured Quechuist, who might have belonged to Andean nobility. The date on the manuscript, probably an edited copy of a previous one, is 1871.
147. See José Durand, *Ocaso de sirenas y esplendor de manatíes*, 2nd ed. (Mexico City: Fondo de Cultura Económica, 1983).
148. See Certeau, *La escritura de la historia*, chaps. 1, 2, and 5.
149. Millones's is the exception.
150. See Osorio, "La sintaxis básica del relato," 116.
151. In Meseses' version the Indians see Valverde as "toad" and "son of the devil" (speech 192). Conversely, in most versions the Spaniards call the Indians "barbarians," "brutes," and "infidels."
152. See Antonio Cornejo Polar, "La literatura peruana: totalidad contradictoria," *Revista de crítica literaria latinoamericana* 9.18 (1983).
153. See Miguel León Portilla, *Visión de los vencidos* (Havana: Casa de las Américas, 1969). See also his *El reverso de la Conquista* (Mexico City: Joaquín Mortiz, 1980).
154. Ángel Rama, *The Lettered City*, trans. John Chasteen (Durham, NC: Duke University Press, 1996).
155. This text is treated in the Overture.

Chapter 2: The Sutures of Homogeneity: Discourses of Impossible Harmony

1. See Benedict Anderson, *Imagined Communities: Reflections on the Origin and Spread of Nationalism* (London: Verso/New Left, 1983); see Julio Ramos, *Desencuentros de la modernidad en América Latina: Literatura y política en el siglo XIX* (Mexico City: Fondo de Cultura Económica, 1989).
2. See Alberto Flores Galindo, *Buscando un Inca: Identidad y utopía en los Andes*

(Havana: Casa de las Américas, 1986); and Manuel Burga, *Nacimiento de una utopía: Muerte y resurrección de los incas* (Lima: Instituto de Apoyo Agrario, 1988).

3. See especially José Durand, *El Inca Garcilaso, clásico de América* (Mexico City: Sepsetentas, 1976); Alberto Escobar, "Historia y lenguaje en los *Comentarios Reales*," in *Patio de Letras* (Lima: Caballo de Troya, 1965); Max Hernández, "El Inca Garcilaso: El oficio de escribir," *Plural* 217 (1989) and *Memoria del bien perdido: Conflicto, identidad y nostalgia en el Inca Garcilaso de la Vega* (Madrid: Encuentros, 1991); Susana Jákfalvi-Leiva, *Traducción, escritura y violencia colonizadora: Un estudio sobre la obra del Inca Garcilaso* (Syracuse: Maxwell School, 1977); Martin Lienhard, "La crónica mestiza en México y el Perú hasta 1620: Apuntes para su estudio histórico-literario," *Revista de crítica literaria latinoamericana* 9.17 (1983); Enrique Pupo-Walker, *Historia, creación y profecía en los textos del Inca Garcilaso de la Vega* (Madrid: Porrúa-Turanzas, 1982); Margarita Zamora, *Language, Authority and Indigenous History in the Comentarios Reales de los Incas* (Cambridge: Cambridge University Press, 1988); Nicolás Wey-Gómez, "¿Dónde está Garcilaso? La oscilación del sujeto colonial en la formación de un discurso transcultural," *Revista de crítica literaria latinoamericana* 17.34 (1991); César Delgado Díaz del Olmo, *El diálogo de los mundos: Ensayo sobre el Inca Garcilaso* (Arequipa: UNSA, 1991); and Manuel Burga, *Nacimiento de una utopía. Muerte y resurrección de los incas* (Lima: Instituto de Apoyo Agrario, 1988).

4. José Durand, *El Inca Garcilaso, clásico de América*, 11. This idea initially appeared in the first chapter, "El Inca Garcilaso, historiador apasionado," in 1952.

5. An example: the many "persons" mentioned above and others all appear in the dedicatory of Garcilaso's translation of the *Dialogues*, which he includes at the end of the prologue to the *History*. There are many more examples. Citations from Garcilaso de la Vega, El Inca, *Royal Commentaries of the Incas and General History of Peru*, trans. Harold Livermore (Austin: University of Texas Press, 1966).

6. Durand, *El Inca Garcilaso, clásico de América*, 48. The title article first appeared in 1953.

7. Garcilaso, *Royal Commentaries of the Incas*, 607.

8. See Burga, *Nacimiento de una utopía*, 276-79.

9. See Jorge Guzmán, *Contra el secreto profesional: Lectura mestiza de Vallejo* (Santiago: Universitaria, 1991), 26-29. Guzmán emphasizes the duality oro/huaca in order to establish his perception of mestizaje and its implicit problems.

10. For example, "they call it *huaca*, which is a sacred place" (Garcilaso, *Royal Commentaries of the Incas*, chap. 3).

11. See Regina Harrison, *Signs, Songs, and Memory in the Andes: Translating Quechua Language and Culture* (Austin: University of Texas Press, 1989), espe-

cially chap. 2, where she makes several references to Garcilaso's translations of *huaca*.
12. Qtd. in Durand, *El Inca Garcilaso, clásico de América*, 54.
13. Durand, *El Inca Garcilaso, clásico de América*, 23–24.
14. John H. Rowe, "El movimento nacional inca del siglo XVIII," *Revista universitaria* 107 (1954), reproduced in *Túpac Amaru II-1780: Antología*, ed. Alberto Flores Galindo (Lima: Retablo de Papel, 1976). Rowe notes that reading Garcilaso was a stimulating force for the Inca renaissance of the eighteenth century but warns that it was later editions attributed to Barcia that proved to have a greater impact because they included prologues that mentioned the restoration of the Inca Empire (27ff). Cornejo consulted *Primera parte de los Commentarios Reales . . . Escritos por el Inca Garcilaso de la Vega . . . segvnda impresión, enmendada: Y añadida la Vida de Inti Cusi Titu Iupanqui . . .* (Madrid: Oficina Real, 1723). It contains a "Prólogo . . . de Don Gabriel de Cárdenas," which is the pseudonym for Andrés González de Barcia Barballido y Zúñiga. The prologue ends with a set of citations in Latin that prophesy the restoration of the Incas, supposedly with the collaboration of England. Since this fragment is in poor Latin and it comes from an indirect source, it probably had little impact on the neo-Inca nobility. Additionally, the same prologue (clearly procolonialist and highly Catholic) relates another prophecy, this time from Indian "diviners" who announce the total destruction of the empire. On Garcilaso's lasting effect, see José Tamayo Herrera, *Historia del indigenismo cuzqueño* (Lima: Insituto Nacional de Cultura, 1980), 80–82.
15. See Luis Alberto Sánchez, *Balance y liquidación del Novecientos* (Lima: Universo, 1973). Also Luis Loayza, *Sobre el 900* (Lima: Hueso húmero, 1990).
16. Gonzalo Portocarrero and Patricia Oliart, *El Perú desde la escuela* (Lima: Instituto de Apoyo Agrario, 1989). Since the surveys took place some years before the publication of this book, the aggressive instigation of the idea of "modernizing" or "Europeanizing" Peru could have changed the percentages, although perhaps not in a numerically significant way.
17. José de Riva-Agüero, "El Inca Garcilaso de la Vega," *Obras completas*, vol. 2, (Lima: Universidad Católica, 1962), 45. The cited text is better known as "Elogio del Inca Garcilaso" and was reedited several times. Citations are from the 1938 edition. All translations are Jentsch's.
18. Menéndez Pelayo, *Orígenes de la novela*, vol. 2 (Buenos Aires: Emecé, 1945), 151–52. Riva-Agüero's quote is from the first edition.
19. José de la Riva-Agüero, *La historia en el Perú* (Lima: Imprenta Nacional de Federico Barrionuevo, 1910).
20. He says, "In the tumultuous disarray of the Conquest, and the recent example of the limitless polygamy of the native princes, simple concubinage was very acceptable and public, and almost proper in the eyes of all, Spaniards and Indians alike" (Riva-Agüero, "Elogio," 10).

21. Riva-Agüero, "Elogio," 9, Cornejo's emphasis. See Cornejo, *La formación de la tradición literaria en el Perú*, which alludes to the similarity of this passage to the story "Amor indígena" by Ventura García Calderón that tells of the rape of an Indian woman by a superior (where he "repeats the joy of the Spanish grandfathers who toppled women along the roads for an hour of pleasure") and the devoted march ("with the desperate pleas of a slave") of the raped Indian behind her proud rapist.
22. Riva-Agüero, "Elogio," 19. This defense of Captain Garcilaso's marriage would have angered the Inca, since he criticized Spanish men who abandoned Indian women to marry Spaniards.
23. See Uriel García, *El nuevo indio* (Cuzco: Rosas, 1930).
24. See Julio Ortega, "Para una teoría del texto latinoamericano: Colón, Garcilaso y el discurso de la abundancia," *Revista de crítica literaria latinoamericana* 14.28 (1988): 101–15.
25. One should note on one hand the official's manipulation that makes the letter "say" what it obviously cannot tell (that the Indians "ate" the melons), and on the other the subtle irony that permeates the whole "tale": the one who masterfully *writes* the story in which the Indians considered the Spaniards gods for knowing the secret of writing is the same one who defines himself as Inca-Indian. In one respect the power of writing has changed hands, or at least scriptural hegemony is disputed territory.
26. See Pupo-Walker, *Historia, creación y profecía en los textos del Inca Garcilaso de la Vega*; Hernández, "El Inca Garcilaso: El oficio de escribir"; José Juan Arrom, "Hombre y mundo en dos cuentos del Inca Garcilaso," in *Certidumbre de América* (Madrid: Gredos, 1971); and Raquel Chang-Rodríguez, "Elaboración de las fuentes en 'Carta canta' y 'Papelito jabla lengua,'" in *Kentucky Quarterly* 24:4 (1977). Arrom has since expanded his study in *Imaginación del Nuevo Mundo* (Mexico City: Siglo XXI, 1991).
27. Pupo-Walker, *Historia, creación y profecía en los textos del Inca Garcilaso de la Vega*, 177.
28. Ricardo Palma, "Carta canta," in *Tradiciones peruanas* (Madrid: Calpe, 1923), 26–28; see Arrom and Chang-Rodríguez. For more on the tradición genre, see Estuardo Núñez, *Tradiciones hispanoamericanas* (Caracas: Biblioteca Ayacucho, 1979). Terracini, *I codici del silenzio*, 225–26, notes that the same story appears in Lope de Vega's play *The New World*.
29. See Cornejo, *La formación de la tradición literaria en el Perú*, chap. 2.
30. See Ricardo Palma, *Neologismos y americanismos* (Lima: Impreso Carlos Prince, 1896). The polemic between Palma and the Royal Spanish Academy is documented in the *Boletín de la academia peruana de la lengua*, 20 (1985).
31. Chang-Rodríguez, "Elaboración de las fuentes en 'Carta canta' y 'Papelito jabla lengua.'"
32. See José Carlos Mariátegui, *Seven Interpretive Essays on Peruvian Reality*, trans. Marjory Urquidi (Austin: University of Texas Press, 1971).

33. See Anderson, *Imagined Communities: Reflections on the Origin and Spread of Nationalism*; and Ramos, *Desencuentros de la modernidad en América Latina*. See also Doris Sommer, *Foundational Fictions: The National Romances of Latin America* (Berkeley: University of California Press, 1991).
34. Alberto Escobar, *La narración en el Perú* (Lima: Majía Baca, 1960), xxiv.
35. Cornejo, *La formación de la tradición literaria en el Perú*, 59.
36. See Pablo Macera, "Lenguaje y modernismo peruano del siglo XVII," in *Trabajos de historia*, vol. 2 (Lima: Instituto Nacional de Cultura, 1977).
37. Jorge Basadre, *Historia de la República del Perú* (Lima: Universitaria, 1968), 1–2.
38. See Julio Cotler, *Clases, estado y nación en el Perú* (Lima: Instituto de Estudios Peruanos, 1978).
39. See Rafael Gutiérez Girardot, *Modernismo* (Barcelona: Montesinos, 1983). See also Richard J. Bernstein, *Habermas y la modernidad* (Madrid: Cátedra, 1988).
40. See Raúl Porras Barrenechea, *Los ideólogos de la emancipación* (Lima: Milla Batres, 1974); and Jorge Basadre, *La iniciación de la República* (Lima: Rosay, 1930); and chap. 4 of *Perú: problema y posibilidad* (Lima: Rosay, 1931); *La promesa de la vida peruana* (Lima: Mejía Baca, 1958); and vols. 1 and 2 of *Historia de la República de Perú*.
41. See Gustavo Gutiérrez, *Dios o el oro en las Indias* (Lima: CEP, 1989).
42. See Basadre, *La iniciación de la República*, 42; and Mariátegui, *Seven Interpretive Essays on Peruvian Reality*, essays 1 and 2.
43. José Ratto-Ciarlo's, *Choquehaunca y la contrarrevolución* (Caracas: Comité del Bicentenario de Simón Bolívar, 1980), 30 (Jentsch's translation). See also Leonardo Altuve Carrillo, *Choquehuanca y su arenga a Bolívar* (Buenos Aires: Planeta, 1991).
44. See Ratto-Ciarlo, *Choquehaunca y la contrarrevolución*, 149–52.
45. *Ensayo de estadística completa de los ramos económicos políticos de la provincia de Azángaro en el departamento de Puno de la República peruana del quinquenio contado de 1825 hasta 1829 inclusive* (Lima: Imprenta de Manuel Corral, 1933). In this and other texts Choquehuanca expresses a clearly proindigenous ideology and takes his thought from the most pragmatic current of the Enlightenment. See Ratto-Ciarlo, *Choquehaunca y la contrarrevolución*, chap. 4.
46. There are three republics mentioned in the handwritten versions; in later ones—for obvious reasons—five.
47. Garcilaso, *Royal Commentaries of the Incas*, chap. 9.
48. See Nathan Wachtel, "Pensamiento salvaje y aculturación: El espacio y el tiempo en Felipe Guamán Poma de Ayala y el Inca Garcilaso de la Vega," in *Sociedad e ideología: Ensayos de historia y antropología andinas* (Lima: Instituto de Estudios Peruanos, 1973).
49. See Ratto-Ciarlo, *Choquehaunca y la contrarrevolución*, chap. 3.
50. Qtd. in Ratto-Ciarlo, *Choquehaunca y la contrarrevolución*, 54–55.

51. See Antonio Cornejo Polar, "La reivindicación del imperio incaico en la poesía de la emancipación en el Perú," *Letterature d'America* 4:19–20 (1983).
52. See Cedomil Goic, "Novela hispanoamericana colonial," in *Historia de la literatura hispanoamericana*, ed. Luis Iñigo Madrigal, vol. 1, *Epoca colonial* (Madrid: Cátedra, 1982).
53. See Pedro Lastra, *El cuento hispanoamericano del siglo XIX* (New York: Giacoman, 1972).
54. See Frederic Jameson, "Third-World in the Era of Multinational Capitalism," *Social Texts* 15 (1986); and Aijaz Ahmad, "Jameson's Rhetoric of Otherness and the 'National Allegory,'" *Social Texts* 17 (1986). See also Doris Sommer, *Foundational Fictions*, and *One Master for Another: Populism as Patriarchal Rhetoric in Dominican Novels* (Lanham, MD: University Press of America, 1984).
55. Octavio Paz, *The Labyrinth of Solitude: Life and Thought in Mexico*, trans. Lysander Kemp (New York: Grove, 1961). The first edition in Spanish published in 1950.
56. See Mikhail Bakhtin, "The Word and the Novel," *Comparative Criticism: A Yearbook* 2 (1980), 213–20; and György Lukács, *Theory of the Novel* (Cambridge, MA: MIT Press, 1974).
57. Rómulo Gallegos, *Doña Barbara*. The first edition was published in 1929. There are various English translations (Jentsch's note).
58. See "El aprendizaje de la lectura: Novela y formación nacional en Hispanoamérica," *Osamayor* 2:4 (1991).
59. Juan León Mera, *Cumandá o un drama entre salvajes* (Quito: Imprenta del Clero, 1879). All translations are Jentsch's. See Manuel Corrales Pascual, "Las raíces del relato indigenista ecuatoriano," *Revista de crítica literaria latinoamericana* 4:7–8 (1978); Hernán Vidal, "Cumandá: Apología del estado teocrático, *Revista de crítica literaria latinoamericana* 6:12 (1980); and Edmond Cros, "Space and Textual Genetics: Magical Consciousness and Ideology in Cumandá" *Sociocriticism* 4–5 (1986).
60. Vidal, "*Cumandá*."
61. Cumandá says, "Listen, white brother . . . our souls are one, our hearts are brothers, our blood is the same, and we should never be separated" (Mera, *Cumandá*, 115). Such texts abound in the novel until the narrator "surprises" the reader with the fact that Carlos and Cumandá are brother and sister.
62. See Corrales, "Las raíces del relato indigenista ecuatoriano," 45, where he points out some tenuous criticism of this group.
63. The "savage" hatred for writing, which in this case ends up in ashes, is not shared by Cumandá. She "kissed the ciphers, as if she could understand them, and immediately remembering what they said, began to sing" (Mera, *Cumandá*, 24). In a way her actions are the same as those of evangelized Indians who repeat sacred texts and liturgy. The oppressor always controls writing, and the oppressed—at best—can only repeat it (in this case, sing it) orally.
64. See Cornejo's foreword in the edition translated by John H. R. Polt (New York:

Oxford University Press, 1998). See also *Birds without a Nest*, ed. Naomi Lindstom (Austin: University of Texas Press, 1996), which is an emended edition of the first English translation by J. G. Hudson published in 1904 (Jentsch's notes). The first edition in Spanish was published in Lima by Carlos Prince in 1889. On Matto and *Torn from the Nest*, see Francisco Carrillo, *Clorinda Matto de Turner y su indigenismo literario* (Lima: Universitaria, 1967); Alberto Tauro, *Clorinda Matto de Turner y la novela indigenista* (Lima: San Marcos, 1976); and Fernando Arribas-García, "*Aves sin nido*: ¿Novela indigenista?" *Revista de crítica literaria latinoamericana* 17:34 (1991). See also Antonio Cornejo Polar, "*Aves sin nido*: Indios, 'notables' y forasteros," in *La novela peruana* (Lima: Horizonte, 1989); and "Clorinda Matto de Turner: Para una imagen de la novel peruana del siglo XIX," *Escritura* 2:3 (1977). In English, see Efraín Kristal, *The Andes Viewed from the City: Literary and Political Discourse on the Indian in Peru* (New York: Peter Lang, 1987).

65. The narrator states, "Would that God, in the exercise of His goodness, might one day ordain the extinction of the native race, which, resplendent once in imperial greatness, now drinks the fetid cup of degradation! God grant its extinction, since *it can never* recover its dignity or exercise its rights!" (Matto, *Torn from the Nest*, 12, Cornejo's emphasis). This idea is repeated in the dialogue between Isidoro Champi and his wife: "We were born Indians, the slaves of the priest, slaves of the governor, slaves of the headman, slaves of all those who manage to get the whip hand . . . Indians! Yes, only death offers us the sweet hope of freedom" (162).

66. First edition, 1895. It is curious that Rosalía does not appear in this novel.

67. Margarita's education seems to have as its only objective her integration into Lima's high society through marriage. Virtue is praised throughout, while stressing the growing immorality of this social group.

68. Manuel González Prada, "Discurso en el Politeama," in *Pájinas Libres* (Madrid: Pueyó, n.d.), 78.

69. It is announced in *Torn from the Nest* that Lucía is expecting, but the novel ends before the birth takes place, and this subject is completely absent in *Herencia*.

70. See Antonio Cornejo Polar, "Matalaché: Las muchas formas de la esclavitud," in *La novela peruana*. See also Tomás G. Escajadillo, *La narrativa de Lópex Albújar* (Lima: CONUP, 1972).

71. Nataniel Aguirre, *Juan de la Rosa*, trans. Sergio Gabriel Waisman (New York: Oxford University Press, 1998). All translations are Jentsch's. The original text was first published in 1885 in Paris.

72. See Alba María Paz Soldán, *Una articulación simbólica de lo nacional: Juan de la Rosa de Nataniel Aguirre* (University of Pittsburgh Press, 1986). Paz Soldán also edited and wrote the foreword to the English translation used here (Jentsch's note). See also Walter Navia Romer, *Interpretación y análisis de Juan de la Rosa* (La Paz: Universidad de San Andrés, 1966).

73. Cf. José Santos Vargas, *Diario de un comandante de la independencia americana, 1814–1825*, ed. Gunnar Mendoza (Mexico City: Siglo XXI, 1982).
74. See Navia, *Interpretación y análisis de Juan de la Rosa*, 59–64.
75. See Paz Soldán, *Una articulación simbólica de lo nacional*, chap. 3.
76. A similar episode is related later when Clara, also a mestiza, sings a *harahui* from the Ollanta maidens' chorus in Quechua as she remembers her sweetheart killed in the rebellion.
77. The novel places the mestizos' "good Quechua" within the narration's time frame but states that by the time it was written down this tradition had been lost. Thus when the narrator remembers another "*harahui* in the style of Ollanta" and begins to transcribe it in Quechua, he stops abruptly: "But what am I doing? Can my young readers even begin to understand that tongue, already as foreign to them as Syriac or Caldean?" This is part of the criticism the old colonel levels at Bolivia's social processes following the time of the war of independence.
78. Note that he discovers his parentage through writing and reading. It is reading (not the oral tradition transcribed in the novel) that allows this discovery.
79. Note that the protagonist, even after learning his paternal surname, keeps the one that refers to his mother's given name (not her surname), including the form "*de la*," which has a clear connotation of belonging and filiation.
80. On the importance of the mother figure in Latin American culture, see Sonia Montecino, *Madres y huachos: Alegorías del mestizaje chileno* (Santiago: CEDEM, 1991).
81. It is clear that in *Torn from the Nest* the protagonist's role is played by Lucía Marín, rather than her husband. This is echoed in the Yupanqui family as well.
82. Paz Soldán comments on the absence of the father in primogeniture families.
83. The most notable of these, the 1879 War of the Pacific, is not mentioned at all in this text nor in *Torn from the Nest*.
84. Ángel Rama, *Rubén Darío y el modernismo: Circunstancia socio-económica de un arte americano* (Caracas: Universidad Central de Venezuela, 1970); Françoise Pérus, *Literatura y sociedad en América Latina: el Modernismo* (Havana: Casa de las Américas, 1976); and Ángel Rama, *Las máscaras democráticas del modernismo* (Montevideo: Fundación Rama, 1985). See also Julio Ramos, *Desencuentros de la modernidad en América Latina*.
85. This term appears in the law that charges Gregorio Reynolds to write his poem for the centennial of Bolivian independence.
86. It is significant that the two poems studied here were unfinished and published in partial form, albeit for different reasons.
87. Gregorio Reynolds, *Redención* (La Paz: Renacimiento, 1925). Vol. 1 was the only one published and ironically concludes with canto 4, dedicated to the conquest. (All translations are Jentsch's.)
88. The most curious segment is the one associating the *Antis* with the *Atlantes*:

"The two letters of the Gnostic alphabet, / a parenthesis open to the secret / of the endless treasure of the *Atlantes*" (53). Tihuanancu, according to the original.

89. José Vasconcelos's *The Cosmic Race*, a great expression of syncretist theory relating to the future of Latin America, was written the same year as *Redención*.
90. For example: "the Inca is Cadmus, Triptolemus, Theseus" (88); "[Inca] students learn the quadrivium" (119); Pachacuti is "a devotee of Mars and Minerva" (121); an imperial festival "Is a Biblical and pagan festival / worthy of Galahad and Helicon. Shulamite and Daphnis—honey and perfume, bee and blossom—pass through the gardens of Arcadia . . . / Arcadia or Trianon?" (138).
91. From José Santos Chocano, *Obras completas*, ed. Luis Alberto Sánchez (Mexico: Aguilar, 1954). First edition published in 1924. (All translations are Jentsch's.)
92. The fact that the epic was never finished only serves to revive the scandal begun when it was found that the Peruvian and Venezuelan governments had paid Chocano advances equivalent to some $35,000 each in the form of advanced sales of the book. See Luis Alberto Sánchez, "Advertencia" in José Santos Chocano, *Obras Completas* (Mexico City: Aguilar, 1954); and *Aladino o vida y obra de José Santos Chocano*, 2nd ed. (Lima: Universo, 1975), chap. 22. The centennial of Ayacucho in Peru, which took place under the dictatorship of Augusto Leguía, was enveloped in a bitter polemic created by Chocano's and Leopoldo Lugones's defense of authoritarianism. This polemic later spread throughout the continent.
93. See under "Concerning Patriotic Speeches and Proclamations" in this chapter.
94. Germán Wettstein, "Lenguage alegórico e ironía pedagógica en el quehacer político de Bolívar," *Casa de las Américas* 21.143 (1984): 31. He transcribes Bolívar's letter to José Joaquín Olmedo (one of Chocano's sources) in which he claims that the Incaist theory is false. He states that although the liberating armies are "avengers of his blood [they are also] descendents of those who annihilated the Inca's empire."
95. The surrender is to Sucre, but in stanza L Sucre gives it over to Bolívar: "the Banner / of the Conquest should be in your hands alone."
96. See Heraclio Bonilla et al., *La independencia en el Perú* (Lima: Instituto de Estudios Peruanos, 1972); and Cotler, *Clases, estado y nación en el Perú*.
97. This is curious in view of the frequency with which Chocano treats the ideal of mestizaje in his other poetry, to the point of making it a basic component of his poetic personage. See Cornejo, *La formación de la tradición literaria en el Perú*, chap. 3.
98. This theme is treated naïvely (according to the "summary") in canto 5. Panama, where the American nations join, will be the seat of the League of Nations and "the Capital of the World."

99. Chocano explains that this "pantheistic" constant was part of Bolívar's basic philosophy. This is debatable. Reynolds also uses this device, especially in the first two cantos. On personification and ghostly apparitions, see Olmedo's "Canto a Bolívar" verses 353–73 in *Poesía de la Independencia*, ed. Emilio Carilla (Caracas: Biblioteca Ayacucho, 1979).
100. The "Final Hymn [to] the Glorification of Spain" appears in this same section.
101. Leguía's letter (in which he refers to Chocano as "crown poet") appears as a prologue in Chocano, *Obras Completas*.

Chapter 3: Stone of Boiling Blood: The Challenges of Modernization
1. This topic is discussed in the last part of chapter 2.
2. On the Vanguard in Latin America, see Hugo Verani, *Las vanguardias literarias en Hispanoamérica: Manifiestos, proclamas y otros escritos* (Roma: Bulzoni, 1986); Nelson Osorio, *Manifiestos, proclamas y polémicas de la vanguardia literaria hispanoamericana* (Caracas: Biblioteca Ayacucho, 1988); and Jorge Schwartz, *Las vanguardias latinoamericanas: Textos programáticos y críticos* (Madrid: Cátedra, 1991). Osorio's *La formación de la vanguardia literaria en Venezuela* (Caracas: Academia Nacional de Historia, 1985) is particularly illustrative.
3. See Ángel Rama, *Transculturación narrativa en América Latina* (Mexico City: Siglo XXI, 1982), especially section 2; José Deustua and José Luis Rénique, *Intelectuales, indigenismo y descentralismo en el Perú* (Cuzco: Bartolomé de las Casas, 1984); Alberto Flores Galindo, "Los intelectuales y el probema nacional," in *7 ensayos: 50 años de historia* (Lima: Amauta, 1979); and Mirko Lauer, *El sitio de la literatura peruana: Escritores y política en el Perú del siglo XX* (Lima: Mosca Azul, 1989), chap. 1.
4. On the relationship between Vanguard and literary institutions, see Peter Bürger, *Teoría de la vanguardia* (Barcelona: Península, 1987), although in the Andean region this institutionality is weak, and consequently any confrontation with it is less visible.
5. See Beatriz Sarlo, *Una modernidad periférifca: Buenos Aires 1920–1930* (Buenos Aires: Nueva Visión, 1988); and Marshall Berman, *Todo lo sólido se desvanece en el aire* (Mexico City: Siglo XXI, 1988).
6. Luis Monguió, *La poesía postmodernista peruana* (Mexico City: Fondo de Cultura Económica, 1954).
7. Jentsch's translations.
8. Alberto Escobar, *Antología de la poesía peruana* (Lima: Nuevo Mundo, 1965), 15–18.
9. See José Carlos Mariátegui, *La polémica del indigenismo*, comp. Manuel Aquézolo (Lima: Mosca Azul, 1976), 76. (All translations are Jentsch's.) In his 1925 "Nationalism and Vanguardism," in *The Heroic and Creative Meaning of Socialism*, trans. Michael Pearlman (Atlantic Highlands, NJ: Humanities Press,

1996), Mariátegui maintains that "the vanguard proposes the reconstruction of Peru on an Indian foundation [and] seeks more truly Peruvian and more remotely ancient materials for its work." His thoughts on Vallejo appear in the corresponding section of *Seven Interpretive Essays on Peruvian Reality*, trans. Marjory Urquidi (Austin: University of Texas Press, 1971), whose first edition in Spanish was published in 1928. On the question of the relationship between the Vanguard and Indigenism, see David Wise, "Vanguardismo a 3800 metros: el caso del *Boletín Titikaka*," *Revista de crítica literaria latinoamericana* 10.20 (1984). See also Beatriz Sarlo, "Vanguardia y criollismo: La aventura de *Martín Fierro*," *Revista de crítica literaria latinoamericana* 8.15 (1982); and Alberto Escobar, *El imaginario nacional. Moro, Westphalen, Arguedas: Una formación literaria* (Lima: Instituto de Estudios Peruanos, 1989), 17.

10. César Vallejo, *Poemas humanos / Human Poems*, trans. Clayton Eshleman (New York: Grove, 1968), 63.

11. See Antonio Cornejo Polar, *Sobre literatura y crítica latinoamericanas* (Caracas: Universidad Central, 1982), *La novela peruana* (Lima: Horizonte, 1989); and *Literatura y sociedad en el Perú: La novela indigenista* (Lima: Lasontay, 1980). See also Kemy Oyarzún, "Latin American Literary Criticism: Myth, History, Ideology," *Latin American Research Review* 22.2 (1988).

12. Mariátegui had to defend himself against this accusation on several occasions by coining a phrase he repeated with slight variations: "in these cosmopolitan and ecumenical journeys for which we are so reproached, we are increasingly discovering ourselves" (Mariátegui, *The Heroic and Creative Meaning of Socialism*, 74).

13. Here Mariátegui obviously is not referring to the Latin American school of that name, but to the new poetry of his day, including the segment of the Vanguard that he considered decadent.

14. From his 1924 "Poetas nuevos y poesía vieja," in *Peruanicemos al Perú* (Lima: Amauta, 1970), 18–19. (All translations are Jentsch's.)

15. From his 1926 article "Poesía nueva," anthologized in César Vallejo, *Desde Europa: Crónicas y artículos (1923–1938)*, ed. Jorge Puccinelli (Lima: Fuente de Cultura Peruana, 1987), 140–41 (Jentsch's translation). It is important to add that Vallejo was developing a very pessimistic view of the Peruvian, Latin American, and European poetry of his day. See his "Contra el secreto profesional" (1927) and "Autopsia del surrealismo" (1930) from the same anthology.

16. See also César Vallejo, *Crónicas*, ed. Enrique Ballón (Mexico City: UNAM, 1984). Mariátegui's chronicles are compiled in *Cartas de Italia* (Lima: Amauta, 1969), but other letters and references to his time in Europe are found in his *Obras completas*, especially in *La escena contemporánea* (Lima: Amauta, 1969).

17. See Antonio Cornejo Polar, "César Vallejo: La universalización de una experiencia nacional," *La Torre* 3.12 (1989); "Vallejo: Mestizaje, transculturación,

modernidad," *Páginas* 14:19 (1989); and *La formación de la tradición literaria en el Perú* (Lima: CEP, 1989). See also Peter Klarén, *La formación de las haciendas azucareras y los orígenes del Apra* (Lima: Instituto de Estudios Peruanos, 1970).

18. Pablo Palacio's work (two short novels and a book of short stories) has been collected in *Obras completas* (Guayaquil: Casa de la Cultura, 1976). Citations from *Un hombre muerto a puntapiés* and *Débora* (Santiago: Universitaria, 1971). His collection of short stories appeared in 1927. Jorge Icaza, *Huasipungo*, 11th ed. (Buenos Aires: Losada, 1977). The first edition was published in 1934. (All translations are Jentsch's.)

19. See Antonio Cornejo Polar, "'Un hombre muerto a puntapiés': Poética y narración," in *Recopilación de textos sobre Pablo Palacio*, ed. José Donoso Pareja (Havana: Casa de las Américas, 1987).

20. He says, "Realism in literature distances us from reality. The realist experiment has merely served to show that we can only encounter reality along the path of fantasy. . . . But fiction is not free. More than uncovering the fantastic, it seems destined to unveil the real. Fantasy serves us little when it does not approach reality." Mariátegui, *The Heroic and Creative Meaning of Socialism*.

21. Gonzalo Zaldumbide, *Egloga trágica* (Puebla: Cajica, 1961). The first, incomplete edition was published in 1913. Obviously the issues are not all ones of form: Zaldumbide clearly expressed the position of the old, landholding aristocracy.

22. Augustín Cueva, "En pos de la historicidad perdida: Contribución al debate sobre la literatura indigenista en el Ecuador," *Revista de crítica literaria latinoamericana* 4.7–8 (1978): 38.

23. Cueva, "En pos de la historicidad perdida," 30. Cf. Ángel F. Rojas, *La novela ecuatoriana* (Mexico City: Fondo de Cultura Económica, 1948); Manuel Corrales Pascual, *Jorge Icaza, frontera del relato indigenista* (Quito: Casa de la Cultura Euatoriana, 1974); Armin Shönberger-Rosero, "Introducción histórico-social a la obra de Icaza," *Bibliografía Ecuatoriana* 7 (1976); and Agustín Cueva, *Jorge Icaza* (Buenos Aires: Centro Editor de América Latina, 1968), and the compilations of his essays *Sobre nuestra ambigüedad cultural* (Quito: Universitaria, 1974) and *Lecturas y rupturas* (Quito: Planeta, 1986). See also his *Narradores ecuatorianos del 30*, Jorge Enrique Adoum, ed. Pedro José Vera (Caracas: Biblioteca Ayacucho, 1980).

24. Jorge Icaza, *El chulla Romero y Flores*, ed. Ricardo Descalzi and Renaud Richard (Madrid: Colección Archivos, 1988). The studies in this edition illustrate the different positions criticism has taken in relation to Icaza's work and specifically his language. First edition published in 1958.

25. Arguedas used this phrase on several occasions. See *Encuentro de narradores peruanos* (Lima: Casa de la Cultura, 1969), 43.

26. The dialogs or exclamations in Quechua or very mestizo Spanish highlight this phenomenon. Having successfully represented collective characters in

this way is clearly to Icaza's credit but is, at the same time, limited by the brevity of these segments. The fact that the narrator shares the "plebian" norm is evident in *El chulla Romero y Flores*.

27. This is a problem similar to the one found in testimony. It may be useful to employ, with some modification, the current criticism on this genre. See *Testimonio y literatura*, ed. Rene Jara and Hernán Vidal (Minneapolis: Institute for the Study of Ideologies and Literature, 1986); and *La voz del otro: Testimonio, subalternidad y verdad narrativa*, ed. John Beverley and Hugo Achugar (Lima-Pittsburgh: Latinoamericana Editores, 1992). The material in the latter was previously published in *Revista de crítica literaria latinoamericana* 18.36 (1992).

28. Vallejo, "Himno a los voluntarios de la república," *España en el corazón*, 253. The dedicatory to Fernando Chávez, *Plata y bronce* (Quito: Editorial Conejo, 1985), reads, "For the one who will never read these pages because an absurd inequality blinded his eyes . . . beneath an infinite gravestone of racial misunderstanding." Ángel Rojas says that the novelist is alluding to his protagonist, but also refers more generically to all indigenous peoples and expresses an anguished consciousness of the fact that "in our case the Indigenist novel is . . . condemned to partial sterility."

29. See Beatriz Sarlo, *Una modernidad periférifca: Buenos Aires 1920–1930*; and Marshall Berman, *Todo lo sólido se desvanece en el aire*.

30. It goes without saying that these social strata are subjects of a vast and rich symbolic and verbal production that is literary in nature, all within the scope of orality and other artistic and cultural conventions.

31. Manuel González Prada, "Discurso en el Politeama," in *Pájinas libres* (Madrid: Pueyó, n.d.), 78.

32. César Vallejo, *The Black Heralds*, trans. Richard Schaaf and Kathleen Ross (Pittsburgh: Latin American Literary Review Press, 1990), 105.

33. It is interesting to note that rain, a source of life in the countryside, is associated with death in the city. This is a constant theme in Vallejo and is most dramatically rendered in the verse "I will die in Paris with hard dirty rain" from "Black Stone on a White Stone" from *Human Poems*.

34. Pío Jaramillo Alvarado, *El indio ecuatoriano* (Quito: Talleres Gráficos del Estado, 1936), 12–14. The much shorter first edition was published in 1922.

35. Jaime Mendoza, *El macizo boliviano* (La Paz: Arnó, 1935), 189.

36. With respect to the condemnation of the mestizo, we need only reflect on Tamayo's theories of the "cholo" (chap. 16) or Valcárcel's ambiguity on this topic. This contrasts with José Uriel García's praise of him in *El nuevo indio*, although here mestizaje is primarily spiritual.

37. In his opinion Inca rule (which he considers a "communist" regime) solved the material problems of its people "but by killing all individual aspiration [and] mortally debilitating the spirit," which explains why the Indian of today

"lacks personality." Below we shall see that Mariátegui, too, considers Inca society to be "Communist," but he extracts from this conclusions diametrically opposed to those of Jaramillo.

38. For example, Jaramillo speaks of his "ethnic inferiority aggravated by four centuries of slavery" (Jaramillo, *El indio ecuatoriano*, 331).

39. Luis E. Valcárcel, *Tempestad en los Andes* (Lima: Populibros Peruanos, 1927). (All translations are Jentsch's.) Valcárcel himself later tempered the proposals contained in this book. See his *Memorias* (Lima: Instituto de Estudios Peruanos, 1981).

40. See José Tamayo Herrera, *Historia del indigenismo cuzqueño: Siglos XVI–XX* (Lima: Instituto Nacional de Cultura, 1980); and José Luis Rénique, *Los sueños de la sierra: Cusco en el siglo XX* (Lima: CEPES, 1991). See also Augusto Salazar Bondy, *Historia de las ideas en el Perú contemporáneo* (Lima: Moncloa, 1965); Luis Enrique Tord, *El indio en los ensayistas peruanos, 1848–1984* (Lima: Ed. Unidas, 1978); and Carlos Iván Degregori et al., *Indigenismo, clases sociales y problema nacional* (Lima: CELATS, 1978).

41. Some of these are pointed out by Mariátegui and Luis Alberto Sánchez, who wrote the book's foreword and colophon.

42. It is symptomatic that in his first works, José María Arguedas contrasts Indians and whites, then later examines the opposition between the highlands and the coast, and in his last novel frequently associates the coast with the feminine. See Antonio Cornejo Polar, "La obra de José María Arguedas: Elementos para una interpretación," *La novela peruana* (Lima: Horizonte, 1989); and *Los universos narrativos de José María Arguedas* (Buenos Aires: Losada, 1973).

43. In the foreword to the third edition of *El nuevo indio* he declares that "the storm in the Andes was accomplished without thunder or lightning" through "the great indigenous flood that fell over Lima" and transformed Peruvian society (Jentsch's translation).

44. This is Uriel García's reading and one reason why his *El nuevo indio* was taken as a response to Valcárcel's thesis.

45. Although it is tempting to comb this thesis for influences from Andean culture (as anthropologists did after the "discovery" of the Inkarri myth), all indications are that Valcárcel was operating under the aegis of the cultured Indigenist elite. See José María Arguedas and Josafat Roel Pineda, "Tres versiones del mito de Inkarrí," in *Ideología mesiánica en el mundo andino*, ed. Juan Ossio (Lima: Ignacio Prado Editor, 1973).

46. Alcides Arguedas, *Pueblo enfermo* (Barcelona: Tasso, 1919), first edition 1909. See Pedro Lastra, "Sobre Alcides Arguedas," *Revista de crítica literaria latinoamericana* 6.12 (1980).

47. Tamayo, *Historia del indigenismo cuzqueño*, chaps. 2, 17.

48. Jaramillo, *El indio ecuatoriano*, 331–36.

49. Hildebrando Castro Pozo, *Nuestra comunidad indígena* (Lima: Lucero, 1924); and *Del ayllu al cooperativismo socialista* (Lima: Barrantes Castro, 1936).
50. Mariátegui had taken this position many years before. In "Nationalism and Vanguardism" he says, "In place of a Platonic love for the Incan past, the revolutionary *indigenistas* show an active and concrete solidarity with today's Indian" (Mariátegui, *The Heroic and Creative Meaning of Socialism*, 71).
51. See Tamayo, *Historia del indigenismo cuzqueño*, 246–54.
52. For example, "the lot of the Indian [is] basic to a program for the reform and reconstruction of Peru" (Mariátegui, *Seven Essays*, 158). There are many more examples. In a 1929 article by the same name he called it "the Indigenist question" (Mariátegui, *The Heroic and Creative Meaning of Socialism*, 94–109).
53. The bibliography on Mariátegui is extensive. See *Anuario Mariateguiano* (Aalborg, Denmark: VBN).
54. See Cornejo, *La formación de la tradición literaria en el Perú*, 127–37.
55. He says for example, "the Incan past has come into our history vindicated not by traditionalists, but revolutionaries" (Mariátegui, *Peruanicemos al Perú*, 121).
56. There are dozens of other references to this subject. Perhaps the most important are the two 1927 articles "Heterodoxia de la tradición" and "La tradición nacional," in Mariátegui, *Peruanicemos al Perú*, 117–23.
57. See especially Mariátegui, *Seven Essays*, chap. 1.
58. Mariátegui treated this point on several occasions, but perhaps his most convincing argument can be found in his polemic with Luis Alberto Sánchez: "No one who looks carefully at the confluence or melding of 'indigenism' and socialism should be surprised. Socialism orders and defines the vindication of the masses, the working class. And in Peru the masses—the working class—are four-fifths indigenous. Our socialism would not be, well, Peruvian—or even socialism—if it did not first find solidarity with the indigenous recovery of justice" (Mariátegui, *La polémica del indigenismo*, 75).
59. This is the thesis of the neo- and ultraliberal ideology expressed by Mario Vargas Llosa and others. In "Questions of Conquest," *Harper's* magazine (December 1990), he says, "Perhaps there is no realistic way to integrate our societies other than by asking the Indians to pay that price (renunciation of their culture, their language; their beliefs, their traditions and customs, and the adoption of the culture of their ancient masters). Perhaps the ideal—that is, the preservation of the primitive cultures of America—is a utopia incompatible with this other and more urgent goal—the establishment of [modern] societies." See Mario Vargas Llosa, *The Storyteller* (New York: Farrar, Straus, Giroux, 1989).
60. See Alberto Flores Galindo, *La agonía de Mariátegui* (Lima: DESCO, 1982); and Jorge Gaete Avaria, *Historia de un lenguaje infortunado: Mariátegui y el marxismo* (Caracas: CELARG, 1989).

61. The full text as it appears in *Amauta* 3.17 (September 1928) reads, "Clearly we do not want Socialism in the Americas to be a blueprint or a copy. It should be a heroic creation. We must give birth, within our own reality and in our own language, to Indo-American socialism" (Jentsch's translation).
62. See Miguel Ángel Rodríguez Rea, *La literatura peruana en debate* (Lima: Ediciones Antonio Ricardo, 1985); and Carlos García-Bedoya Maguiña, *Para una periodización de la literatura peruana* (Lima: Latinoamericana Editores, 1990).
63. Mariátegui thought that it was the Vanguard that had seen the contradictions inherent in the bourgeois order and put this before the public, but at a cost when they did not replace the "absolute bourgeois" with someone new. See his 1926 article "Arte, revolución y decadencia," later anthologized in *El artista y su época*, 18 (1967). Now we would say that the problem that Mariátegui detects is the existence in all modernism of an antimodernist attitude, especially in the realm of art.
64. There are dozens of references to this topic. Perhaps the most obvious is *The Black Heralds*, considered "the dawn of a new poetry in Peru," precisely because this "probably mark[s] the beginning of Peruvian, in the sense of indigenous, poetry" (Mariátegui, *Seven Essays*, 250–51).
65. See "Nationalism and Vanguardism:" the Vanguard proposes the reconstruction of Peru on an Indian foundation . . . Vanguardism . . . seeks more truly Peruvian [than vice-royal] and more remotely ancient materials for its work" (Mariátegui, *Meaning* 70–71). See also "Literature on Trial" in *Seven Essays*.
66. Alcides Arguedas, *Raza de bronce: Wuata Wuara*, ed. Antonio Lorente Medina (Madrid: Archivos, 1988), 347–48 (Jentsch's translation).
67. Jorge Icaza, *The Villagers (Huasipungo)*, trans. Bernard Dulsey (Carbondale: IL: Southern Illinois University Press, 1964), 216.
68. José María Arguedas, *Todas las sangres* (Buenos Aires: Losada, 1964), 470–71, Jentsch's translation). See Cornejo, *Los universos narrativos de José María Arguedas*.
69. The idea of modernity is very conflictive in these novels: They sometimes tend, as in the case of Valcárcel's Indigenist thought, toward a restoration of the past.
70. See Cornejo, "La novela indigenista: Un género contradictorio," *Texto crítico* 5.14 (1979), and "La novela indigenista: Una desgarrada conciencia de la historia," *Lexis* 4.1 (1980).
71. See the section on this novel in chapter 2.
72. See José María Arguedas, *Yawar fiesta*, trans. Frances Horning Barraclough (Austin: University of Texas Press, 1985), chap. 2.
73. See chapter 2.
74. Alcides Arguedas, *Raza de Bronce*, 348 (Jentsch's translation).
75. Ariel Dorfman, *Imaginación y violencia en América* (Santiago: Universitaria, 1970), 202.

76. Ciro Alegría, *Broad and Alien Is the World*, trans. Harriet de Onís (London: Merlin, 1973). The first edition in Spanish was published in 1941. See Goran Tocilovac, *La comunidad indígena y Ciro Alegría* (Lima: Biblioteca Universitaria, 1975); Eduardo Urdanivia, *Análisis e interpretación de El mundo es ancho y ajeno* (Lima: Universidad de San Marcos, 1974); *La obra de Ciro Alegría* (Arequipa: Universidad de San Agustín, 1976); *Ciro Alegría: Trayectoria y mensaje* (Lima: Varona, 1972); Alejandro Losada, "Ciro Alegría como fundador de la realidad hispanoamericana," *Acta litteraria* 17.1–2 (1975); Henry Bonneville, "Ciro Alegría y el mestizaje," in *Literatura de la emancipación Hispanoamericana y otros ensayos: Proceedings of the 15th Congress of the Instituto Internacional de Literatura Iberoamericana* (Lima: Universidad de San Marcos, 1972); and the section on Ciro Alegría in Julio Rodríguez-Luis, *Hermenéutica y praxis del indigenismo* (México City: Fondo de Cultura Económica, 1980). See also *Anuario Bibliográfico Peruano: 1967–1969* (Lima: Biblioteca Nacional, 1976).

77. Rumi is described as follows: "It was a delight to see the gay picture the village made, and still more delightful to live there.... Those who had made it their business to live here had known for centuries, that happiness comes from justice, and justice from the common good" (Alegría, *Broad and Alien Is the World*, 6).

78. Alegría's image of the community owes much to Mariátegui. See Tomás G. Escajadillo, "Ciro Alegría, José María Arguedas y el indigenismo de Mariátegui," in *Mariátegui y la literatura* (Lima: Amauta, 1980).

79. See Tomás Escajadillo, "Los principios estructuradores de *El mundo es ancho y ajeno*" in *Alegría y El mundo es ancho y ajeno* (Lima: Universidad de San Marcos, 1983).

80. This communitarian model, typical of the Indians (who for some are "barbaric") is at the root of the inversion that Alegría proposes with respect to D. F. Sarmiento's classic opposition between civilization and barbarism, and which the former considered as the basic (and faulty) structure of *Doña Bárbara*: "the truth is otherwise ... the man of the country is the civilized one ... and the one from the city is truly barbaric, though he often hides his claws under his gloves. The most pathetic aspect of this phenomenon is that it is precisely the supposedly barbaric country folk who have stood up, asking for schools, bread, machinery, rights, law to the true barbarian in the city, who denies them all this deliberately and has no respect for human dignity and life." See "Nota sobre el personaje en la novela hispanoamericana," in *La novela hispanoamericna*, ed. Juan Loveluck (Santiago: Universitaria, 1969), 133 (Jentsch's translation).

81. See Concha Meléndez, "*El mundo es ancho y ajeno*," in *Asomante: Estudios hispanoamericanos* (San Juan: Universidad de Puerto Rico, 1943); and Matilde Billariño de Olivieri, *Las novelas de Ciro Alegría* (Santander: Bedía, 1956).

82. Alegría, *Broad and Alien Is the World*, 199.

83. The clearest example of this is Castro's decision to drain a "magical" lagoon against the express wishes of the elder *comuneros* in order to increase arable land.
84. Alegría, *Broad and Alien Is the World*, 414.
85. Ciro Alegría, *El mundo es ancho y ajeno* (Caracas: Bibiloteca Ayacucho, 1948), 9 (Jentsch's translation).
86. See *Encuentro de narradores peruanos*, 240–53; and see Hayden White, *Tropics of Discourse: Essays in Cultural Criticism* (Baltimore: Johns Hopkins University Press, 1978), chap. 1.
87. The exception would be where the narrator retells fables or popular legends. See Cornejo, *La novela peruana*.
88. See Guillermo Mariaca, *La palabra autoritaria* (La Paz: Tiahuanakos, 1990).
89. See Ángel Rama, "El área cultual andina," in *Transculturación narrativa en América Latina*.
90. *Yawar Fiesta* and *Todas las sangres* are examples of the first, and *The Fox from Up Above and the Fox from Down Below*, trans. Frances Horning Barraclough (Pittsburgh: University of Pittsburgh Press, 2000) and the bilingual collection of poetry *Katatay/Temblar* of the second. See Arguedas' anthropological works in Ángel Rama, *Formación de una cultura nacional indoamericana* (Mexico City: Siglo XXI, 1975). On literature and migration, see Mirko Lauer, *El sitio de la literatura*.
91. See Tomás G. Escajadillo, "La narrativa indigenista: Un planteamiento y ocho incisiones," diss., Universidad Nacional Mayor de San Marcos, 1971; see the bibliography that appears in José María Arguedas, *El zorro de arriba y el zorro de abajo*, ed. Eve-Marie Fell (Madrid: Archivos, 1990); and that of William Rowe in *Revista peruana de cultura* 13 (1970); see José María Arguedas, *Deep Rivers*, trans. Frances Horning Barraclough (Austin: University of Texas Press, 1978); and Julio Ortega, *Texto, comunicación y cultura: Los ríos profundos de Arguedas* (Lima: CEDEP, 1982).
92. See Roland Forgues, *José María Arguedas: Del pensamiento disléctico trágico: Historia de una utopía* (Lima: Horizonte, 1984).
93. See Cornejo, "José María Arguedas: Una espléndida historia," in *Rencontre de Renards: Colloque international sur José María Arguedas* (Grenoble: AFERPA, 1989).
94. The quote is from his speech "I Am Not an Acculturated Man," upon winning the Premio Inca Garcilaso de la Vega in 1968. Qtd. in Arguedas, *The Fox from Up Above and the Fox from Down Below*, 268–69. For Arguedas's biography, see Mildred Merino de Zela, "Vida y obra de José María Arguedas," *Revista peruana de cultura* 13 (1970), amended in the Venezuelan edition of *Los ríos profundos* (Caracas: Biblioteca Ayacucho, 1978); Sybila Arredondo, "Vida y obra de José María Arguedas y hechos fundamentales del Perú," in *José María Arguedas, Obras Completas*, ed. Sybila Arredondo (Lima: Horizonte, 1983); and Christian Fernández, "The Death of the Author," in *The Fox from*

Up Above and the Fox from Down Below, 290–306. There are many autobiographical texts. The most interesting are in *El zorro de arriba y el zorro de abajo* (Buenos Aires: Losada, 1971); and the Proceedings of the *Primer Encuentro de Narradores Peruanos* (Lima: Casa de la Cultura del Perú, 1969).

95. Arguedas speaks to this in one of his first short stories: "Till one day they tore me away from my heaven, to bring me to all this noise and commotion, to people I don't care for and don't understand.... While I live here, bitter and pale, like an animal from the cold plains, taken to the coast, to burning and alien sands." From "Warma Kuyay (Puppy Love)," trans. Hardie St. Martin, in *The Eye of the Heart*, ed. Barbara Howes (New York: Avon, 1973). This story first appeared in *Amor mundo y todos los cuentos* (Lima: Moncloa, 1933).

96. On the writing of Quechua, specifically literary writing, see Julio Noriega, "Buscando una tradición escrita y poética quechua en el Perú," diss., University of Pittsburgh, 1993. The first chapter, "El quechua: Voz y letra en el mundo andino," appears in *Revista de crítica literaria latinoamericana* 19.37 (1993).

97. See José María Arguedas, "La novela y el problema de la expresión literaria en el Perú," *Mar del sur* 3.9 (1950). A corrected version appears as the foreword to the Chilean edition of *Yawar fiesta* (Santiago: Universitaria, 1968).

98. The topic of modernity in the nineteenth century appears in Julio Ramos, *Desencuentros de la modernidad en América Latina* (Mexico City: Fondo de Cultura Económica, 1989).

99. It is significant that at first the letter is destined for "the world" and later for "the sky."

100. See Edwin Rodrigo and Luis Montoya, *La sangre de los cerros / Urqukunapa yawarmin: Antología de la poesía quechua que se canta en el Perú* (Lima: Universidad de San Marcos-Mosca Azul, 1987).

101. This is the relationship between the protagonist/narrator, who exercises his discourse within the world of the novel as an adolescent, and the narrator/narrator or "basic speaker," who organizes the entire text and has an adult consciousness. In the fiction of the novel the latter would only evoke his childhood and youth. Upon doing so, he substantiates it.

102. See Mikhail Bakhtin, *Problems of Dostoevsky's Poetics*, ed. and trans. Caryl Emerson (Minneapolis: University of Minnesota Press, 1984); and *Estética de la creación verbal* (Mexico City: Siglo XXI, 1985).

103. See Nathan Wachtel, *Sociedad e ideología* (Lima: Instituto de Estudios Peruanos, 1973).

104. Qtd. in César Delgado Díaz del Olmo, *El diálogo de los mundos:Ensayo sobre el Inca Garcilaso* (Arequipa: Universidad de San Agustín, 1991), 48.

105. The Inca wall seems humiliated by the filth on the street, the presence of modern buildings, and above all because it is part of the houses inhabited by the hated "*señores*" of Cusco.

106. See Iris Zavala, *La posmodernidad y Mijail Bajtín: Una poética dialógica* (Espasa-Calpe, 1991).

107. Arguedas, *The Fox from Up Above and the Fox from Down Below*, 259–60.
108. See Leonidas Morales, "José María Arguedas: El lenguaje como perfección humana," *Estudios Filológicos* 7 (1971); and Alberto Escobar, *Arguedas o la utopía del lenguaje* (Lima: Instituto de Estudios Peruanos, 1984).
109. See Martín Leinhard, *Cultura popular andina y forma novelesca: Zorros y danzantes en la última novela de Arguedas* (Lima: Latinoamericana Editores-Tarea, 1981). There are similar characteristics in other works, even *Todas las sangres*, which is the farthest from this problematic, in spite of the "choral" character found there. See Cornejo, "Estructura e ideología de *Todas las sangres*," *Revista de crítica literaria latinoamericana* 6.12 (1980).
110. See John Beverley and Hugo Achugar, *La voz del otro: Testimonio, subalternidad y verdad narrativa* (Lima: Latinoamericana Editores, 1992), intro.; and Benita Parry, "Problems in Current Theories of Colonial Discourse," *Oxford Literary Review* 9.1–2 (1988).
111. See Walter Mignolo, "La semiosis colonial: La dialéctica entre representaciones fracturadas y hermenéuticas pluritópicas," in *Crítica y descolonización: El sujeto colonial en la cultura latinoamericana*, ed. Beatriz González and Lúcia Costigan (Caracas: Academia Nacional de Historia, 1992). See also Michael Taussing, *Shamanism, Colonialism and the Wild Man* (Chicago: University of Chicago Press, 1987), 42; and Elzbieta Sklodowska, *Testimonio hispanoamericano: Historia, teoría, poética* (New York: Peter Lang, 1992), chap. 3.
112. Domitila Barrios de Chungara and Moema Viezzer, *Let Me Speak! Testimony of Domitila, a Woman of the Bolivian Mines*, trans. Victoria Ortiz (New York: Monthly Review Press, 1978); Gregorio Condori Mamani, Paul Gelles, and Gabriela Martínez Escobar, *Andean Lives: Gregorio Condori Mamani and Asunta Quispe Huamán* (Austin: University of Texas Press, 1996). The latter was originally transcribed in Quechua (Condori and Quispe are monolingual) and translated into Spanish. The English version was translated from the Quechua.
113. Apart from open discussion with Betty Friedan and other feminists from the First and Third Worlds, she is uninformed regarding matters such as lesbianism, prostitution, and—although she contributes somewhat here—machismo.
114. She was director of the Comité de Amas de Casa de [la mina] Siglo XX, which participated decisively in the struggle of miners and others.
115. One should note that their editors do not use the word "testimony" but rather "autobiography" in the subtitle and "life history" in the "Preliminary Note." These definitions are valid for Condori's and Quispe's accounts.
116. For the Quechua text of this and subsequent quotes from Condori, see Ricardo Valderrana and Carmen Escalante, *Gregorio Condori Mamani: Autobiografía* (Cusco: Centro Bartolomé de las Casas, 1977); or the notes to either edition of *Escribir en el aire* (Jentsch's note).

117. Valderrama and Escalante guarantee that this is a "true story" and that they have confirmed it with other sources, though they point out small errors in remembering names, exact dates, and some omissions of relative importance, such as Condori's not mentioning that he receives a small pension from Social Security (Valderrama and Escalante, *Gregorio Condori Mamani*, 15–17).
118. Condori makes only two references to unions: when Emiliano Huamantica keeps him from being fired from the factory and (like wishful thinking) when he says that he would like to see all Cuscan porters unionize.
119. Condori is, however, confused about more ancient history. For example he says, "The Chileans had grabbed hold of Tacna-Arica . . . way back in those distant times of Christopher Columbus" (Condori, *Andean Lives*, 39).
120. Carmen Escalante and Ricardo Valderrama, *Nosotros los humanos/Ñuqanchik runakuna: Testimonio de los quechuas del siglo XX* (Cusco: Bartolomé de las Casas, 1992). (All translations are Jentsch's.)
121. It should be noted that Inca and Inkarri are delimited and that the sense of filiation with the former is somehow mixed with Christian dogma. Escalante and Valderrma allude to this and other connected themes in their introduction (Cornejo's note). For the Quechua text of this and subsequent quotes from *Nosotros los humanos*, see the original text or the notes to either edition of *Escribir en el aire* (Jentsch's note).
122. E.g.: "litis" = *litip*; "demanda" = *dimandata*; "declaración" = *diklarakuchkantaq*.

Overture

1. Jacques Derrida, *Of Grammatology*, trans. Gayatri Chakravorty Spivak (Baltimore: Johns Hopkins University Press, 1976).
2. The iron-clad grid is an allusion to Algirdas Greimas's "square."
3. Surely Arguedas said it best: "Vallejo was the beginning and the end." From "Last Diary?" in *The Fox from Up Above and the Fox from Down Below*, trans. Frances Horning Barraclough (Pittsburgh: University of Pittsburgh Press, 2000), 236.
4. This is Jentsch's original translation. Others may be found in *Spain, Let This Cup Pass from Me*, trans. Alvaro Cardona-Hine (Los Angeles: Red Hill, 1978); *Spain, Take This Cup from Me*, trans. Clayton Eshleman and José Rubia Barcia (New York: Grove, 1974), 29, 31; *César Vallejo: Selected Poems*, trans. H. R. Hays (New York: Sachen), 107, 109 (Jentsch's note).
5. The first edition's title page reads, "César Vallejo / (1894–1938) / *España, / aparta de mí este cáliz* / Poemas / (Foreword by Juan Larrea. Illustrations by Pablo Picasso) / Soldiers of the Republic manufactured the paper, / composed the text and maneuvered the machinery. / Ediciones Literarias del Comisariado. / Army of the East. / War of Independence. In the year 1939." Lost for many years, a copy of this edition was discovered by Juan Gilabert in the library of the monastery of Montserrat. The details of this finding can be

found in "La primera edición de *España, aparta de mí este cáliz*," *Revista de crítica literaria latinoamericana* 5.10 (1979). Julio Vélez discovered other copies in the same library.
6. This appears in Vélez and Merino, "Abisa a todos los compañeros, pronto," *Nuevo hispanismo* 1 (1982), which later became a chapter in *España en César Vallejo*, vol. 1 (Madrid: Fundamentos, 1984), 128–37.
7. The manuscript of the report was found bound into one of the copies of the first edition discovered by Vélez in the monastery of Montserrat. He published it in *César Vallejo: 1892–1938 [Catálogo de la] Exposición celebrada con motivo del cincuentenario de la muerte del poeta* (Madrid: ICI, 1988). Vallejo made its release conditional on his responses being transcriptions of articles already published.
8. Antonio Ruiz Vilapana, *Doy fe . . . Un año de actuación en la España nacionalista* (Paris: Imprimérie Coopérative Etoile, n.d.), 38–39 (Jentsch's translation). All bibliographic references give the date of this edition as 1937. The editions out of Buenos Aires (La Nueva España), Cali (Editorial América), and Panama (La Moderna) were from the same year. Vallejo would have been familiar with the one used here or the manuscript of the book. Vélez and Merino state that Ruiz left Spain with the originals on September 30, 1937.
9. A photographic copy of the manuscript was published in the journal *Visión del Perú* 4 (1969). This issue is better known as *Homenaje Internacional a César Vallejo*.
10. César Vallejo, *Poesía Completa*. ed. Juan Larrea (Barcelona: Barral, 1970), 181 (Jentsch's translation).
11. Vallejo, *The Black Heralds*, trans. Richard Schaaf and Kathleen Ross (Pittsburgh: Latin American Literary Review Press, 1990), 117.
12. The symbol of the spoon appears, for example in Vallejo's "The Miserable Supper" (*The Black Heralds*), LVIII (*Trilce*), "Lánguidamente su licor" (*Poemas en Prosa*), and "The fact is the place where I put on my" (*Human Poems*).
13. In the first version he has the name Santiago.
14. Ortega emphasizes that "writing fulfills . . . a central function . . . as natural and cosmic writing" in this poem. Julio Ortega, *La teoría poética de César Vallejo* (Lima: Del Sol, 1986), 80. Jean Franco points out the importance of the images of writing in *Spain, Let This Cup Pass from Me* in *César Vallejo: La dialéctica de la poesía y el silencio* (Buenos Aires: Sudamericana, 1984), 343–45.
15. César Vallejo, *Poemas humanos / Human Poems*, trans. Clayton Eshleman (New York: Grove, 1968) 235. This text has been read as Vallejo's *ars poetica*, though without reference to the theme of orality. See Julio Ortega, *Crítica de la identidad: La pregunta por el Perú en su literatura* (Mexico City: Fondo de Cultura Económica, 1988), 93–117.
16. See José Pascual Buxó, "Vallejo: El estatuto oral de la epopeya," *Hispania* 72.1 (1989). According to Buxó all Vallejo's poetry attempts to "replace as much a possible the complex structures of written communication with the incom-

plete but strongly expressive utterances of oral language" (Buxó, "Vallejo," 69). Buxó takes the phrase "directly and immediately" from Vallejo himself and uses it expertly to analyze *Spain, Let this Cup Pass from Me* as an oral-popular epic poem.

17. Buxó, "Vallejo," 72. See chapter 3.
18. See Carlos Pacheco *La comarca oral* (Caracas: Casa de Bello, 1992).
19. See chapter 1.
20. See Michel de Certeau, *The Writing of History*, trans. Tom Conley (New York: Columbia University Press, 1988).
21. See chapter 3.

INDEX

Acosta, Father José de, 72–73
Adorno, Theodor, 2
agraphic culture, 5, 29, 41
Aguirre, Nataniel: *Juan de la Rosa*, 94–102
Alegría, Ciro: 143–44; *Broad and Alien Is the World*, 141
Almagro, Diego de: in Oruro version, 48, 51
Amaru, Tupac, 1: as viewed by Condori, 159–60; execution of, 66; in *Ayacucho y los Andes* (Chocano), 107; revolt of, 67, 80, 95
Arguedas, Alcides, 126, 138–39; and the "indigenous problem," 130. *See also individual works*
Arguedas, José María, 121, 138–39, 145–54, 156, 165, 172. *See also individual works*
Aristotle, 7
Arzanz, Bartolomé: *Historia de la villa imperial de Potosí*, 34
Atahuallpa [also written Atabaliba, Atabaliva, Atahualpa], 14–15, 36–41, 44–46, 48–54, 56–57, 59, 70, 98, 160, 165; and evangelization of the Americas, 25–26, 27–31; as mythical figure, 158–59, 161, 170; reaction to the Bible, 16–25; theatrical retellings of the death of, 31–34
autos sacramentales, 34–35
Ayacucho, battle of, 103, 106, 109–10
ayllu, 131, 138; and reinterpretation of indigenous myths, 161–62

Bakhtin, Mikhail, 6; assertions regarding dialogue, 58, 152–53
Ballón, Enrique. *See* diglossia
Balmori, Hernando: and Oruro version, 35–36, 39–40, 42, 46, 48, 50–51, 53–54
Barrios de Chungara, Domitila: *Let Me Speak!*, 155–56
Bello, Andrés, 74
Bendezú, Edmundo, 2
Benjamin, Walter, 7
Benzoni, Jerónimo, 19
Beyersdorff, Margot: *La Adoracion de los Reyes Magos*, 48
bilingualism, 6; and heterogenization of subject, 148–52; in Arguedas, J. M., 146; in Icaza, 120–23; in *tradición* (Palma), 72–75; in versions of the Cajamarca "Dialogue," 17, 26–27, 30, 41–44
Bolivian literature, 10, 35, 126–27. *See also* Aguirre, Nataniel; Arguedas, Alcides; Barrios de Chungara, Domitila; Mendoza, Jaime; Reynolds, Gregorio
Burga, Manuel. See *comparsa*

Cabello de Balboa, Miguel: criticism of Valverde, 20
Calatayud, Alejo, 95–96, 99
Catari, Tupac, 95
Certeau, Michel de, 56
chala: as metaphor for paper, 47, 49–51
chicha: spilling of, 24
Chimpu Ocllo, Isabel, 70

Chocano, José Santos: *Ayacucho y los Andes*, 103, 106–10; "Poet of America," 113
Choquehuanca, José Domingo, 76; relationship to his Inca heritage, 79–82
Cieza de Léon, Pedro, 21; condemnation of Valverde, 20
Columbus, Christopher: and imaginary of his time, 55; portrayal in *Rendición* (Reynolds), 104
comparsa: of the Inca/Captain, 32–34
Condori Mamani, Gregorio, 155, 157–60
"cosmic race," 8, 110
Costumbrismo, 74, 83–84, 128
coya (palla): 35, 51
Cueva, Agustín, 120

"Dead Idyll" (Vallejo), 124–26
Deep Rivers (J. M. Arguedas), 145–53, 172
Derrida, Jacques: and authenticity of language, 165
Diccionario de la legislación peruana, 79
diglossia: 2, 5–6, 13
Doña Barbara (Gallegos), 84
Durand, José, 61, 66

Ecuadorian literature, 10, 84–85, 118–21, 126. *See also* Icaza, Jorge; Jaramillo, Pío; Mera, Juan León; Palacio, Pablo
El Primer Nueva Crónica y Buen Gobierno (Guaman Poma), 24–25, 31, 39
Escobar, Alberto, 27, 74, 115
Estete, Miguel, 20, 22

Felipillo [pseud. Martinillo], 14–15, 26, 45, 50

García, Uriel, 71, 130–31
García Canclini, Néstor, 2
Garcilaso de la Vega, El Inca, 18, 30, 34, 104; as dissenting voice in describing the Cajamarca "dialogue," 25–28; "civilizing" effect of the conquest, 80–81; influence on image of Atahuallpa, 38; mestizo writing, 59–71. *See also* individual works

Gómara, Francisco López de, 18–19, 21, 71–72
González Prada, Manuel, 91, 124, 129
Guaman Poma de Ayala, Felipe, 24–26, 30, 39, 51, 55, 59, 81. *See also individual works*
Guatemalan literature, 36

Herencia (Matto), 90
Hernández, Max, 30–31
huaca, 64–65
Huascar, 31, 37
Huayna Capac, 70, 80
Human Poems (Vallejo), 170–71

Icaza, Jorge, 122, 138; *Huasipungo*, 118, 120–21, 139
indigenism, 5, 71, 114–16, 118, 121–22, 124, 127–29, 131–34, 151, 154; and "Vanguardist Indigenism," 135–36; Indigenist novels, 136–45. *See also* Alegría, Ciro; Arguedas, Alcides; Arguedas, José María; García, Uriel; Icaza, Jorge; Mariátegui, José Carlos; Matto de Turner, Clorinda; Valcárcel, Luis E.
Iriarte, Francisco, 42; Chillia version, 52; Llamellín version, 42–43, 45, 52; Manás version, 53

Jameson, Frederic, 83
Jaramillo, Pío, 126–27, 130, 132

Kapsoli, Wilfredo: Pomabamba version, 40, 50, 52

La Florida del Inca [*La traducción del indio de los Diálogos de Amor*] (Garcilaso), 61
Lara, Jesús, 34–35, 38–39, 46, 54
Leguía, Augusto B., critique of Chocano, 110, 118
"lettered city," 4, 58. *See also* Rama, Ángel
Lienhard, Martin: and "alternative literature," 2, 5
"Literature on Trial" (Mariátegui), 135
López Albújar, Enrique: *Matalcaché*, 93
López de Palacios Rubios, Juan: *requerimiento* drafted by, 18

Los heraldos negros [*The Black Heralds*] (Vallejo), 115, 118, 168–70
Losada, Alejandro: regionalization of literature, 4

MacCormack, Sabine: on Atahuallpa's relationship to books, 22–23
magical realism, 2, 5
Manco Capac, 80–81, 109
Mariátegui, José Carlos, 79, 126, 131, 134; relationship to Indigenism and Vanguardism, 116–18, 135–36. *See also individual works*
Mártir de Anglería, Pedro, 72
Marxism, 7, 126, 131–32, 172; Mariátegui's divergent conception of, 134–35; simplified class warfare in *Let Me Speak!* (Barrios), 156–57
Matto de Turner, Clorinda: *Torn from the Nest*, 89–94. *See also Herencia*
Mendoza, Jaime, 126–27
Menéndez Pelayo, Marcelino: questioning Garcilaso, 67–68
Meneses, Teodoro, 34–35, 37, 52
Mera, Juan León: *Cumandá*, 84–89
Mestizaje, 8; conflicting roles in literature, 127; in *Ayacucho y los Andes* (Chocano), 108—9; in *Juan de la Rosa* (Aguirre), 96–98; in *Rendición* (Reynolds), 105–6; in *Torn from the Nest* (Matto), 92; lineage of Garcilaso, 69–71; manifestation in writing of Garcilaso, 60–66
Mexican literature, 36. *See also* Paz
Mignolo, Walter, 2
Millones, Luis: Carhuamayo version, 52
mimesis, 9–10, 144, 152
misti, 32, 40, 138, 146, 148, 162
Modernism [*modernismo*], 72, 168; as literary voice of independence centennial, 103; detachment from social reality, 113–18, 121–22
Murúa, Martín de, 18, 20–22

naturalism, 120, 137–38
Neoclassicism, 75, 82
Neo-Platonism, 63

"new Indian," 8, 131. *See also* García, Uriel
"new narrative," 2
ñudo. See *quipu*

Olguín, Milly. *See* Iriarte, Francisco
Ong, Walter, 41
Ortiz, Fernando: influence on Rama, 5

Pacheco, Carlos, 5
Palacio, Pablo: "Un hombre muerto a puntapiés," 118–20; Vanguardism, 122
Palma, Ricardo, 71–75, 84, 113
Pardo, Luis, 32, 74
Paz, Octavio, 83
"Pedro Rojas" (Vallejo), 58, 165–69, 171–72
Philip II, 64
Pizarro, Francisco, 15, 19, 23, 25, 29, 32, 36–39, 45–46, 49; apparition in *Ayacucho y los Andes* (Chocano), 108–9; condemnation to death in versions of the Cajamarca "dialogue," 51; in Condori, 159; in cosmology of Choquehuanca, 80–81; mixture of language of, 42–43
Pizarro, Pedro, 20
Porras Barrenechea, Raúl: on Garcilaso's ethnicity, 66
Positivism, 3, 68, 126–27; in Varcárcel's concept of race, 129
"possible consciousness," 91
Pueblo enfermo (Alcides Arguedas), 130
Pupo-Walker, Enrique, 71

quillca: the Bible as, 24
quipu, 25
quipucamayo, 68
Quispe Huamán, Asunta, 157, 160
Quispicondor, 40

Rama, Ángel, 2, 4–5, 103
Ratto-Ciarlo, José, 82
Raza de bronce (Alcides Arguedas), 139
realism, 113, 130, 144; anticipating a just future, 137–39; criticism of, 118–22
"Reality and Fiction" (Mariátegui), 120
Reynolds, Gregorio: *Rendición*, 103–6, 109–10

Rincón, Carlos, 2
Riva-Agüero, José de la: 67, 71; "Elogio del Inca," 68–70
Rivarola, José Luis, 43
Romanceros, 17
Romanticism, 85–86, 88, 90, 121, 131, 149, 168; conception of the "I," 6–9
Royal Commentaries of the Incas (Garcilaso), 26–28, 31, 60–64, 67–68, 71–72, 81

San Martín, General José de, 76–79, 81
Santa Cruz Pachacuti, Joan, 24
Seven Interpretive Essays on Peruvian Reality (Mariátegui), 132–33
Spain, Let This Cup Pass from Me (Vallejo), 168, 170

Tamayo, Franz, 126, 130
taqui, 32–33
Tarapaki, Victoriano: *Nosotros los humanos*, 161–62
Tayta, 161–62
Terracini, Lore: semiotic violence, 53
testimonio, 2, 5–6
The Fox from Up Above and The Fox from Down Below (J. M. Arguedas), 153
The General History of Peru (Garcilaso de la Vega), 61–62, 66
Titu Cussi, Diego, 24, 30
tradición. See Palma, Ricardo

Valcárcel, Luis E., 126; *Tempestad en los Andes*, 128–31
Vallejo, César, 45, 58, 123–26, 154, 165–72; relationship to Modernism, 115–18. See also individual works
Valverde, Father Vicente, 40, 52, 165, 170; "dialogue" with Atahuallpa, 14–29, 40, 170; use of the Bible as a political tool, 46
Vanguard movement, 103, 114, 119–20, 122, 124, 151, 168–69, 171; relationship to indigenism and Modernism, 116–18. See also indigenism: and "Vanguardist indigenism"; Mariátegui, José Carlos; Palacio, Pablo
Vargas Llosa, Mario, 4
Vasconcelos, José. See "cosmic race"
viracocha, 22, 29–30, 69

wanka, 34–36, 39, 41, 44–46, 51–54, 56–59; exemplification of conflict between orality and writing, 48
Wachtel, Nathan, 36, 40

Xerez, Francisco de, 20, 23

Ynstruçion del Ynga (Titu Cussi), 30

Zárate, Agustín de, 18, 21
Zavaleta Mercado, René, 2
Zumthor, Paul, 41